Doing Ethics in Context

DOING ETHICS IN CONTEXT

South African Perspectives

Edited by
Charles Villa-Vicencio and John W. de Gruchy

THEOLOGY AND PRAXIS: VOLUME TWO

ORBIS BOOKS
Maryknoll, New York

DAVID PHILIP
Cape Town and Johannesburg

The Catholic Foreign Mission Society of America (Maryknoll) recruits and trains people for overseas missionary service. Through Orbis Books, Maryknoll aims to foster the international dialogue that is essential to mission. The books published, however, reflect the opinions of their authors and are not meant to represent the official position of the society.

First published 1994 in southern Africa by David Philip Publishers (Pty) Ltd, 208 Werdmuller Centre, Claremont 7700, South Africa, and in the United States of America by Orbis Books, Maryknoll, NY 10545

ISBN 0-86486-266-0 (David Philip)
ISBN 0-88344-990-0 (Orbis Books)

Printed by The Rustica Press, Old Mill Road, Ndabeni, Cape, South Africa

CIP data for this book are available upon application to the Library of Congress

D2768

Contents

Contributors

JAN BOTHA is a Senior Lecturer in the Department of Religious Studies at the University of Stellenbosch.

DOT CLEMINSHAW is a human rights activist with a particular interest in women's issues.

JAMES COCHRANE is Associate Professor of Theology and Head of the Department of Theological Studies at the University of Natal, Pietermaritzburg.

JOHN DE GRUCHY is Professor of Christian Studies in the Department of Religious Studies at the University of Cape Town.

DAVID FIELD is a Ph.D. student in the Department of Religious Studies at the University of Cape Town.

WILMA JAKOBSEN is an ordained priest in the Church of the Province of South Africa at St George's Cathedral, Cape Town.

PETER KASENENE is Associate Professor and Head of the Department of Theology and Religious Studies at the University of Swaziland.

LOUISE KRETZSCHMAR is a Senior Lecturer in the Department of Systematic Theology and Theological Ethics at the University of South Africa.

GILBERT LAWRENCE is the Director of Health Services, Western Cape Regional Council.

WELI MAZAMISA is a Lecturer in the Department of Religious Studies at the University of Cape Town.

MALUSI MPUMLWANA is the Director of the Institute of Pastoral Studies in Grahamstown.

NJONGONKULU NDUNGANE is the Bishop of the Kimberley and Kuruman Diocese of the Church of the Province of South Africa.

ZOLANI NGWANE is a Ph.D. student at the University of Chicago Divinity School.

KLAUS NÜRNBERGER is Professor of Theology in the Department of Theological Studies at the University of Natal, Pietermaritzburg.

DAWID OLIVIER is a Senior Lecturer in the Department of Systematic Theology and Theological Ethics at the University of South Africa.

ROBIN PETERSEN is a Ph.D. student at the University of Chicago Divinity School.

BARNEY PITYANA is a senior research officer in the Department of Religious Studies at the University of Cape Town.

NEVILLE RICHARDSON is a Senior Lecturer in the Department of Theological Studies at the University of Natal, Pietermaritzburg.

WILLAM SAAYMAN is Professor of Missiology at the University of South Africa.

AUGUSTINE SHUTTE is a Senior Lecturer in the Department of Philosophy at the University of Cape Town.

MOLEFE TSELE is a Ph.D. student at the Lutheran Theological Seminary, Chicago.

CHARLES VILLA-VICENCIO is Professor of Religion and Society in the Department of Religious Studies at the University of Cape Town.

Introduction

Theology and praxis in South Africa require that the student of ethics be exposed to a vast range of ethical models, methods and ways of doing ethics. To facilitate this, an effort is made in the chapters that comprise this volume to capture the broad, pluralistic character of theology and ethics in South Africa. No attempt is made to systematise the different perspectives, insights, theological traditions, cultures or social locations that give rise to this diversity. Any attempt to do so in a study of this kind can only undermine the multi-cultural, pluralistic context of academic pursuit that makes theological study in South Africa such a rich and rewarding experience.

The contributors to this volume stand within different theological traditions. Some are women and some are men. Some are black, others are white. Some are established theologians, others are beginning their theological careers. They teach, study or minister in a range of churches, seminaries and universities. This makes the book an ecumenical effort that reflects the inclusivity and diversity of the Christian tradition.

The explosion of knowledge and events in recent history has left ethicists overwhelmed by the mass of data generated by scholars posing ethical questions. Traditional answers to ethical questions are, in turn, being questioned by people in virtually every walk of life. Can we in this situation talk of a coherent and integrated approach to the study of ethics? Is it still possible to say what is 'right' and what is 'wrong'? Whose interests are being served ultimately by traditional answers to complex ethical questions? Why do people of different social classes, genders and races perceive ethical concerns in different ways? These are some of the questions for which answers are sought in the essays in this volume.

The larger part of the book deals with ethical theory. Some people who are actively engaged (and even risk their lives) in the struggle for a better society may be impatiently tempted to suggest that the urgency of the moment is such that theory should be ignored. The response of José Miguez Bonino to this kind of suggestion is pertinent:

I understand and share this impatience. But I am also convinced that we underestimate the theoretical task and turn our backs on theory only at considerable cost to ourselves and to the effectiveness of our action. The cost in human life that we pay for simple pragmatism is too high.[1]

Theoretical discussion is necessary for a number of reasons. Firstly, there is no way of escaping it. Whether we are aware of it or not, we all operate with certain presuppositions and assumptions which inform our decision-making. There is a need to critically examine and assess the implicit theory that informs our actions. Secondly, by exposing ourselves to the assumptions and theories of others, we are compelled to assess and evaluate our own ethical views critically. We learn in the process to act in a more thoughtful and sensitive manner — and therefore also more effectively. Thirdly, by sharing in theoretical debate we have an opportunity to challenge the presuppositions and ethical assumptions of others. Finally, we become part of what Selznick calls the 'moral commonwealth' which forms the basis of ethical behaviour in any age.[2] In brief, the moral presuppositions of society, which many people accept without question, are at least partly sustained by a theoretical foundation. This foundation needs to be constantly reviewed, debated and modified by ethicists, philosophers, social scientists and people in every walk of life who are daily confronted with the need to make ethical decisions. The study of ethics equips us to participate in this debate. In exposing us to a plurality of ethical views, it can help us overcome our own dogmatism, which gives rise to the kind of self-righteousness and arrogance that tears societies apart. Community, which is at the heart of the biblical message, reminds us of the need to be co-creators and negotiators of values and ethical practices that enable us to live together in justice and social harmony.

The chapters that follow are divided into four parts. The first part deals with introductory themes. Louise Kretzschmar provides a basic introduction to the study of ethics. Augustine Shutte's chapter addresses questions of philosophical ethics both within the tradition of the West and in relation to African thought. Jan Botha, in turn, writes on the Bible and ethics.

The second part of the volume comprises five ethical theories. Barney Pityana writes on natural law ethics. Klaus Nürnberger analyses the Protestant debate on law and gospel. Charles Villa-Vicencio reflects on an ethic of responsibility, drawing on the situational ethics debate and the *Grenzfall* ethics of Barth and Bonhoeffer. Neville Richardson considers the ethics of character and community, and Robin Petersen writes on Karl Marx and the post-Marxian contribution to theological ethics.

Part three deals with contextual ethics. Zolani Ngwane writes on ethics in liberation theology. Molefe Tsele's chapter is concerned with ethics in Black theology. Peter Kasanene reflects on ethics in African theology, and Wilma Jakobsen on ethics in feminist theology. All these chapters address both the broader international debate and the South African debate.

The final part of the book includes several shorter pieces on specific ethical issues. These are considered under two categories. The first concerns medical ethics, which is introduced by Gilbert Lawrence, with contributions by Dot

Cleminshaw on abortion, Willem Saayman on AIDS, and Dawid Botha on euthanasia. The section on political ethics is introduced by Charles Villa-Vicencio. Malusi Mpumlwana writes on the violence debate, Njongonkulu Ndungane on human rights, James Cochrane on economic justice, John de Gruchy and David Field on ecology, and Weli Mazamisa on reparation and land. The South African aspects of the debate on all of these issues are considered.

Should these contributions succeed in generating ethical debate, they will have served their purpose. A brief bibliography is provided at the end of most chapters. By drawing on these and other sources, students will be able to offer their own critique of what is found between the covers of this book. They will hopefully begin to formulate their own ethical approach to decision-making and begin to wrestle with some of the ethical problems facing society. Ethics is, however, never reflection for the sake of reflection. It requires people to analyse, think and critically reflect in order to act and share in the process of making the world a more just and decent place in which to live. This action must, in turn, give rise to further reflection and self-critique. Doing ethics involves participation in an action—reflection—action continuum.

The editors acknowledge the assistance of Pat Lawrence, David Field, Steve Martin, Noel Stott and Gita Valodia. Our sincere appreciation goes also to all the contributors to this volume.

[1] José Miguez Bonino, *Toward a Christian Political Ethics* (Philadelphia: Fortress Press, 1983), p. 9.

[2] Philip Selznick, *The Moral Commonwealth: Social Theory and the Promise of Community* (Berkeley: University of California Press, 1992).

PART ONE
Introductory Themes

1

Ethics in a Theological Context

LOUISE KRETZSCHMAR

Theological ethics draws on a number of different disciplines. At the same it retains a distinctively Christian theological character. While this particular study is written from within the Christian tradition, an attempt is made in what follows to address such general questions as the nature of ethics, the relationship between ethics and other disciplines, and the factors which influence our perceptions of what is right and wrong or good and evil. Finally, the task of theological ethics will be examined.

What Is Ethics?

Many people are of the opinion that ethics has merely to do with individual actions such as drinking, smoking, pornography, and stealing. This perception of ethics is both limited and superficial. It is limited in the sense that it concentrates on the activities of individuals, ignoring the interface between individuals and the social realm. It is superficial because, even at the personal level, it pays insufficient attention to motives and psychological drives, failing to take into account the extent to which personal and social ethical problems are interrelated. An adulterous relationship that leads to a divorce, for example, may on first sight appear to be an ethical issue between two persons. On closer examination, however, it is clear that it impacts on the marriages, children, wider families, friends and associates of the couple involved. As such, it has a wide interpersonal and social impact.

A further reason why an exclusively individualistic understanding of ethics is invalid is that such a perception of ethics is unbiblical. The Hebrew prophets, for example, stressed that both personal and social morality are vital to true religion (see Amos 5:21–24; Mic. 6:6–8; and Isa. 1:11–17). Jesus, in turn, did not restrict his ministry to preaching that individuals should be saved. He ministered to individuals as persons with a variety of social and psychological needs, not simply as souls that needed to be saved (Luke 4:1–44). He healed the sick and cast out demons (Matt. 4:23–25); he severely criticised the Pharisees and Sadducees who were the religious *and* political leaders of his day (Matt. 23:1–36); he fed the hungry (Matt. 14:13–21); and he forgave sins (Luke 5:17–26; 19:1–10). The early church, too, combined personal and social ethics (Acts 2:43–47; 4:32–35; 11:27–30; 1 Cor. 16:1–9; James 2:1–26; 5:1–61; and John 3:13–18).

A Definition of Ethics

How, then, can ethics be defined? It is not easy to come up with a definition of ethics that satisfies everyone because definitions of ethics emerge from people's understanding of what constitutes an ethical problem. Further, because we live in different contexts, our definitions reflect these contexts. Essentially, ethics has to do with what we perceive to be right or wrong, good or bad.

Differently stated, ethics is often regarded as an understanding of what 'ought' to be. The use of the word 'ought' implies that there is a radical distinction between what 'is' and what 'ought to be'. Ethics may also be seen as a code or set of principles by which people seek to live their lives. William Barclay defines ethics as 'the science of behaviour. Ethics is the bit of religion that tells us how we ought to behave.'[1]

Klaus Nürnberger defines theological ethics as 'a reflection on what ought to be and on how we can be liberated and motivated to bring it about'.[2] This definition implies that reflection and rational analysis are not enough; one must also be 'liberated' and 'motivated' in order to put what one believes into practice. In this view, it is not enough to say what ought to be the case; a Christian ethic also implies that there is a way in which people, situations and structures can be transformed. To put it differently, people need to be saved from sin, despair and oppression through the redeeming work of Christ in order that they may be empowered to be different and act differently. Thus, the essential difference between a purely human or philosophical ethic and a Christian ethic is that the latter seeks to move, by the grace of God, beyond analysis to personal liberation and redemptive action in the world.

A Christian theological ethic, then, can be defined as follows: an understanding of what ought to be, a willingness on the part of individual believers to be saved and to become disciples of Jesus Christ, and a commitment on the part of both individual believers and communities to preach and practise their faith with reference to human, social and physical reality.

The problems that confront our modern world are legion. They exist at a personal or psychological level, at a social or structural level, in the realm of philosophy and ideology, and at a global or international level. Because the Christian ethic is a normative rather than a purely descriptive ethic, it seeks to answer the question 'How should we live?' rather than 'How do we live?' The Christian ethic is also normative in the sense that it considers certain values and actions as inherently right or good and their opposites as wrong or evil.

The Christian ethic is further concerned not merely with theological theory but with theological praxis. Praxis is the ongoing critical and creative interplay between reflection and action (or theory and practice). Theory needs to be informed by action, and action by theory. Theological ethics, then, is not a matter of abstract theorising; it is a process through which believers seek to provide answers to the real questions that people are asking about their faith and its application to their personal and social existence.

Ethical Methodology

How do people arrive at ethical judgements or decisions? What criteria (yardsticks or approaches) have they used? Did they use a *deontological* approach based on norms — that is, on their view of what is right or wrong, good or bad. For instance, the statement 'abortion is wrong because it amounts to killing and it is wrong to kill' reflects a deontological approach. Such an approach is centred on rules or principles of what is right or wrong, in and of itself, despite the consequences.

Another approach is a *teleological* one, in which a person takes a decision on the basis of the consequences of an action. Teleological judgements are made on the basis of the goal or result of an action being considered to have moral worth. For example, in the case of a woman falling pregnant as a result of being raped, it may be argued that the consequences for the woman, her family and the child are so negative that abortion could be justified. Thus, utilitarianism (from the Latin *utilis*, meaning useful) makes moral judgements on the basis of the usefulness of an action. Something is judged to be good if it results in 'the greatest good for the greatest number'.

Often people make decisions purely on the basis of whatever emotion is dominant at that time, or on the basis of what they perceive to be in their own interests. Others may claim personal intuition ('I just knew') or the guidance of the Holy Spirit ('God told me to do it'). In making ethical decisions, people are also strongly influenced by relationships (personal or social). Thus, someone might say, 'If I have an abortion I will be ostracised by my community.' As indicated throughout this volume, people use a variety of ethical criteria and methods in making ethical decisions.

The Scope of Theological Ethics

The study of ethics is important, even vital. Unless we are aware of what we believe and why we believe it, it will be easy for other people to manipulate us into accepting their belief systems, commitments and actions. Further, in order to relate meaningfully with the world around us, we need to understand what others believe and why they believe it. Understanding does not constitute agreement, but it does imply the willingness to listen and enter into a dialogue with those around us. For those who are committed to the proclamation and practical expression of a Christian theological ethic, a proper understanding of their own beliefs and those of others is a necessary first step.

The Relationship Between Ethics and Other Academic Disciplines

Ethics is in many ways an eclectic discipline which freely draws upon a number of different sources; therefore it is best pursued in an interdisciplinary manner.

This being the case, it is necessary to examine briefly the relationship between ethics as well as other theological disciplines and a variety of other academic disciplines.

Theological Disciplines

In addition to theological ethics, the theological disciplines include biblical studies, missiology, church history, systematic theology, practical theology and cognate disciplines such as the science of religion and religious studies. Space does not permit a detailed examination of the points of agreement or disagreement between all these disciplines. I will restrict myself to a few comments that indicate the relationship (indeed interdependence) between them.

Biblical Studies. Theological ethics often draws heavily on the Bible as a source of moral teaching and authority. Indeed, the creeds or statements of belief of many churches affirm the Bible as 'the supreme and final authority for faith and life'. What is less clear is how the Bible's moral injunctions are to be interpreted. This is the case for at least two reasons. Firstly, the Bible was written over a long period of time and reflects a development in the religious perceptions and experiences of both the Jews and the Christians. This immediately raises the question as to how the prescriptions of an ancient and historically diverse book can be applied to our contemporary situation. Secondly, the Bible itself has, over the centuries, been the subject of intense debate. Various schools of thought have sought to develop a paradigm (framework of understanding) according to which it can be reliably interpreted. More recent examples include structuralism, evangelicalism, liberation theology, feminist theology and post-modernism.

The problem of the Bible and ethics is dealt with elsewhere in this volume. A single observation must therefore suffice. Ethicists need to ask how the ethical teachings of the Bible can, firstly, be understood in terms of the context in which they were written and, secondly, be applied to the various contexts in the modern world.

Missiology. Missiology addresses the question concerning the mission or task of the church. Various answers to this question have been given. These include the saving of souls; preaching the gospel; healing the sick; ministry to the marginalised; empowering the poor; liberating the downtrodden.[3] Ethical debate is clearly related to all these issues.

Church History. The history of ethics is obviously quite closely related to church history. For example, an analysis of the economic systems as either legitimated or resisted over the years cannot be undertaken without a consideration of the various social and ecclesiastical contexts that have pertained since the first century. Similarly, an analysis of sexual ethics cannot be undertaken without a knowledge of the interrelationship between socio-cultural and theological perceptions of, amongst other things, the nature and role of women in church and society.

Systematic Theology. Theological perceptions of matters such as the nature of humanity, the nature and task of the church, the meaning of Christ's incarnation, the origin and purpose of the natural world, and the end (or goal) of existence, profoundly influence our notions of what is right and wrong, or good and bad.

For instance, questions about homosexuality cannot be pursued in isolation from our conception of the nature of human beings. The hotly debated question of whether women should be ordained is determined in part by whether we perceive Christ's incarnation and ministry as an affirmation and example of what constitutes redeemed humanity or as evidence for God's essential masculinity. Ecological issues cannot be distanced from our doctrines of creation and redemption. Finally, our vision of the nature and realisation of God's kingdom (or rule) profoundly affects our notions of present and ultimate justice, judgement, reconciliation and salvation.

Practical Theology. Practical theology focuses attention on the self-understanding and activities of the local church (and the church as an institution) with respect to preaching, teaching and discipleship, celebration or worship, church government and administration, counselling, and its service those to both within the church and in the community at large.

Science of Religion. The science of religion has been significantly influenced by the impact of the social sciences, not least by social anthropology. This has resulted in an attempt by scholars to 'bracket' or suspend their beliefs in order to understand with empathy the views and values of people of different religions, as well as one's own religion. The science of religion has opened up an awareness of the differences between religions, which is especially relevant in South Africa today. The fact that our Muslim, Jewish and Hindu neighbours see things differently can illuminate a Christian ethical perspective. Ethical reflection can only benefit from exposure to different world-views, religions and ideologies.

Theological ethics is, thus, closely related to biblical studies, missiology, church history, systematic theology, practical theology, and the science of religion.

The Other Academic Disciplines

The interdisciplinary methodology of theological ethics also means that it interacts with a number of other disciplines. Discussion is limited in what follows to a consideration of aspects of philosophy, history, the natural sciences, and the human or social sciences.

Philosophy. For much of Western history, philosophy has exercised an enormous influence on theology and, therefore, on theological ethics. In particular, the Greek philosophers Plato and Aristotle had a significant impact on the early church fathers and, later, on Augustine and Aquinas. Throughout the Middle Ages, and up to the twentieth century, philosophies such as those of Descartes, Hume, Kant, Hegel, Feuerbach, Marx and Whitehead have had a major impact on Western perceptions of humanity and the world in which we live. The influence of these philosophers (and attendant movements such as the Enlightenment, rationalism, idealism, deism, secularism and positivism) has been extended throughout the world.

More recently, the influence of philosophy on religious thought has become more diffuse because a host of differing world-views originating from Latin America, Africa and Asia have challenged, or mingled with, predominantly Western philosophies. This has led to the widespread acceptance of views such as relativism. According to this view there are no ethical absolutes; ethics is always relative to particular persons or circumstances. Recognising that no one philosophical system is presently dominant in theological debate, theological ethics can only become better equipped to cope with the challenges of decision-making by being located within philosophical debate.

History. Mention has already been made of church history. History, in its broader dimensions, is equally important for ethics. This means that it is not satisfactory to refer to all that falls outside of the parameters of church history as secular history, because the study of secular history (what some feminists call 'herstory') cannot be so neatly separated from religious history. Thus, if one studies the Reformation, there are a number of approaches that can be adopted. For example, one may study the socio-economic and doctrinal aspects of the Reformation from a Marxist perspective, or the new theological teaching and its social consequences from a Calvinist, Lutheran or Anabaptist perspective. Furthermore, any doctrinal studies cannot ignore the social context within which these beliefs emerged, nor can economic analyses ignore the ideological context in which economic changes occurred.

Perhaps the central reason why a knowledge of history is important is that it can provide a context within which theological ethics can be identified and evaluated. This is necessary both because roots are important to us as persons and groups and also because what might be valid in one age might be less valid or even unethical in another. For example, it could be argued that Calvin supported the emergence of capitalism because the Protestant city-state of Geneva was an industrial and financial centre. Calvin regarded the financiers who provided capital and credit to small businesses as offering a service to the city's inhabitants. Thus, although he insisted that certain restrictions be placed on the lending of capital (for instance, he stated that those in financial difficulties should not be charged interest!), he did not object in principle to interest being charged on loans.[4] Arguably, Calvin was also well aware that the future of Protestantism in Geneva was dependent on the ability of the city to survive in a religiously and economically hostile environment.

These examples show how a knowledge of particular historical contexts is vital if we are to arrive at a proper understanding and evaluation of ethical comment and values.

Natural Sciences. Technically speaking, the debates between theology and 'modern' science date back to the sixteenth century when the use of the inductive method of scientific inquiry began to be advocated and employed. But it was with the publication of Charles Darwin's *Origin of Species by Means of Natural Selection* (1859) and *The Descent of Man* (1871) that the scientific and religious world was thrown into controversy. The repercussions of this conflict were intense and long-lasting, particularly for Christian doctrines about the origins and nature of the world and humanity.

Several important debates followed, one of which concerned primary and secondary causality. Darwin, for instance, never claimed that his evolutionary theories constituted an explanation for the origin of the world but only for the evolution of matter. Furthermore, because science was for so long dominated by the philosophy of positivism, a broad divide was thought to exist between science and religion. Positivism taught that only science can provide knowledge of phenomena and true knowledge. Metaphysics and religion were dismissed as false and illusionary.[5] The irony is that whereas prominent scientists no longer adhere to the philosophy of positivism (especially since the rise of quantum physics earlier this century), positivism is still dominant in popular thinking.[6]

The enormous growth of the natural sciences since the nineteenth century has changed the face of our world. The basic disciplines of physics, chemistry, zoology and botany have branched out into a host of others, including nuclear physics, ecological management, space technology, electronics and the like. Such developments have solved certain problems, but also created others. Ethical issues arising from the burgeoning of modern science and technology include whether rapid and uncontrolled industrialisation and the use of nuclear energy can be regarded as advantageous; whether humanity can actually bring to a halt the frightening levels of environmental pollution and the rapid destruction of natural habitats for fauna and flora; and why the world persists in making extensive use of non-renewable fossil fuels. Put differently, science and scientists can certainly not be regarded as morally neutral.

Medical science, in turn, has made possible contraception, abortion, organ transplants and the treatment of a host of illnesses including diabetes, certain forms of cancer, polio, tuberculosis and malaria. As a result of these developments, medical ethics is a vital, fast-growing and complex field of theological ethics. In South Africa, the present state of the health care services makes a proper understanding and application of the ethical implications of medical science an urgent necessity.

The Human or Social Sciences. Since the nineteenth century the work of anthropologists (such as Lévi-Strauss, Evans-Pritchard and Frazer), sociologists (such as Durkheim, Weber and Marx), and psychologists (such as Freud, Jung and Erikson) has radically altered the way that humans perceive themselves, their world and God.[7]

Anthropologists have exposed us to a number of host cultures in which the religions, kinship structures, economies and political systems may be significantly dissimilar to our own. For Christians, this exposure has raised a number of issues, including the relationship between Christian faith and culture. What is essentially Christian and what is merely Western? How can the Christian faith be 'Africanised' or 'Asianised'? Is there anything distinctive or authoritative about Christian ethics, or are all ethical systems culturally derived and of equal validity? Are all religions roughly equivalent and equally valid ways to God, or do Christians continue to affirm that Jesus is 'the way, the truth and the life' (John 14.6)?

Psychologists have shown us that our personalities include not only a conscious but also an unconscious dimension; and that the unconscious, if continually unrecognised and repressed, can exercise a much greater influence on our lives than the conscious. Although psychologists may disagree about the precise nature and influence of the unconscious, their work raises questions about the extent to which theology has concentrated its energies on the conscious and rational aspects of our personalities at the expense of other dimensions. This could explain, for example, why apparently ethical persons behave in wholly unethical ways when they believe their interests to be threatened; why moral individuals create immoral social structures; and why religion can function either as a liberating and healing mechanism or in a repressive and destructive manner.[8]

At its best, the discipline of psychology raises the question of the impact of religion on our lives and personalities. How do various religions function in psychological terms? Is religion, as Freud believed, evidence of neurosis or, as Jung believed, a means of attaining human health and integration? Which religions (or forms of a particular religion) lead to emotional and mental health and which lead to character disorders and psychological illness?

Sociology has, over the past hundred years, developed into a complex and controversial discipline. Essentially, though, it is concerned with the way in which societies function: how they control their members, how they socialise children, how they develop during periods of social transition, how their economic, political and cultural systems come into being and are perpetuated.

Sociologists of religion have been primarily concerned with the social function of religion. Thus, a distinction is made between the manifest and latent functions of religion. Manifest functions are those that are identified by the adherents themselves (such as the need for salvation), whilst the latent functions are those identified by sociologists (for example, the contribution religion makes to social cohesion, control or change). This raises the question whether, in South Africa, religion functions as a mechanism of social control (as Karl Marx argued) or as a means of social cohesion (Durkheim) or, under certain circumstances, as a means of social transformation (Max Weber).[9]

Another important dimension of sociology, as it impacts on theological ethics, is the influence of our social background on the development of our ethical beliefs and actions. More is said about this later, but at this point it is important to note that our social location — that is, our racial, class, culture and gender loyalties — certainly influence our theological ethics.

To sum up, theological ethics cannot be pursued in isolation. Not only the theological disciplines but also a host of other disciplines can inform and challenge our ethical analyses, values and actions.

Factors That Influence Ethical Judgements and Decisions

Consideration has been given to the relationship between theological ethics and other theological and academic disciplines. We now turn to a consideration of other factors which impact on our decision-making.[10] People often think that they arrive at their ethical viewpoints in an entirely rational, objective and neutral manner. In actual fact, there are a great many additional (often dominant) factors that influence the way we perceive ethical issues and the way we act upon these perceptions. One of these factors is the influence of our personal experience and family background, the other is the impact of our social context.

Personal Experience and Family Background

The experiences of children of growing up in a family (or as orphans) have a deep and lasting influence on their personalities. Even if people have a fairly 'normal' childhood, there is a host of factors that influence their personalities and their perceptions. If, on the other hand, children experience great trauma, this cannot but affect them profoundly. The exact influences of childhood experiences cannot be predicted, because the personality of each child is different and three children from the same home may end up with very different moral perceptions. Nevertheless, personal and family experiences are very important factors in the development of moral values, especially because many of these experiences occur before children are able to verbalise or fully understand what is happening to them. Consequently, these experiences and perceptions are often stored in the subconscious and may never be integrated with the rest of their personality.

A number of examples can be cited. The quality of their parents' marriage will have some influence on their emotional reaction to the idea of getting married themselves or making commitments. Their relationship with siblings may lead them to feel that they are loved and accepted or that they need to fight for their place in the sun. Children who witness continual domestic violence, or are themselves victims of physical, emotional or sexual abuse, end up severely traumatised and emotionally scarred. Children who have experienced forced removals instituted by the government or grew up without a father because of migrant labour will almost certainly later have strong feelings and views about injustice and economic exploitation. Children growing up in white racist homes may find it difficult in later life to see blacks as individual persons rather than as a threatening group.

In all these instances, the moral perceptions of children about sexual, social, political and economic ethics may be formed long before they are capable of rational decision-making. If early perceptions are not identified and reviewed, they may continue to exercise an unconscious but extremely powerful effect on a person's moral judgement.[11] In short, the moral or immoral actions of each individual impacts on the lives of other individuals, particularly in the context of the family.[12]

The importance of personal influences is not restricted to our childhood or early adolescence. The choices we make as teenagers or adults also have a greater or lesser impact on the rest of our lives. Decisions related to our studies, jobs, church involvement, close friendships, ongoing relationships with family members, marriage and so on have an enormous impact on our lives. They affect our world-views, the circles we move in, our relationship with God, our careers and family circumstances, what we do in our spare time, and our socio-economic circumstances.

All this means that we need to be aware that our ethical decisions may be made on the basis of unconscious factors (deep inner drives and needs) rather than conscious ones. Thus, the conscious reasons we give for our views or actions are not necessarily the most important ones. They may simply be rational justifications for deeper, hidden reasons of which we may not even be aware or which we feel we cannot possibly admit to ourselves, let alone to others. This does not mean that such influences are deterministic in nature. If we acknowledge their existence and influence and seek to deal with the effects that they have had on our personalities (for example, through some form of counselling), we can be delivered from their power over us. However, denying their existence or repressing their attendant emotions will only increase the impact that our past has on both our present and our future.

Social Context and the Convictions of Social Groups

In our century, particularly as a result of the discoveries of the human or social sciences, much more attention has been given to the role that our entire social context plays in the formation of our moral notions and behaviour. All of us owe some allegiance to various groups within our society and all these groups have identities and interests which they are concerned to protect. This means that it is not sufficient to look at the moral beliefs of individuals; we also need to look at the moral convictions of social groups. Niebuhr put it like this:

> Individual men may be moral in the sense that they are able to consider interests other than their own in determining problems of conduct, and are capable, on occasion, of preferring the advantages of others to their own ... But all these achievements are more difficult, if not impossible, for human societies and social groups.[13]

Group interests can be defined as the concerns, values, hopes and ambitions that are shared by a particular community. Social groups generally share certain common perceptions, interests and values. For example, the theological questions asked by those groups which daily experience hunger, homelessness and hopelessness will differ significantly from, those groups whose basic human needs for food, shelter and the means to achieve their aims are satisfied. Similarly, the poor and the rich will respond differently to passages in the Bible such as Matthew 19:16–26 (the rich young ruler) and Acts 2:37–47 (the communalism of the early church).

This brings us to the issue of ideological commitments and the fact that theology and ideology are very closely linked since groups often seek to justify their interests by claiming that these interests have divine authority or support. The word 'ideology' has a number of technical meanings which we shall not unpack here.[14] Suffice it to say that, in a general sense, an ideology is a world-view or a mindset to which a person or group is committed. Such ideologies include nationalism, capitalism, socialism, racism, integration and separatism. Ideologies are expressions of those socio-cultural, political or economic realities to which we are committed. Ideologies, then, reflect our basic world-views.

The word 'ideology' is also used in a negative or pejorative sense. In this sense, ideologies reflect the basic interests, fears and ambitions of a specific group. Ideologies are developed by groups to justify or legitimate their attitudes, interests and actions. Thus, ideologies often obscure (or cover up) the real reasons of the group propounding them. For example, in the 1960s Dr Verwoerd argued that 'separate development' would benefit black South Africans because it would preserve their identity and ethnic institutions. The real reason behind the ideology of apartheid, as history has shown us, was to promote white and, particularly, Afrikaner interests at the expense of black interests. Within the present debate about South Africa's political and constitutional future a number of ideological frameworks and commitments are to be seen. These include a unitary democracy, federalism or regionalism, individual rights, and group and, especially, minority group rights.

All this should warn us that groups are always able and willing to use religion to justify and legitimate their own interests. We all want to have God on our side. Thus, British imperialism devised the notion of the 'white man's burden', slave owners used the letter to Philemon to argue that Paul supported slavery, and certain men have used selected Pauline texts to prevent women from exercising God-given spiritual gifts such as leadership, prophecy, teaching and pastoring. In all these instances, selected aspects of religion were (and are) used to support the *status quo* and to legitimate the interests of the powerful against the critique and resistance of marginalised, ignored, exploited and patronised groups.

But religion has not only been used to prop up the *status quo*. There is also another side to the story, namely that religion has acted as a subversive force. Thus, certain of the sixteenth-century Anabaptists were part of the Radical Reformation and sought to give socio-political and economic expression to their religious faith. The English Civil War of 1642–1660 was led and supported by Puritans, Separatists, Presbyterians and Baptists. More recently in South Africa, proponents of Black and liberation theologies have been in the forefront of the struggle against apartheid.

This should prompt the question whether social groups are misusing religion to justify and promote their own interests, and whether it is right for Christians to lend their support to particular persons, policies or parties. It is useless to argue that 'religion and politics should not mix' for they are, inevitably, interconnected. Believers cannot exist outside a social context. Even those groups or churches that seek to distance themselves from social affairs are making a political choice. For by withdrawing, they are lending *de facto* support to the groups that are presently in power. Even if they are unaware of it, they are supporters of the political *status quo*. The difference between religious persons or groups that are actively involved in political issues and those that withdraw from active participation is not that the former are political and the latter are apolitical. Rather the former wish to see and promote change whilst the latter wish to retard or avoid change.[15]

The ethical issue that Christian individuals and groups need to face is not whether they should be involved in politics (since all are in some sense already involved). The key questions are how they should be involved, whom they should support, and on what basis they can claim that their choices are compatible with their Christian faith. Christians should also be aware of the influence of their racial, cultural, class and gender loyalties on their moral judgements and in the way they interpret the Bible.[16]

The Bible

The point has already been made: it is one thing to say the Bible is a source of ethical values; it is quite another to agree on the interpretation of biblical passages. The technical term for interpretation is hermeneutics. In this regard, two vital components of biblical interpretation are a consideration of the biblical context itself and the contexts of modern interpreters.

Why is the biblical context important? Because we cannot simply make use of isolated texts to support our ethical viewpoints. We need to take into account the contexts in which such verses occur as well as other, related texts to be found elsewhere in the pages of the Bible. For example, with reference to the matter of birth control, it is not enough to cite God's command 'Be fruitful and multiply and fill the earth' (Gen. 1:28) without also bearing in mind other verses which relate to the purpose of marriage (Gen. 2:18–25; 1 Cor. 7:1–40; and Eph. 5: 1–33 – not just v. 22), responsible parenting (1 Tim. 5:8) and celibacy (Matt. 19:12; 1 Cor. 7:17).[17]

What, then, of the context of the modern interpreter? In recent years, liberation theologians have insisted that the personal and social experiences of people, as well as their racial, class, gender and cultural loyalties, significantly influence the way in which they interpret biblical texts. No one comes to the Bible with a completely 'open' mind. Whether we admit it or not, we all view the Bible through a certain 'set of spectacles'. Consequently, the more we become aware of our own ideological commitments (and the more we are exposed to the interpretations of those who come from different contexts from ourselves), the more we will be able to learn from the text rather than manipulate it for our own (often unacknowledged) individual and social purposes.

The Church

The church, too, has been a major source of moral authority, particularly for individual Christians but also for the wider society. Clearly, in countries where Christians are in the minority, the church's influence has been more circumscribed.

In what ways has the church exercised moral authority? Firstly, as a major social institution. This was particularly evident during the Middle Ages when the Roman Catholic Church exercised both spiritual and temporal authority in Europe.[18] In terms of the Constantinian model instituted by the Roman emperor in 313, church and state formed a unity in which the latter was undoubtedly the senior partner. Under certain popes such as Innocent III, the balance of power tilted towards the church, and it was able to exercise enormous influence over the national states of Europe. During this time, the church as an institution made and unmade kings and queens, declared crusades, and held complete moral sway over the socio-religious lives of millions of people through its control of baptism, marriage and burials and its influence over education, the arts, law and medicine. In effect, the church was the moral authority within Europe.

After the Reformation of the sixteenth century, the monolithic Constantinian unity of church and state was broken up, and social, political and economic rivalry increasingly created a divided and progressively secular Europe. Rationalism, deism, the rise of modern science, the effects of the industrial revolution, the emergence of democratic ideals, and various forms of secularism successively broke the absolute moral and intellectual power of the Christian church.[19]

By the beginning of the twentieth century, there was a bewildering variety of religious denominations in Europe, and the majority of the population no longer attended church on Sunday. The moral authority of the church as an institution had been severely weakened. Its authority was now indirect, rather than direct, and its moral judgement was more often ignored.[20]

Church authority is ultimately, however, communicated to most Christians through their own local community or church. These local churches are not, however, simple channels of the major ideas and influences of the universal church. They are shaped and influenced by their own location within the community of which they are a part. However, some churches have mistakenly sought to escape from their social responsibilities within the community and have ended up preaching and propagating what has been called a privatised form of the Christian faith.

Privatisation can be defined as the limitation of the gospel to the private, spiritual concerns of the individual. A privatised understanding of the gospel is inherently dualistic (it creates a false distinction between spiritual and material reality) and individualistic (it concentrates on individual reality whilst ignoring social reality). It spiritualises the gospel by, for example, stressing that salvation and reconciliation have to do with our relationship with God alone and not also with our relationships with one other. It is a-contextual because it interprets the Christian faith in purely abstract and theoretical terms rather than asking how our faith can actually be lived out in the context of all the practical problems that beset us. Those churches which espouse a privatised gospel either avoid the public sphere or respond to it in an uncritical and ineffective manner, thereby rendering themselves vulnerable to manipulation by group interests. Consequently, 'a privatised gospel both fails to bring about holistic spiritual renewal in the lives of individual believers and it is unable to promote either ecclesiastical or social transformation'.[21]

There are, however, those churches who do seek to involve themselves both in their local communities and in the process of transforming the evil and unjust social structures in the nation at large. Unfortunately, because South Africa is so divided, as a result of racism and the effect of laws such as the Group Areas Act, different churches in South Africa perceive their role in society in rather different ways. Also, the people to which they seek to minister experience very different problems.

What does it mean to be a Christian in these different situations? How can the churches exercise both moral restraint and leadership? What should Christians be saying and doing in the contexts in which they live? We return to these questions in a subsequent section, but it should be clear that to a greater or lesser extent our moral values are influenced by the church — both as an institution and as a force in the local community. The issue of whether the influence of the church is positive or negative depends entirely on the particular circumstances, individuals and groups involved.

Theology

A major source of moral teaching is to be found in the theology or tradition of the church. The word 'theology' is made up of two Greek words, *theos* (God) and *logos* (word). Theology has, thus, been defined as 'words about God' or as 'God-talk'. Such a definition, however, overemphasises the aspects of thought, discussion, and writing about God, and underemphasises the practical implications of believing in God. Therefore many theologians now talk about 'doing' theology – that is, not simply seeking to describe who God is or what God wills, but actually being involved alongside God in the world. As the Latin American theologian Gustavo Gutiérrez puts it: 'the theology of liberation offers us not so much a new theme for reflection as a *new way* to do theology. This is a theology which does not stop with reflecting on the world, but tries to be a part of the process through which the world is transformed.'[22]

It can be seen, then, that definitions of theology have enormous implications for our understanding of theological ethics. If it is the task of the church to be actively involved in the process of the redemption of the world, the ethical task of identifying 'what is and what ought to be' is a vital component of this process.

Whereas Catholics have long emphasised the importance of tradition, Protestants have often stressed the authority of the Bible as superior to that of tradition. As a Protestant myself, I believe that the Bible (and not theology or church tradition) is the highest authority, but it would be naïve to think that Protestants do not, in practice, accord a very important place to tradition. This fact is clearly reflected in the theological praxis of the many denominations within Protestantism. Calvinists, Lutherans, Methodists and Presbyterians, for example, all place great importance on the theologies of Calvin, Luther and Wesley as well as on catechisms such as the Augsburg (1530), Heidelberg (1562–3) and Westminster (1648) confessions. Even Charismatics and Pentecostals have their own traditions and theological emphases that characterise the beliefs and practices of their churches.

In addition to being understood as a synonym for theology, the word 'tradition' can also be used in a more general sense. In this instance it would mean 'what is traditionally thought and done'. All local churches have their own ways of doing things and are, more often than not, extremely reluctant to try anything new. In terms of the ethical understanding and activities of churches, this can have both positive and negative consequences. For example, if a church has a tradition of using 30 per cent of its monthly income for the help of those who are in need, it will be compelled to develop ministries that identify, care for and empower the poor, sick and helpless. This would be a positive manifestation of a church's tradition. But there are also negative manifestations of tradition. For example, churches that have always understood mission purely in terms of personal evangelism will find it difficult to develop ministries that more closely resemble the ministry of Jesus.[23] This will be even more difficult for middle-class or ruling-class churches whose members less often are poor, uneducated, unable to pay for health care, unemployed and socially marginalised. Very few of the members of such churches will want to move out of their 'comfort zones' and actually practise their faith as did Jesus and the early disciples.

Theology and church tradition, then, also play an important role in shaping our moral perceptions and actions.

The Holy Spirit

The early church was empowered and led by the Holy Spirit. 'The New Testament view of Christian ethics', says David Cook, 'is dependent on the view that God's Holy Spirit dwells in the hearts and minds of Christian believers.'[24] In fulfilment of Jesus' promise (John 14:16–17), the Holy Spirit empowered the disciples (Acts 2:1–4), enabling them to preach, heal, and defy the Sanhedrin in the name of Jesus of Nazareth (Acts 2:14–4:22). It was the work of the Holy Spirit that led to thousands being converted (Acts 2:41, 47; 5:14). The Holy Spirit guided the disciples (Acts 11:1–18) and enabled a relatively small group of Christians to 'turn the world upside down' (Acts 17:6).

Ever since then, the guidance of the Holy Spirit has been cited as a moral basis for actions. A variety of terms has been used: the conscience, the 'still, small voice', intuition and the like. Essentially, then, the moral guidance of the Spirit is experienced as an inner moral voice (Jer. 31:31–34; Acts 8:29) which, at times, is clear to a number of believers (Acts 13:2). It is the task of the Holy Spirit to teach, guide and lead believers into all truth (John 14:25–31; 15:21–16:15). Consequently, the accuracy of this voice depends on the degree of spiritual maturity attained by the person claiming to be led by the Spirit.[25]

In recent years, the rise of the charismatic movement has re-emphasised themes such as the baptism of the Spirit, the filling of the Spirit, dreams and visions, special revelations, and the *charismata* (or grace-gifts) of 1 Corinthians 12:1–11, Romans 12:1–8 and Ephesians 4:1–16. The problem is that these gifts can be distorted and abused. It is significant that Paul's letter to the Corinthians seems to have been prompted precisely by the abuse of the gifts of the Spirit. How does one know that it is the Spirit that is speaking and not simply our own wishful thinking? In addition, the experiences themselves constitute insufficient evidence since ecstatic experiences are common in a number of different religions. For this reason, Christians have often emphasised that claims to extraordinary guidance from the Spirit must be tested against the Bible because the guidance of the Spirit in one's heart cannot conflict with the guidance of the Spirit in the Word of God and in the Christian community.

The Task of Theological Ethics

From the preceding pages it should be clear that the scope of theological ethics is not a narrow or circumscribed one. A holistic and contextual approach to the Christian faith needs to be developed in order for us to properly understand and effectively practise a genuinely Christian ethic.

Theological ethics is inescapably linked to the *missio Dei*, the mission of God in the world. God's love for and involvement with the world (not just human beings) begins with creation, continues through the Fall and all of human history, is revealed repeatedly throughout the Old Testament and especially in Christ, is reflected in the establishment of the church and its mission of living out the rule of God in the world, and ends in the final realisation of God's rule, or kingdom. This raises the question: What is the task of ethics? It encompasses at least the following dimensions: analysis, the proclamation of salvation or liberation, and practical action. Even though the last dimension specifically concentrates on action, all the dimensions involve Christians in the task of reflection, declaration and action. In short, theological ethics means that we must be thinking about, speaking about and doing the will of God in the world.

Analysis

The first task of ethics is to identify the nature, extent and causes of the many ethical problems that exist in our world. This process needs to be both descriptive and analytical; that is, it both states what the problems are and explains why such problems arise. In this process of analysis, the context of the problem needs to be taken into account since the application of the Christian faith to social reality is not a generalised process.[26] What are some of the types of problems confronting us, needing to be analysed and understood?

To begin with, a description and analysis of the situation of individual persons is necessary. Many people experience the world as a lonely or threatening place, they are alienated from it and one other, they are marginalised, they are unsure whether there is any purpose to their existence, they experience grief, worry and uncertainty. In the deepest recesses of their being, they ask questions such as 'Is there a God?'; 'Why did God allow my child to die?'; 'Who am I?'; 'Is there forgiveness for me?'; 'How can I give and receive love?' As a result of rapid social change, many have experienced a loss of spiritual values. People seek, unsuccessfully, to fill this spiritual void with promiscuity, alcohol, work, being busy, drugs, consumerism, a lust for power, mindless entertainment, and so on. Despite the many technological advancements in our world, we are still confronted with the age-old questions 'Where do I come from?', 'What am I doing here?', and 'Where am I going?'

The next step in the process of analysis is an examination of our social or structural context. Why is it that poverty, violence, injustice, hunger and exploitation persist in our world? What have been the social and religious effects of urbanisation, industrialisation and mechanisation? Why are certain people or groups in power and others are marginalised? How do the powerful use their positions, and is it valid for those who are exploited to rise up against their oppressors?

For far too long, churches have sought to stick 'band-aid' plasters on the festering sores in our society instead of examining the root causes for our social sickness. Despite the example of Jesus, there are even those who have said that the concern of the gospel is primarily, or exclusively, to save souls. To counteract such distortions, ethicists or religious believers need to engage in thorough social analysis. In order to make an impact on the social context within which they live, Christians need to examine exactly what constitutes 'good works' and Christian service (Eph. 2:8–10). Otherwise they will never be able to effect social transformations, and will remain preoccupied with social welfare.

Social welfare, though meaningful and vital, is not a sufficient expression of Christians' love for their neighbours. Social analysis will, in addition, enable the churches to be more aware of the existence and influence of the religious legitimations used by social groups to further their own interests — often at the expense of the gospel.[27]

The next element of the task of ethical analysis is theoretical analysis. There are a great many philosophies, ideologies and ideas current in our world today. Christians need to ask which of these are compatible (or partly compatible) with their Christian convictions and which are incompatible. For example, reductionist approaches, such as those common in certain biological and sociological schools of thought which reduce human persons to nothing but chemical reactions or instinctual behaviours, cannot be regarded as compatible with the Christian understanding of humanity as having free will and being ultimately responsible to God.[28]

There is a complex theoretical debate, current especially in South Africa at present, about which economic system Christians should advocate as most likely to solve the problems of high unemployment, poverty, a weak economy, high taxation, insufficient housing, the concentration of wealth in the hands of a few, and inadequate access to land. Should we opt for a market-driven economy or state intervention? Is capitalism or socialism — or some combination of the two — the right solution? What ethical principles should the churches suggest for consideration in economic theorising, and do the churches have the credibility that will prompt political and economic leaders to pay heed to their suggestions?

A further level of analysis is ecclesiastical. This is necessary because it is not enough to say that the church must witness to the world; at times the church is part of the problem rather than part of the solution. For example, it has already been argued that as a result of a privatised understanding of the gospel churches are unable to apply their faith adequately to their personal and social circumstances.

Another example of the need for ecclesiastical analysis flows from the fact that theology (as well as theological education) has sometimes been pursued in a wholly abstract and irrelevant way. For example, what is the point of South African theological students becoming experts on Augustine, Calvin, Barth and Bultmann if they are about to minister to a congregation drawn from a poor and uneducated community? Such an understanding of theology is particularly irrelevant if the theological insights of the past are neither studied in relation to the social contexts in which they emerged nor related to present-day contexts. Churches that seek to 'love God and their neighbour' in a way that is abstracted from the actual social crises obtaining all around them are not recognisably Christian. In short, the nature of theology and theological ethics needs to be re-examined and pursued in a contextual manner.

Having stressed the importance of context, we also need to say that a contextual approach must be balanced by an ecumenical and international approach. Theological ethics in South Africa can benefit from exposure to the writings and activities of ethicists from the rest of the world, and ethicists from one denomination can certainly benefit from the views of ethicists from other theological (and religious) traditions. Moreover, the insights of persons that belong to different social groups need to be taken into account. For instance, theological ethicists who have their social roots in the white, English-speaking, middle classes need to be exposed to the approach of blacks who are rooted in the working classes. The tragedy of the South African situation is that our churches have for so long been divided along class, cultural and racial lines. In addition, the voices of women have been ignored or muted, thus enabling theology and ethics to be pursued from a purely male perspective. In all these instances, the need for ecclesiastical analysis is apparent.

The final element of ethical analysis is the necessity for a global perspective. People today cannot live in isolation from their immediate or even their more distant neighbours. High levels of pollution in one country affect the water, air and land of other countries. Uncontrolled deforestation and the use of chemicals that contribute to global warming affect the weather patterns of the entire globe. The wanton disposal of nuclear waste, the destruction of the earth's fauna, flora and natural habitats, and the lack of attention to sustainable development threaten the very future of our existence. Finally, the international money markets and the economic power of the 'first world' often impact negatively upon the everyday existence of people in the 'developing world'.

These few examples indicate that the task of ethical analysis is a large and complex one. It covers a range of vitally important dimensions in our lives, including the personal, social, theoretical, ecclesiastical and global.

The Proclamation of Salvation or Liberation

Despite the obvious importance of analysis, the task of ethics is not complete once problems have been identified and analysed. This is because Christians claim that people and structures can be transformed. The second dimension of the task of ethics has to do with the church's proclamation of the message of salvation, or liberation. 'Liberation' is not understood theologically to encompass socio-political liberation alone. It includes personal, psychological, cultural, political, economic and even theological liberation. People need to be delivered from the many forms of sin and bondage that are daily manifested in our broken world. Sin, indeed, is not simply sin against God (Ps. 51:4), nor is it only adultery, lying, envy or drunkenness (Gal. 5:19–21). Sin can also be manifested in social relations and structures. Injustice, the abuse of power and the exploitation of workers, for example, are also defined by the Bible as sin (see Isa. 1:16–20; Amos 2:6–8; 5.10-24; and Mic. 2:1–5). The gospel is, thus, a message about the kind of transformation that God seeks to bring about in our own personalities, our interpersonal relationships, our social context, our thoughts and paradigms, our churches and, indeed, in all of creation.

Lost, confused, sinful and broken people need to hear that God is present with us and sins can be forgiven; that the grace and love of God can be experienced in the here and now; that a new start can be made; and that their personalities and lives can be radically changed. The Christian gospel is a proclamation of the redemption offered in Jesus Christ and the call to discipleship. However, this proclamation will be totally ineffective unless Christians themselves actually evidence the love, wisdom and compassion of Christ in a practical way to those to whom they preach.

The proclamation of the gospel does not end with the personal appropriation of salvation, for the world in which we live is desperately in need of salvation and renewal. The message of salvation also needs to be extended to the social and structural dimensions of existence.[29] But the Christian gospel of salvation is incomprehensible unless there is some prior understanding of what sin, or evil, is. Although the word 'sin' is not a particularly popular term in our modern-day context, examples of sin and its consequences are not hard to find. Any honest examination of the daily newspapers or television newscasts — or our own hidden motives — reveals the all-too-painful facts of human lust, injustice, dishonesty, indifference, cruelty, and our desire to exploit one other and the natural world.

· Christians can identify those elements of social existence that result in life, prosperity, safety, justice and compassion. Unfortunately, there is insufficient space in this chapter to comment on what the message of salvation should be with regard to the many issues raised in the previous sections. But the meaning of social liberation can be illustrated with respect to the issue of what constitutes good government.

Christian ethicists insist that rulers are not a law unto themselves. Rather they are responsible to the community which they govern, and they will be held accountable for their deeds. Romans 13:1–4 does not constitute a licence for rulers to do as they please but it means that they are to punish evil and reward good, and not, as is all too often the case, the other way round. Jeremiah 22:13–30 outlines the characteristics of good and bad government. Concerning Josiah, we are told:

> ... did not your father eat and drink, and do justice and righteousness?
> Then it was well with him. He pled the cause of the afflicted and the
> needy; then it was well. Is this not what it means to know me? declares
> the Lord (Jer. 15b–16).

But to Jehoiakim, the prophet of the Lord said:

> Woe to him who builds his house without righteousness and his upper
> rooms without justice. Who uses his neighbour's services without pay and
> does not give him his wages... But your eyes and your heart are intent
> only upon your own dishonest gain, and on shedding blood and on
> practising oppression and extortion. (Jer. 22:13, 17)

Since no nation can prosper without leaders of integrity, compassion, wisdom and justice, it is the prophetic role of the church to speak out against those who abuse their power.

The Christian gospel is, then, concerned with the liberation of persons and groups from the bondage of all forms of sin. It is equally concerned with the movement towards the healing and transformation of persons and societies.

Practical Involvement

As the task of ethics goes beyond the safe descriptive analysis of the academy, it remains incomplete unless it also seeks to become, in some way, part of the process of finding solutions. This is why it is necessary to speak of theological praxis, in which theory and practice, analysis and action, intellectual development and practical transformation are welded together.

This brings us back to the question of what the Christian gospel involves. It is clear that God seeks from us not merely intellectual assent, but faith. And faith without works, the letter of James tells us, is dead (James 2:14–26). But how are Christians to relate to 'the world'? According to William Barclay, Christians must avoid the following three tendencies: to be totally immersed in the world; to completely renounce the world; or to totally withdraw from the world. Rather, the Christian must combine 'involvement and detachment'.[30] Detachment is necessary because Christians need to be in the world without being like it, otherwise they cannot serve it (Rom. 12:1–2). Involvement is also necessary because without it our faith has no practical application.

This was why Evangelicals in England during the revival of the eighteenth century turned their attention to abolishing slavery, preventing child labour, providing education, building hospitals, and reforming the prisons. Christians in South Africa, likewise, could reflect their commitment to Christ by involving themselves in the restructuring of the country's education and health systems, transforming local government structures, the police force and the defence force, reforming the legal system, and providing housing for the homeless, to mention but a few urgent needs. In order to be effective, this task cannot be accomplished by individual Christians acting in isolation. Rather, capable and committed Christians need to form groups and develop proper strategies in order to tackle the many different needs of the country.

Christians need to act as 'salt and light' in society by preserving what is good and exposing what is evil (Matt. 5:13–16). They need to speak out for truth, justice, mercy and peace. They need to expose corruption, cruelty and indifference. In this way they will be living according to the rule of God and act as signposts of the kingdom of God.

Another dimension of practical action is that of empowerment. Not only do Christians need to be motivated and empowered to move out of their 'comfort zones', but they need to empower others. Jesus did this by paying attention to the people whom everyone else ignored and by delivering them from whatever held them in bondage. Thus, lepers were healed, prostitutes and tax-collectors were forgiven, and women were taught (Luke 17:11–19; 10:38–42; 7:36–50; 19:1–10; and John 11:17–37).

Individual people and social groups are in dire need of liberation from fear, uncertainty and the desire to control or oppress others. Once, by God's grace, inner healing and transformation begin to occur, compassion and service can emerge. Thus personal healing and empowerment must precede the attempt to enable others to be empowered, otherwise it becomes a new and subtle form of manipulation and disempowerment. The churches must stand alongside people to empower them and to assist them to devise possible solutions to their problems. But churches, too, need to be delivered from oppressive structures, false teachers and repressive forms of religion (cf. Luke 13:10–17).

Theological ethics, therefore, adopts a world-transforming rather than a world-escaping approach to social and physical realities. This means that God's work of salvation is not to be restricted to a heavenly future. As our Creator, Lord, Saviour, Mother, Father and Friend, God seeks to engage us in the task of the restoration and re-creation of the fallen and broken world in which we currently live. In other words, Old and New Testament passages which reflect God's concern for the sick, poor and powerless (for example, Isa. 58; Mic. 6:6—8 and Luke 8:40—56) have concrete meaning for our lives in the present. God's concern for righteousness, justice, mercy and the correct use of political and spiritual authority (see Matt. 25:31—46; Jer. 7:1—7; 22:13—30; and Luke 11:37—54) should be evidenced in the personal and social dimensions of our lives.

Conclusion

Theological ethics is a fascinating, complex and important field of study. It interacts with all the theological disciplines as well as a number of other academic disciplines including philosophy, history, natural science and the social sciences. A number of factors influence people in the formation of their ethical perceptions, which impact upon their behaviour and actions. These factors involve personal and family experiences, our social contexts, the Bible, theology, the church and the Holy Spirit. Drawing on these sources and reflecting on these contexts, the task of ethics includes analysis, salvation and practical action.

[1] William Barclay, *Ethics in a Permissive Society* (London: Fontana/Collins, 1971), p. 13.

[2] Klaus Nürnberger, 'Theological Ethics' in I. H. Eybers, A. König and J. A. Stoop (eds), *Introduction to Theology*, 3rd ed. (Pretoria: NG Boekhandel, 1982), p. 218.

[3] Cf. David J. Bosch, *Witness to the World* (London: Marshall, Morgan and Scott, 1980), and *Transforming Mission: Paradigm Shifts in Theology of Mission* (Maryknoll: Orbis, 1991).

[4] Cf. Ernst Troeltsch, *The Social Teaching of the Christian Church*, Vol. 2 (Chicago: University of Chicago Press, 1981), p. 648.

[5] See John Macquarrie, *Twentieth Century Religious Thought* (London: SCM, 1981), pp. 95—115.

[6] See ibid., pp. 240—251; Thomas S. Kuhn, *The Structure of Scientific Revolutions* (Chicago: University of Chicago Press, 1970).

[7] See Macquarrie, *Twentieth Century Religious Thought*, pp. 155—168. See also Gregory Baum, *Religion and Alienation*, (New York: Paulist Press, 1975).

[8] Cf. Reinhold Niebuhr, *Moral Man and Immoral Society* (New York: Scribners, 1960).

[9] See Charles Villa-Vicencio, *Trapped in Apartheid* (Cape Town: David Philip, 1988), and R. Bocock and K. Thompson, *Religion and Ideology* (Manchester: University Press, 1985).

[10] See also John Macquarrie, *Principles of Christian Theology* (London: SCM, 1977), pp. 1—40.

[11] See Gerard Hughes, *God of Surprises* (London: Darton, Longman and Todd, 1985), and Elizabeth O'Conner, *Journey Inward, Journey Outward* (New York: Harper and Row, 1968).

[12] Compare Jer. 31:29—30 with Exod. 20:5—6 and 34:6—7. See also the trauma of Jacob and his family in Gen. 25—50.

[13] Niebuhr, *Moral Man and Immoral Society*, p. xi.

[14] See Charles Villa-Vicencio, 'Church and Ideology in Africa', *Missionalia*, 8:2 (1980), pp. 70—81, and James Leatt and Klaus Nürnberger (eds), *Contending Ideologies in South Africa* (Cape Town: David Philip, 1986).

[15] See Charles Villa-Vicencio, 'Theology in the Service of the State: The Steyn and Eloff Commissions', in Charles Villa-Vicencio and John W. de Gruchy (eds), *Resistance and Hope: South African Essays in Honour of Beyers Naudé* (Cape Town: David Philip, 1985), pp. 112—125.

[16] See Richard Longenecker, *New Testament Social Ethics for Today* (Grand Rapids: Eerdmans, 1984).

[17] Cf. Norman L. Geisler, *Ethics: Alternatives and Issues* (Grand Rapids: Zondervan, 1971), pp. 211–218.

[18] In the Balkans, Russia and Greece, the Russian and Greek Orthodox churches held equal moral sway.

[19] Owen Chadwick, *The Secularization of the European Mind in the Nineteenth Century* (Cambridge: Cambridge University Press, 1975).

[20] Millions of Catholics, for example, ignore the Vatican's moral judgement regarding contraception and practise artificial methods of birth control.

[21] Cf. Louise Kretzschmar, 'The Privatization of the Christian Faith Amongst South African Baptists: With Particular Reference to Its Nature, Causes, and Consequences' (PhD thesis, University of Cape Town, 1992), p. 1.

[22] Gustavo Gutiérrez, *A Theology of Liberation* (London: SCM, 1974), p. 15.

[23] David J. Bosch, 'Mission in Jesus' Way: A Perspective from Luke's Gospel', *Missionalia,* 17:1 (April 1989), pp. 3–21.

[24] David Cook, *Moral Maze* (London: SPCK, 1983), p. 60.

[25] Kenneth Leech, *True Prayer: An Introduction to Christian Spirituality* (London: Sheldon, 1980).

[26] See Albert Nolan, *God in South Africa* (Cape Town: David Philip, 1988) p. 1.

[27] See John W. de Gruchy and Charles Villa-Vicencio (eds), *Apartheid Is a Heresy* (Cape Town: David Philip, 1983).

[28] See Cook, *Moral Maze*, pp. 37–41.

[29] See John W. de Gruchy, *Theology and Ministry in Context and Crisis: A South African Perspective* (London: Collins, 1986).

[30] Barclay, *Ethics in a Permissive Society*, pp. 172–175.

Select Bibliography

Barclay, William. *Ethics in a Permissive Society*. London: Fontana/Collins, 1971

Cook, David. *Moral Maze*. London: SPCK, 1983

Nolan, Albert. *God in South Africa*. Cape Town: David Philip, 1988

Villa-Vicencio, C. *A Theology of Reconstruction: Nation Building and Human Rights*. Cape Town: David Philip, 1992

Wellman, Carl. *Morals and Ethics*, 2nd ed. New Jersey: Prentice-Hall, 1988

Wogaman, J. Philip. *A Christian Method of Moral Judgment*. London: SCM, 1976

Wogaman, J. Philip. *Making Moral Decisions*. Nashville: Abingdon, 1990

2

Philosophical Ethics

AUGUSTINE SHUTTE

Most contemporary philosophical ethics is of very little relevance either to the struggle in South Africa or to Christian moral theology. There is, however, one recent philosophical development which I feel holds out some hope on both counts. This chapter will be an attempt to present and explain this new approach to ethics, and try to show its theological and human relevance in South Africa at this time.

Christian faith is our personal response to the person of Jesus. The original response of this kind was that of his first followers in their experience of his resurrection. Through reflection on this experience by the apostolic community — a reflection expressed in the writings of the New Testament — the first Christian theology was produced. As *fides quaerens intellectum* (faith seeking understanding), this theology used the thought-forms and concepts of their own culture and time. And this will also be true for Christians trying to understand and express their faith in other times and cultures. Because of this, the philosophy that is produced in different times and cultures will always be important for Christian theology.

Philosophy is our attempt to become aware of our fundamental beliefs about the world and how to live in it, to formulate these beliefs in a precise and systematic way, and to provide reasoned arguments for their truth. In this way we hope to produce a coherent and critically grounded world-view (metaphysics) and a system of values that indicates how we ought to live (ethics). And clearly such an intellectual activity will have the utmost importance for our attempt to understand our faith. For faith in Jesus has a meaning for us that affects the way we see the world, and consequences for how we live in it. So philosophy can help us appropriate all this more fully. At the same time it forces us to become critically aware of our own culture and its assumptions about what is real and what is worthwhile. And it provides us with concepts by means of which we can express our beliefs in a more precise and systematic way.

European Philosophical Ethics

This is certainly so in the case of philosophical ethics, particularly at the present time. There is a development in ethics in contemporary European philosophy that is, in my view, both big with relevance for theology and also strikingly consonant with central themes of traditional African thought. In this chapter I propose to present a sketch of this new approach to ethics, as well as bring out the similarity with African thought. I will conclude with a pointer to its theological relevance.

The tradition of European philosophical ethics has two main roots, the Greek idea of nature and the biblical idea of law. In medieval philosophy these two elements are brought together in the notion of natural law (with its classical expression in the work of Thomas Aquinas). The modern period, characterised by the rise of the natural sciences (with a different conception of nature) and by secularisation (abstracting the idea of law from its religious setting), saw the break-up of the medieval synthesis, and the continuing but separate existence of its two elements in the empiricist and rationalist streams of modern philosophy.

The separation of the ideas of nature and law in relation to morality in the modern period has resulted in the two main contemporary forms of philosophical ethics, the utilitarian and the deontological. Utilitarianism is consequentialist in that it ties morality to the consequences of our acts, whether they produce more pleasure than pain. Deontological ethics is, as the name implies, concerned with the principle on which we act: is the principle of our action capable of being universalised in a law-like way?

Each of these approaches to morality embodies something that should be regarded as central to morality. Utilitarianism is concerned that the consequences of our acts should contribute to human welfare, such welfare being determined by some reference to natural feelings of pleasure and pain. Deontological ethics is concerned with the normative and overriding force of morality and seeks to secure this by connecting morality to rationality. Each, however, by emphasising one central aspect in isolation from the other, distorts morality. Human nature is not, as utilitarianism implies, merely an object which the sciences are able to investigate. Nor is reason, as the idea of duty for duty's sake implies, an abstract system of principles separate from our concrete human nature. The source of both errors is the scientific idea of nature, which comes eventually to be applied to human nature too. We must now consider this a little more carefully.

Forgetfulness of the Human Person

European philosophy in the modern period (roughly from the end of the fourteenth to the beginning of the nineteenth century) is characterised by a huge forgetfulness of the human person. The philosophers of the period were so hypnotised by science (and also by the technology that it made possible), so extroverted into the observable and measurable world, that they quite forgot themselves. I do not only mean that they were more interested in the world of 'nature' than in human beings. This forgetfulness of the human person continues even after the rise of the human sciences, history, sociology, psychology and the rest. In fact it is here that it becomes more clearly apparent — and more dangerous.

When I speak of forgetfulness of the human person I am thinking of the fact that persons are subjects as well as objects. As knowing subjects, human persons are the producers, the creators of science; as acting subjects, we are the agents who change the world by technology and work. Science, however (not only the human sciences), studies us (and technology increasingly manipulates us) as objects. And in doing so it misses the most important aspect of human nature, the fact that we are knowing and acting subjects. This is inevitable for science, since every science has to take for granted that we are able to think and choose, and so able to devise and practise scientific method. But it is precisely our ability to think and choose that makes us moral beings. No wonder that a forgetfulness of this aspect of our human nature should make it impossible either to relate morality to human nature or to give an adequate account of morality.

It is as subjects, then, that human persons are the originators of both science and moral action in the world. Ironically it is precisely in the modern period that our subjectivity is most fully displayed, in our growing understanding and control of our environment. In fact I want to suggest that it is these developments that make possible an insight into human nature that was not possible before. As psychologically acute as Aquinas is, he still approaches human nature within a broadly cosmological vision of the world, as occupying a particular place in the hierarchy of being, as one species among others.

It is the discovery of human subjectivity that has enabled contemporary Thomist philosophers such as B. Lonergan, K. Rahner, A. MacIntyre, H. McCabe, H. Meynell and others to reconnect morality with human nature in a renewal of Aquinas's theory of natural law. Such a development is at odds with the dominant forms of contemporary European philosophy both as regards its materialist (or dualist) understanding of human nature which derives from its connection with the sciences, and as regards its utilitarian (or deontological) conception of ethics. It is, however, far more open than other kinds of European philosophy to non-European forms of thought. In particular — and this is the main theme of this chapter — the conception of human persons on which this new form of ethical naturalism is based exhibits a striking consonance with certain ideas about human nature that are central to traditional African thought.

I now propose to discuss this contemporary Thomist approach in some detail, and in particular the way it relates to traditional African thought. I shall then make explicit how this particular form of philosophical ethics can be useful for doing moral theology in a South African context.

The Discovery of Subjectivity

The emergence of an awareness of human subjectivity begins as far back as Immanuel Kant in the European philosophical tradition. In Kant, however, it is expressed in strongly dualistic terms. The rational subject of thought and action (and hence of morality) is sharply separated from the phenomenal self that is part of nature and history. Hegel sought to close this gap, making humanity both the ultimate product and the subject of nature and history. In the process, however, he appears to reduce reality to ideas, and history to the development of a single universal Spirit.

It is only with Søren Kierkegaard and the development of the existentialist and phenomenological movements in European philosophy that human subjectivity begins to be explored in a thorough and concrete way. At the same time the human sciences, especially the social sciences, begin to provide a mass of varied insights into the environmental influences on persons and the causal links that connect them to sub-human nature. In spite of its growing insight into the links between human subjects and the natural and social worlds, modern science operates with a radically materialist view of the world, a view in which subjects could only exist as an exception. For this reason any recognition of human subjectivity would entail dualism.

During the modern period the philosophical tradition centred on Aquinas went underground, being kept alive solely by the Catholic Church, in which it had been canonised as the 'perennial philosophy'. As such, it was simplified and vulgarised and reduced to a form that could be easily assimilated by those training to be priests. In the twentieth century, however, there has taken place a 'resurrection' of authentic Thomist philosophy, begun by philosophers and historians of philosophy such as Maritain and Gilson, but then continued in a creative way by thinkers such as Karl Rahner and Bernard Lonergan.

Aquinas had inherited the Aristotelian conception of human nature, in which soul and body were related as form and matter in the one human individual. Aquinas understood this in a way that avoided both the body–soul dualism of Plato and the materialism of the pre-Socratics. Nevertheless, the language he had inherited from the Greek philosophers was always open to misunderstanding in a dualistic way, especially in the modern period, where the only alternative to materialism was understood to be substantial dualism of a Cartesian kind.

Reformulating Aquinas

Contemporary Thomists such as Rahner, who have learnt from existential and phenomenological philosophy as well as from the human sciences, have reformulated Aquinas's understanding of human nature in a way that makes our subjectivity central while at the same time avoiding any form of dualism.

The subjectivity of persons is their capacity to originate thought and action. As such, they are both self-conscious and self-determining. In human self-consciousness the self is both the one who knows and the one who is known, both subject and object at once. The same is true of human self-determination; we are both the subject who acts and the object who is acted upon. We bring ourselves to act. As subjects, then, human persons are self-enacting, self-realising. As such, we transcend the influences on us of all external causes whatsoever; we are free. This is not to say that the causes that science discovers, whether social or natural, cease to operate in us. That would be absurd. They are necessary but not sufficient to explain what we think and do.

As subjects, then, human persons are constituted by this twofold *internal* relationship to themselves, through which we both know ourselves and affirm ourselves as self-realising. But that is not all we are. We also exist in relationship to what is other than oneself, to our natural and social environment and, especially, to other persons. This is the relationship that is studied in so many varied ways by the sciences.

Taken together, the sciences reveal the forms of our dependence on what is other than ourselves for our existence and our character. Such dependence is radical; without it we cannot think or act, be self-conscious or self-determining.

Without a sensible environment we can have no sensations; without sensations, no images; without images, no thoughts. Without thought there can be no self-awareness. And similarly, without feelings we can have no emotions; without emotions we cannot choose; without choices we cannot act. No action means no self-realisation. We are dependent on what is other than ourselves for our self-consciousness and self-determination. Such dependence is not sufficient to make us self-enacting, self-realising beings, but it is necessary.

Intersubjectivity

This necessity is especially evident in our relationship to other persons. In addition to the variety of ways in which our dependence on our social and natural environment is revealed by the different sciences, there is a unique form of dependence on other persons for the exercise, development and fulfilment of precisely that capacity that makes us persons and subjects, the capacity for self-awareness and self-determination. It is especially this unique intersubjective relationship between persons, and the forms it takes in human life and growth, that have been the centre of interest for contemporary Thomist philosophers influenced by existential and phenomenological philosophy. There is not space here to provide a detailed picture of the account of intersubjectivity given by Thomist philosophers such as J. Donceel, R. Johann, W. Luijpen, M. Nedoncelle, J. Toner and others.[1] Here I want to stress just one aspect of intersubjectivity that this body of work reveals.

It is an important, though paradoxical, feature of the dependence of human persons on others for their development as persons that it is precisely through this dependence that their capacity for self-determination is developed. Self-determination and dependence on others appear to be strict alternatives. And so they are, in sub-personal relations and also in those social relationships that are not properly intersubjective. The more one is influenced by another, the less self-determining one is. When, however, the relationship between persons is strictly personal, a relationship of subject to subject, quite the opposite is the case. The more I am influenced by the other, the more the act is my own and the more self-determining I become.

One can get an idea of this paradoxical growth of freedom-in-dependence by considering examples where it does not occur. A good example is that of 'wild children', children who have grown to physical maturity quite apart from any contact with other persons. In the few cases where careful study has been possible, it is apparent that these children have quite failed to develop as persons, as responsible subjects of thought and action. Something similar is found in cases of 'hospitalism', where babies have grown up in institutions without the normal personal attention from a caring parent. They were in contact with nurses but, because of the number of babies to each nurse, relationships between nurse and baby could only be purely functional and not properly personal.

The Thomist authors already referred to present extremely rich analyses of the various forms taken by the intersubjective transaction between persons that brings about the development of our capacity for self-realisation. What emerges from this body of work is that it is only in certain kinds of relationship with other persons that this capacity is developed, those in which one is known and affirmed as the person one is by one who both knows and is able to affirm himself or herself. Why this should be so we are not able to go into here. There are, however, two features of this account of the necessary conditions for personal growth which are relevant to our interests in this chapter.

The first is the reciprocity involved in the interpersonal transaction productive of personal growth. In order to develop as a person I need to be known and affirmed by one who has self-knowledge and the ability to affirm himself or herself.

His or her affirmation of me enables me to come to know and affirm him or her. And this brings about knowledge and affirmation of myself. As the transaction proceeds, it is always the case that the more I know and affirm others for their own sake, the more I become able to know and affirm myself. And the more I am able to know and affirm myself, the more I will naturally come to know and affirm others for their own sake too.

Secondly, if it is true that a certain kind of dependence on other persons is necessary for me to develop as a person, namely as a free, self-determining subject, then we have discovered a way of understanding human persons that does justice to their subjectivity, and so is not materialist, but is not dualistic either. As subjects, human persons are self-determining and hence transcend the influence of the kind of causes the sciences can discover. As *human* subjects, however, we depend on the influence, the strictly personal causality, of other persons for the exercise and growth of this capacity for self-realisation towards fulfilment.

Traditional African Thought

We have thus arrived at a conception of human nature that does justice to our subjectivity, our ability to be the originators of thought and action, and hence should be able to provide a foundation for morality as well. Before we show how this can be done, I want to bring out the connection between this conception of human nature and two ideas that are central to a traditional African understanding of human persons.

A Person Is a Person Through Persons

These are the ideas of *umuntu ngumuntu ngabantu* and *seriti*. The first expression, which can be translated from the Xhosa to mean that a person is a person through persons, presents us with the distinctive African idea of community that underlies so much of African culture and so many traditional practices and institutions. It is a view of community that is sharply opposed to all kinds of individualism. It is, however, equally opposed to collectivism of a European kind.

Menkiti distinguishes the African idea of community from 'an aggregated sum of individuals'. African thought, he says, 'asserts an ontological independence to human society, and moves from society to individuals' rather than, in the manner of European thought, 'from individuals to society'.[2]

Likewise, Leopold Senghor distinguishes the African view of community from the best-known European ones, all of which he labels 'collectivist' in a negatively critical sense. He is especially concerned to differentiate the African view from any form of communism or European socialism, speaking instead of a 'community society' and coining the term 'communalism' to express the African conception. It is, he holds, 'a community-based society, communal, not collectivist. We are concerned here, not with a mere collection of individuals, but with people conspiring together, *con-spiring* in the basic Latin sense, united among themselves even to the very centre of their being.'[3]

The reason that Senghor is so concerned to distinguish the African view of community from all forms of European collectivism is his belief that the latter undermine the dignity and value of individual persons. He speaks of traditional African society being 'based both on the community and on the person and in which, because it was founded on dialogue and reciprocity, the group had priority over the individual without crushing him, but allowing him to blossom as a person.'[4]

It is useful to see dialogue or conversation as the typical activity and, indeed, the ultimate purpose of a community as understood in traditional African thought, since this is a co-operative activity that is achieved simply by the presence of person to person, rather than by them fulfilling any further function, as would be the case in some practical activity such as building a house.

Perhaps the best model for community as understood in African thought is the family. The family has no function outside itself. It is a means of personal growth for its members, and the interaction, the conversation and companionship between the growing and fully grown members is also an end in itself. African culture is famous for its notion of the 'extended family' (now seriously threatened by the advancing tide of European culture in its present degraded form). And the extended family is capable of extension to include anyone, not only those related by blood, kinship or marriage. In the last resort, humanity itself is conceived of as a family, a family which one joins at birth but does not leave by dying. Because of this, no one is a stranger. The world is our common home, the earth the property of all. Because human life only exists by being shared, all that is necessary for that life, for living and living well, is shared by the human family as a whole.

The traditional African idea of community seems to me to accord very closely with the understanding of human nature in contemporary Thomist philosophy presented above. That, too, avoids individualism by insisting on our dependence on other persons for our development as persons. At the same time it avoids the kind of collectivism criticised by African thinkers by showing that it is only in strictly personal relationships with others that persons are able to grow as persons.

Vital Force

The second African idea, that of *seriti*, denotes a kind of force or energy that manifests itself in human life and in the relations between persons, so that the world of persons can be seen as a field of force in which individuals exist as focuses or vortices of the energy of the field. The striking thing from the point of view of European philosophy is that though *seriti* is not the kind of force that could be observed or measured by any instrument, it is not purely mental or spiritual either. Here is Gabriel Setiloane's vivid attempt to describe it:

the human person is like a live electric wire which is ever exuding force or energy in all directions. The force that is thus exuded is called *seriti*. *Seriti* has often been translated to mean dignity or personality. Actually, that describes only the end result of the phenomenon. It is derived from the same word-stem *-riti* as *moriti*, which means 'shadow' or 'shade'. It is a physical phenomenon which expresses itself externally to the human body in a dynamic manner. It is like an aura around the human person, an invisible shadow or cloud or mist forming something like a magnetic or radar field. It gives forth into the traffic or weltering pool of life in community the uniqueness of each person and each object. While physically its seat is understood to be inside the human body, in the blood, its source is beyond and outside of the human physical body. . .[5]

Such descriptions are clearly metaphorical and poetic attempts to describe something that is not simply either material or immaterial. The notion of *seriti* has in fact a sort of metaphysical function in African thought, and is used to explain the phenomena referred to by the expression *umuntu ngumuntu ngabantu*, the dependence of persons on other persons for personal growth. Thus it has a remarkable similarity to the kind of 'personal causality' which manifested itself in the Thomist account of intersubjective relationships between persons, an influence that is not physical in any way, or observable and measurable by any science, but is nonetheless certainly real. '*Seriti* is not neutral. Its very existence seems calculated to promote and participate in relationship with the external world, human, animal, animate, inanimate, and even spiritual.'[6] And even more explicitly:

This manner of understanding human personality explains the interplay which takes place when people come into contact or live together. The essence of being is 'participation', in which humans are always interlocked with one another. The human being is not only 'vital force', but more: 'vital force in participation'. The all-important principle is this 'vital participation' which forms the very soul of the community body and accounts for the miasma which attaches to the group, the clan or the tribe. 'Participation' with its concomitant element of 'belonging' is made possible by '*seriti*', which is ever engaged in interplay with other people's *diriti* whenever they come into contact.[7]

Although traditional African thought is not formulated with philosophical rigour, such descriptions make it quite clear that interpersonal transactions are seen as depending on a kind of energy that, though it is not physical in any scientific sense, is not purely spiritual either. We thus have, in the traditional African understanding of human nature, a view which is neither materialist nor dualist, but which exhibits a remarkable consonance with that of the Thomist authors elaborated above.

If therefore we are able to build an ethics on the foundation of a contemporary Thomist conception of human nature, there is good reason to suppose that it can be applied in an African cultural context. Let us now address ourselves to this matter.

A Contemporary Philosophical Ethics

The contemporary Thomist account of human nature presents human persons as the self-determining subjects of thought and action. It also depicts them as dependent on their environment, especially that constituted by other persons, in all sorts of ways. Finally it reveals the special way in which they are dependent on other persons for the exercise, development and fulfilment of those capacities they possess precisely as persons and subjects.

In my opinion, such a view of human nature combines the Greek idea of human nature, as a unified system of powers or tendencies oriented towards an integrated realisation and fulfilment by means of the deliberate exercise (of the specifically human powers) of intellect and will, with the biblical view of human persons as the image of God and so in some sense responsible for the direction of both natural and historical processes towards goals that they themselves have set.

The essence of the moral life in this view is the development and fulfilment of our human nature, especially our nature as persons — that is, as self-determining subjects of thought and action. As we have seen, however, this is only possible through certain kinds of relationships between persons, which together make for a strictly intersubjective community of persons. Personal growth and personal community go hand in hand. Neither is possible without the other, and together they constitute the goal and the ultimate principle of morality.

With this conception of human nature as a foundation it is not too difficult to construct a conceptual framework for the moral life. The various powers and tendencies of human nature are centred on and united in our power of self-realisation, our subjectivity. It is this, above all, that is the indicator of our moral character. If the moral life consists in the fulfilment of our human nature, then it is this power, especially, that has to be developed. We can fail at other tasks without ruin; to fail at this is to destroy ourselves.

The idea of self-realisation or subjectivity is both general and abstract. We can however quickly make it more concrete. The self of which we are speaking is constituted by the capacities that make up our human nature. There are three sets or systems of such capacities: cognitive, volitional and emotional. Self-realisation consists in the development and integration of these systems in a goal-directed life.

In the cognitive sphere, self-realisation consists in the growth of our self-awareness into ever fuller self-knowledge. In the volitional sphere we must develop our capacity for self-determination into ever more complete self-affirmation. Both self-knowledge and self-affirmation are centred on the emotional system of the self. Self-knowledge consists fundamentally in knowing what our wants are, and their order of importance in our lives. Self-affirmation consists fundamentally in promoting our desires to decisions in accordance with their value.

Self-knowledge is thus the principle of order and unity *within* each system of the self, in the cognitive sphere ranking our beliefs about what is desirable in order of importance so that this ranking can be reproduced in the volitional and emotional spheres in our decisions and desires. Self-affirmation is the principle of order and unity *between* the systems, ordering our decisions and ultimately our desires in conformity with this ranking. Thus, together, self-knowledge and self-affirmation are principles of integration of the self in its progress towards self-realisation.

According to the understanding of human nature we are dealing with, such self-realisation can only come about under a certain kind of influence of other persons. To describe the character of such influence will add yet more concrete detail to our ethical framework. I cannot here explain, but must simply describe, the character of the interpersonal relationships necessary for personal growth.

To grow in self-knowledge and self-affirmation I must be known and affirmed by others who both know and affirm themselves. Through their knowledge and affirmation of me, they enable me to know and affirm them, and through my knowledge and affirmation of them I come to be able to know and affirm myself.

The more I am known and affirmed, the more I am enabled to know and affirm both myself and the other. My knowledge and affirmation of the other and of myself increase in direct proportion to each other. So personal growth and personal community go hand in hand. In the personal community made possible by personal growth there is mutual and reciprocal self-transcendence through knowledge of, and self-donation through affirmation of, each by the other.

Thus in this way we are able to derive, from an insight into the subjectivity of human nature and the necessary conditions for its realisation in human life, a conceptual framework for an ethics, comprising a concrete ideal of individual character, of interpersonal relations and community. Nor is it difficult to see how such a framework may be filled out and made yet more concrete.

In such an ethical task the sciences will also have a role to play. Each of the social sciences, for example, will have something to contribute regarding the kind of social environment that would foster rather than hinder interpersonal transactions of the kind that bring about personal growth and community. And so would novelists and poets and dramatists. Presently I will discuss the relation of such a person-centred ethics to theology.

Ethics in an African Context

I have tried to show how a particular philosophical understanding of human nature can act as the foundation for ethics. In doing so, I have drawn on the work of contemporary philosophers such as Alasdair MacIntyre and others who seek to bring about a return to the naturalist tradition of moral philosophy, as well as contemporary Thomists influenced by existential and phenomenological philosophy.

In a way, what I and these authors hope to achieve is a renewal of the tradition that leads from biblical and Greek ethical thought through Aquinas to the present day. This is the tradition that seeks to link ethics to the facts of human nature on one hand, and the forms of community produced by persons in the course of human history, on the other. I have already suggested that there is much in common between a Thomist understanding of human nature and that contained in some traditional African ideas. This similarity extends to the sphere of morality as well.

In our treatment of the idea of *seriti* we concentrated on the role it plays in the understanding of human nature and community. But it also has an ethical function. In traditional African thought morality is never merely conventional. As Tempels makes clear, 'Objective morality to the Bantu is ontological, immanent and intrinsic morality.'[8] The fundamental norm in the ethics of traditional African thought is human nature itself: 'it is the living *muntu* who, by divine will, is the norm of either ontological or natural law.'[9] It is in fact a natural-law kind of ethics. And, as this nature is understood in terms of *seriti*, of vital force, so the moral life in all its individual, social and political ramifications is understood as the struggle to increase the power of this force. 'The activating and final aim of all Bantu effort is only the intensification of vital force. To protect or increase vital force, that is the motive and the profound meaning in all their practices. It is the ideal which animates the life of the *muntu*, the only thing for which he is ready to suffer and to sacrifice himself.'[10]

The ethical theory outlined above would be quite at home in such a cultural context, in which the good of the individual and that of the group are so inextricably intertwined. One has of course to remember that the social context of the moral life in South Africa is no longer that in which traditional African thought developed but one formed and dominated by European science and technology. The institutions and practices which embodied and expressed traditional moral values and ideals will have to change. A sympathetic reformulation of these ideals and values achieved on the basis of a dialogue between a traditional African outlook and the kind of philosophical ethics I have presented can only help to make such changes creative ones.

A philosophical ethics of the kind that I have outlined would also have a direct application to the kind of all-encompassing struggle that is at present going on in South Africa. However one envisages the goals – in the different dimensions of our life – of this struggle, it must be seen as in some sense a liberation struggle. It is not difficult to see that philosophical ethics in a contemporary Thomist mould embodies the idea of freedom. Indeed, personal growth as I have depicted it is precisely a growth in individual freedom, the freedom of self-realisation that is achieved through the overcoming of internal conflicts of various kinds and the progressive integration of the self.

Such personal growth, moreover, is achieved (if the above account is accurate) only by means of the coming into being of a community of persons characterised by the fullest possible mutuality and reciprocity. It is a community, in short, that is a microcosm of social freedom, the freedom that is the positive side of the absence of domination and subjection, of any kind of conflict. Such an idea of human freedom, in which individual and social freedom are seen as necessarily interconnected, can provide a criterion with which to morally evaluate the aims, means and conduct of a particular liberation struggle such as ours.

The practical task of ethics in a South African context is to critically evaluate the different institutional milieux, in which human life is lived in our society, namely those of family, language, gender, education, work, recreation, culture and government, considering the actual institutions themselves, the practices associated with them and the way in which they are understood and justified. In each case one will be asking the question as to how far personal growth and community are fostered or hindered by them — that is, whether they are genuinely liberating or not.

Relevance to Theology

We come finally to the question of the relevance of such a philosophical ethics as I have presented for theology as such. The foundation for any relevance is, of course, human nature itself. Philosophical ethics must, in my view, be based on an understanding of human nature. Theology is our attempt to understand how this nature can be saved. And if one believes that grace perfects rather than replaces nature, then the dynamics of salvation and the process of personal growth must dovetail in some way or other. God's power (whether in creation or salvation), being transcendent, is incommensurable with human power, and so in no empirical way distinguishable from or additional to it.

Hence faith will be sensitive to the forms grace takes in the ordinary transactions between persons that bring about personal growth and community. And here philosophical ethics of the kind suggested above can be a faithful servant.

[1] See J. Donceel, *Philosophical Anthropology* (New York: Sheed and Ward, 1967); R. Johann, *The Meaning of Love* (New Jersey: Paulist, 1966); R. Johann, 'Person, Community and Moral Commitment', in R. Roth (ed.), *Person and Community* (New York: Fordham, 1975), pp. 155–175; R. Johann, 'Freedom and Morality from the Standpoint of Communication', in R. Johann (ed.), *Freedom and Value* (New York: Fordham, 1976); W. Luijpen, *Existential Phenomenology* (Pittsburgh: Duquesne, 1960); M. Nedoncelle, *Love and the Person* (New York: Sheed and Ward, 1966); and J. Toner, *The Experience of Love* (Washington: Corpus, 1968).

[2] I. Menkiti, 'Person and Community in African Traditional Thought', in R. Wright (ed.), *African Philosophy* (New York: University Press of America, 1979), pp. 165–167.

[3] L. Senghor, 'Négritude and African Socialism', in K. Kirkwood (ed.), *St. Anthony's Papers* No. 15 (Oxford, 1963), p. 16.

[4] L. Senghor, 'Négritude', *Optima*, 16 (1966), p. 5.

[5] G. Setiloane, *African Theology* (Johannesburg: Skotaville, 1986), p. 13.

[6] Ibid., p. 14.

[7] Ibid., p. 14.

[8] P. Tempels, *Bantu Philosophy* (Paris: Présence Africaine, 1959), p. 121.

[9] Ibid., p. 121.

[10] Ibid., p. 175.

Select Bibliography

Lonergan, B. *Insight*. London: Darton, Longman and Todd, 1957
Lonergan, B. *Method in Theology*. London: Darton, Longman and Todd, 1972
MacIntyre, A. *After Virtue*. London: Duckworth, 1982
McCabe, H. *Law, Love and Language*. London: Sheed and Ward, 1968
Meynell, H. *Freud, Marx and Morals*. London: Barnes and Noble, 1981
Rahner, K. *Hearers of the Word*. London: Sheed and Ward, 1969
Rahner, K. *Foundations of Christian Faith*. London: Darton, Longman and Todd, 1978

3

The Bible and Ethics

JAN BOTHA

Introduction

Christian churches are communities of moral discourse and discernment, in which the moral question 'What ought we do?' is asked. In many different ways the Bible is involved in this continuing moral discourse and discernment of the church. As the classical document of Christian origins, the Bible continues to play a role when Christians seek to answer moral and ethical questions.

This chapter discusses the meaning of the terms 'the Bible' and 'ethics' and their possible relation. It distinguishes between the ethics in the Bible and the ethics of modern Christian communities and its relation to the ethics in the Bible. An overview is given of a number of approaches to the 'application' of interpretations of the ethical directions given in the Bible to present-day situations. This is followed by a consideration of a related issue, namely the ethics of interpretations of the New Testament as something different from the ethics of the New Testament.

The Concepts of 'the Bible' and 'Ethics'

Ethos and Ethics

'Ethos' relates to the manner in which a specific group of people express their convictions about what is right and wrong or good and bad through their specific way of life. A group's ethos is more or less the moral aspect of their culture. Such a particular ethos is always socially and historically determined. It is social since it is a community that shares certain values and a certain lifestyle. It is historical since a community develops its typical moral convictions and characteristic lifestyle through a period of time. Since the ethos of a group of people is historical, it continues to change. It differs not only between different communities in different places, but it also differs within the same community in different eras of its existence.

In normal life a group of people usually do not reflect explicitly on their way of living and thinking. They are seldom able to explain their ethos rationally. For them, it speaks for itself, it is the way things are and should be. They are at home in their ethos. They seldom realise that their 'home' is merely their symbolic construction of moral reality. For them it is reality, it is good and bad, right and wrong.

'Ethics', on the other hand, relates to the conscious reflection on ethos, to the explicit process of accounting for moral choices. Those who consciously try to account for choices in terms of whether something is good or bad are busy with ethics.

The Bible

Introducing his book, *Wolf in the Sheepfold: The Bible as a Problem for Christianity,* Robert Carroll writes: 'The Bible is a profoundly problematical collection of books in many senses — religious, cultural, political, intellectual, moral, ethical and aesthetic — as well as posing problems for modern strategies of reading (Marxian, feminist, philosophical, postmodernist, etc.).'[1] A brief look at the development and nature of the Bible immediately makes it clear why it is problematical in all these senses.

There is no such thing as 'the Bible' in any absolute or single sense of the word. Different collections of books are regarded by different communities as authoritative writings and thus as the 'Bible'. The Hebrew Bible contains stories from the mists of the mythological past of several ancient Near Eastern communities. In ancient Israel an awareness developed that there were stories, laws, prophecies and teachings that gave authoritative content to the religious conviction that God concerns Godself with human beings. As a result, certain traditions arose and were passed on from generation to generation, acquiring normative effect for the life and faith of the people of Israel. In this process the traditions and stories were continually reinterpreted and expanded in order to communicate a meaningful message in new circumstances.

During the sixth to the fourth centuries BC, collections of writings began to take shape, resulting — after much further rewriting and retelling — in the first five books of the Hebrew Bible (called the Pentateuch). Similarly, the words and writings of ancient Israelite prophets were written down and passed on until some of them gained fairly general acceptance in Israel more or less during the second century BC. Yet another group of books — the so-called Writings (e.g. Psalms, Proverbs and Job) — although dating back many centuries, was accepted as part of the authoritative list of religious books approximately at the end of the first century BC.

Thus, through many centuries, from many different cultures, from groups living — both in time and space — far away from each other, a collection of books developed and came to be regarded as authoritative for Israelite and later for Jewish people and still later for Christians. It became a 'canon' — that is, an authoritative list of books accepted as Holy Scripture, a collection of writings assigned a normative function by certain religious groups. But even after this process was complete, important differences remained: the Hebrew Bible used by Jews contains only 39 books, while the Old Testament used by Roman Catholic, Eastern Orthodox and Slavonic Christians includes (with differences amongst them) another 18 books, whereas the Old Testament of the Ethiopic Church contains 89 books! These different canons are not a matter of right or wrong: they are the result of a historical process, and each religious group has specific reasons for its choices.

Although the books of the New Testament were all written during the latter half of the first century AD and perhaps in the early second century, it took almost another three hundred years for the Christian church to agree on a final list that was generally accepted. For example, Revelation, 2 Peter, Jude and Hebrews were for many hundreds of years not regarded as Scripture by all the Christian communities. On the other hand, for hundreds of years certain Christian groups have used books such as The Shepherd of Hermas and Clement as Scripture in exactly the same manner that they used the gospels and the letters of Paul.

'The Bible', then, is a collection of books, consisting of two testaments, each with its own long and complicated history. It came into existence during a period of more or less one thousand four hundred years. It was written by different communities living in places such as modern-day Palestine and Israel, Turkey, Rome and Iran. Different ancient Near Eastern cultures, and the Hellenistic and Roman cultures as well, all produced parts of the Bible. What is more, the books of the Bible were originally written in different languages (Hebrew, Aramaic and Greek).

In the light of this history, it is not strange that different and even directly opposing views about many issues can be found in the Bible. For example, the prophetic book of Nahum announces judgement on the city of Nineveh while the prophetic story of Jonah proclaims mercy for the same city. In Isaiah 2:4 we hear a pre-exilic pacifist proclaiming, 'They will hammer their swords into ploughs and their spears into pruning-knives', while the militant post-exilic prophet Joel exclaims: 'Hammer the points of your ploughs into swords and your knives into spears' (3:10). The 'faith and works' tension in the New Testament is well known: for Paul those who rely on works for salvation are under a curse because one can only be saved through faith (Gal. 3:10ff), while James states in no unclear terms that faith by itself, if it has no works, is dead (James 2:17) and serves no purpose. Examples of different and opposite views can be multiplied in both the Old and the New Testament. This is why the Bible is problematical in a moral and ethical sense.

Ethics in the Bible

The distinction between a historical description of the ethics of the communities which produced the biblical documents and the use of their writings normatively in the ethical discourse of later times is of fundamental importance. In the Bible we find many ethical directions. This could be called ethics in the Bible, which is something different from the use of the Bible in ethics (which will be our concern in the next section). The investigation of ethics in the Bible is traditionally the concern of biblical scholarship while ethicists and theologians concentrate on the use of the Bible in ethics.

Given the nature of the Bible and its historical development, a vast array of different moral and ethical directions is found in the pages of the Bible. To elaborate briefly on only one New Testament example, much of the moral exhortation in Paul's letters has been given the technical name 'paraenesis'. Malherbe has identified the following characteristics of this form of literature. 'Traditional material' or 'precepts' are present in it; it gives general rules (which does not mean that it is not related or adapted to the settings in which it is given). Paraenesis focuses on the practical conduct of life; it may be diverse in content and often consists of series of brief unconnected admonitions strung together (see, for example, Romans 12). It contains commands or summonses directed to a specific type of audience, pressing them to maintain a certain way of life rather than convincing them to adopt a new way of life. It sometimes refers to content (for example, traditional maxims or precepts of wisdom, especially moral wisdom); at other times it refers to the form or process of moral teaching (that is, the process of addressing words of encouragement or discouragement about behaviour to a person or persons).[2]

Recent biblical scholarship has made significant progress in the investigation of the different forms of literature containing moral exhortation as well as the content and social functions of these exhortations within the wider cultural and historical contexts of the ancient Near East and the Graeco-Roman world of biblical times. Focusing on the New Testament, Wayne Meeks proposes that we should try to understand the 'moral universe' of the first Christian groups. This is similar to trying to understand a foreign language. He writes: 'What we must do with the scattered fragments of evidence we glean from our sources is not to boil them down to obtain their essence, however we might define that — the code of moral rules, the moral principles, the logic of ethical argument, the ideals and goals of moral perfection. Rather, we must reconstruct, must imagine the world in which these fragments made sense.'[3]

In order to do this, Meeks visualises three aspects. Firstly, we must gather all the information that we have about the social structure of each of the various forms of the early Christian community and try to correlate it with the specific constellations in the symbolic universes exhibited by our sources. Secondly, we must make an analysis of what he calls the 'grammar' of the movement's morals. This consists of an analysis of the logic of the interactive world that Paul and his readers shared and the meaningful structures of the process in which they were engaged before and after the writing of the letters. Thirdly, such a 'cultural–linguistic' inquiry into these communities might help us to escape the temptation of thinking that only what is unusual or unique about the Christian moral universe is important: 'The "essence" of Christianity is not some residue that remains after we have boiled away everything they have "borrowed" from the impure world around them.'[4]

Any responsible and plausible use of the Bible in the ethical discourse of our own contemporary situation presupposes such a historical and sociological investigation into the ethics in the Bible. Because of the nature of the Bible and the vast cultural and temporal difference which separates us from those communities which produced it, this task is immensely complicated. Unfortunately, the level of sophistication and expertise needed for this task tends to occupy biblical scholars to such an extent that many of them become isolated from the debate amongst ethicists and theologians about the use of the Bible in contemporary ethical questions. However, since biblical ethics does not equal Christian ethics, yet another field of inquiry opens up before us.

Approaches to the Use of the Bible in Ethics

As a general introductory remark to his essay on 'The Changing Use of the Bible in Christian Ethics', James M. Gustafson writes:

> There are no recent American writings of academic repute that assume in a simple way that the Bible provides the rules for the governing of the whole human community as if it were the rational norm and ideal of morality applicable to all regardless of their status in Christian faith. This kind of rationalistic moral idealism forgets that the Bible is much more than a moral textbook; it is for writers of various persuasions a source of knowledge of God and a source for God's word of judgment and redemption to man. Thus, the moral teachings are seen within the wider framework of theological affirmations and of the Christian experience of sin and forgiveness through Jesus Christ. The Bible, to put it simply, has a different moral authority for Christians themselves than for others.[5]

Within the Christian community itself, however, a number of approaches are used to 'apply' the New Testament to present-day situations. In his book *What Are They Saying About Scripture and Ethics?*, W. C. Spohn notes that 'they' are saying many different things, and he contends that 'we enjoy an irreducible plurality of theological uses of Scripture in ethics because of the irreducible plurality of literary forms in the Bible itself.'[6]

Four Approaches to the Relation of the Bible to Ethics[7]

A Prescriptive Approach. For those following this approach, the Bible contains or gives 'propositional revelation', and, as such, has authority in matters of both faith and conduct. Consequently, a simple one-to-one relationship is viewed as existing between past and present. The minutest details of the various precepts and laws within the Bible are applied directly and in a prescriptive manner to the present. A literal compliance with the gospel ethic, which presupposes that the Bible contains 'revealed morality', characterises this approach. For example, since it is written in Romans 13:1 that 'everyone should submit to the governing authorities', it is held that Christians should do so always and in all circumstances. It is a law or command of God that has objective status, and believers have only to refer to this command.

Such an approach, however, fails to do justice to the New Testament in two respects. Firstly, it does not take cognisance of the historical, cultural and literary context of the time in which the Bible originated and the totally different context of today's world. Secondly, to view the New Testament simply as a law book is a distortion of this body of literature.[8]

An Ethics of Principles or Ideals. In liberal Protestantism, the notion of revealed morality has taken another form. The individual and specific laws and commands in the New Testament are not to be interpreted as having, in a literal sense, a binding force on the believer. Rather, the ideals or principles that lie behind these laws are upheld as binding. The biblical interpreter must look behind the laws of the New Testament (which are related to specific circumstances) in order to ascertain those universal principles that inspired such laws. Once these universal principles have been discovered, they can then be applied to the present day, to new and changing circumstances.

In terms of this approach, the appeal in Romans 13 to 'submit to the governing authorities' has as a general and universally valid principle behind it the notion that Christians should have respect for authority – whether it be the authority of government, parents, the principal of a school, or the guard at the gate of a zoo. Whatever the circumstances, those having authority within a particular situation should be respected and obeyed by Christians.

This approach has taken on a number of different forms and formulations. Best known perhaps is Reinhold Niebuhr's succinct summary of biblical morality as 'the law of love'. The problem with this approach is that it tends to reduce the wealth and variety of New Testament teaching to a limited number of principles. Furthermore, it does not explain why supposedly universally valid principles that can be derived from the New Testament might be in conflict with each other.

'Revealed Reality' Rather Than 'Revealed Morality'. The revolution in European theology spearheaded by Karl Barth during the first half of the twentieth century gave rise to a different approach to the 'application' of the Bible to present-day matters. Following Barth, theologians have emphasised that the Bible is not the revelation of a morality, but the revelation of the living God. Christian ethics, therefore, has to think not about morality reduced to propositions, but about God and how life ought to be properly related to God's power and presence. The Bible points first of all towards the living God. What is required of ethics is obedience to a person, not a proposition.

In terms of this approach, the exhortation of Romans 13:1 to 'submit to the governing authorities' will then be interpreted and applied in the context of what it supposedly says about God.

Relationality and Responsibility. This approach, which builds directly on the previous one, focuses attention on the Christian's response to the God who has given the gift of faith to the believer. Of particular importance is the view expressed by H. Richard Niebuhr that too much of Christian ethics tries to find 'Christian answers' to problems of morality instead of being open and responsive to the work of the living Lord. The Bible has to be used in such a way that it helps the Christian community to interpret the God whom it knows in its existential faith, and not as providing a revealed morality that is to be 'translated' and 'applied'. Gustafson discusses variations of this ethics of faith-response as propagated by Paul Lehmann with his notion of 'an ethics of the biblical indicative' and by John Sittler with his emphasis on 'the shape of the engendering deed'.[9] Gustafson himself argues for a relationality and responsibility model as the primary way to understand Christian ethics.[10]

The results of historical–critical scholarship have shown that what might have been a valid norm in the context of the biblical world does not necessarily mean that it has equal reference and validity today. For example, the notion in Romans

13:4 that authorities do not carry the sword in vain (interpreted as declaring that they have a divine right and commission to exercise capital punishment) was a valid norm in the first century. Yet the greater part of the modern developed world does not hold this as a valid norm any longer. In the place of acting according to norms or goals, Gustafson's relationality and responsibility approach places God in the very centre of activity. The Christian responds to what God has done and strives to retain a relationship with this God of salvation.

Hartin evaluates these approaches as follows:

> To my mind of all the approaches so far discussed, this approach
> [relationality and responsibility] is the most satisfactory. The person of
> Jesus remains the very centre of life and action of the Christian. Morality
> is no longer limited to the narrow legalistic carrying out of stipulated
> laws. Instead, morality emerges from the very context of the Christian
> faith as a way of life which is led as a response to the gift of faith which
> the believer has received. The Scriptures give us a picture of the
> understanding which God's people had of themselves as they lived their
> lives under God's covenant in a relationship to Jesus.[11]

The Ethics of Interpretation

W. A. Beardslee explains how the 'ethics of hermeneutics' has been influenced by the different approaches to ethics in general which we have just discussed.[12] He sketches the shift that has taken place from the widespread presupposition of New Testament hermeneutics that ethics is rooted in an irreducible 'ought', to a goal-oriented and transformative ethic of political responsibility.[13] To reflect on the ethics of interpretation is to reflect on what kinds of acts of interpretation are responsible in a number of senses. To compose and to interpret texts is to engage in responsible action. This notion has been worked out in some detail by Lundin, Thiselton and Walhout in their book *The Responsibility of Hermeneutics*: 'The actions surrounding, and in a sense performed by, a text are multiple. The author or speaker is responsible for this action, and it is patently false to claim that human action can have nothing to do with purpose, intention, situation or goal.'[14]

On the other hand, once a text comes to occupy a place in tradition and is read in times or places different from those in which it was spoken or written, there begin to emerge further dimensions of action and their effects. Readers may 'use' the text for purposes not envisaged by the author, and because such 'uses' also remain personal actions their propriety may be judged by certain criteria of responsibility. The action model allows us to separate out different levels and dimensions of language use without necessarily opening the door to the mistaken view that the 'meaning' of a text is simply what any reader cares to impute to it. Some actions seem to be more appropriate than others. If language is a tool, what was the tool designed to do? Is it now being used responsibly? It is possible to make a text 'mean' what the reader uses it to mean, just as it is possible to use a chisel as a screwdriver. In such a case of forced misapplication it is not enough to answer, 'But the chisel turned the screw effectively.'

The consequence of this view is that not all interpretative acts of reading are equally responsible. Lundin, Thiselton and Walhout explain the notion of responsible interpretation with yet another metaphor:

> Indeed, interpretative responsibility emerges here as a major and constructive hermeneutical category. It is sometimes fruitless to ask whether a text can be taken to mean something without asking whether we can take it to mean this responsibly. But responsibility also depends on purpose and situation. A piano can be used for firewood, and in most circumstances such actions would be irresponsible. But if one were dying of cold, stranded on an ice floe in the Arctic Ocean, it might conceivably become a responsible act to set fire to a Steinway.[15]

The notion of responsibility as characteristic of current understanding of ethics in general can also be used fruitfully in a consideration of the ethics of interpretation. Responsibility as criterion for ethical evaluation requires consideration of both the nature of the material with which one is dealing (a piano or a text) and the situations in which the acts of interpretation take place.

Ethical Themes in Texts

It is important to distinguish between the ethics of interpretation and ethical themes in literature, or thematic ethical meaning. The exhortations 'everyone should submit to the governing authorities' (Rom. 13:1) and 'pay your taxes' (Rom. 13:6) are examples of ethical themes in the New Testament. This theme could be formulated as 'How must a person behave with regard to rulers?' or 'What is the right or good conduct in the relation between governed and rulers?' The questions of 'what must' and 'the good' are what ethics is all about. As a criterion in terms of which one can decide what is good or what is right, one may ask what is responsible within a given situation.

The ethics of interpretation poses the question 'What ought one to?' or 'What is good or right?' or 'What is responsible?' with regard to the act of interpretation as such. What is it that 'ought' to be done or what is 'good' when we read these exhortations in Romans 13:1–7 or any other text? The ethics of interpretation requires that people take responsibility for their acts of reading. It calls for an interpretation with a view to life. It provides for different modes and methods of reading, demanding methodological sophistication and rigour in accordance with the best that is available.

The method of reading, as such, is not ethical or unethical. Only people can act ethically or unethically. The interpretative acts of people, or the ways people use methods of interpretation, therefore, are subject to ethical reflection. If a community uses a method of interpretation in such a way that it remains an esoteric, 'pure' academic endeavour, isolated from life, or if a community tolerates such practices, it becomes an ethical problem. Thus, the ethics of interpretation asks *who* (which individual or group?) reads *which* Bible (what view of the text does the community hold, what authority does it grant the text?), *how* (using which methods?) and *why* (whose interests are at stake, what does the community want to achieve with its acts of interpretation?).

J. H. Miller, in *The Ethics of Reading*, phrases this question as follows: 'My question is whether ethical decision or responsibility is in any way necessarily involved in that situation and act of reading, and if so, how and of what kind, responsibility to whom or to do what, decision to do what.'[16]

Reflection on the ethics of interpretation is of particular importance when one deals with the Bible, since, as Carroll rightly asserts:

> Whatever the Bible may say about oppression it has in its time served the interests of the oppressor. . . . It is not just the use of the Bible, but also some of the substantive things in the Bible itself. The Bible, in whatever version, may make a good servant; it can be a bad master. Treating it as the divine word exempt from criticism can blind eyes to that truth. Also, the Bible contains some appalling practices of an uncivilized nature and nobody should treat these as normative.[17]

And so the Bible must be used critically. In this critical use of the Bible the ethically responsible conduct of the interpreter is of utmost importance. The Bible must be interpreted within the context of a modern and just scale of religious values.[18]

Conclusion

The moral teachings of the Bible cannot be reduced neatly to one single and simple set of rules. Given the nature of the Bible and the process of its development, it does not make sense for one to expect to find such a system in the writings of the Bible. However, it is the widely held conviction of the Christian church that the Bible is an authority for life and faith. Used critically and responsibly, the Bible is a rich source of age-old wisdom and an important conversational partner in the church's ongoing engagement with the moral question 'What ought to be done?'

[1] Robert Carrol, *Wolf in the Sheepfold. The Bible as a Problem for Christianity* (London: SPCK, 1991).

[2] See A. J. Malherbe, *Moral Exhortation: A Greco-Roman Sourcebook* (Philadelphia: Westminster, 1986).

[3] W. A. Meeks, 'Understanding Early Christian Ethics', *Journal of Biblical Literature*, 105:1 (1985), p. 5.

[4] Ibid., p. 10.

[5] J. M. Gustafson, 'The Changing Use of the Bible in Christian Ethics', in C. E. Curran and S. J. McCormick (eds), *The Use of Scripture in Moral Theology* (New York: Paulist Press, 1984), p. 4.

[6] W. C. Spohn, *What Are They Saying About Scripture and Ethics?* (New York: Paulist Press, 1984).

[7] For more details see J. M. Gustafson, 'The Changing Use of the Bible'; T. W. Ogletree, *The Use of the Bible in Christian Ethics. A Constructive Essay* (Philadelphia: Fortress, 1983); R. Longenecker, *New Testament Social Ethics for Today* (Grand Rapids: Eerdmans, 1984), pp. 1–15; P. J. Hartin, 'New Testament Ethics: Some Trends in Recent Research', *Journal of Theology for Southern Africa*, 59 (1987), pp. 35–42, and 'Methodological Principles in Interpreting the

Relevance of the New Testament in South Africa', *Scriptura*, 37 (1991), pp. 1–16; Spohn, *What Are They Saying?*; and A. Verhey, *The Great Reversal: Ethics and the New Testament* (Grand Rapids: Eerdmans, 1984), pp. 154–159.

[8] Hartin, 'Methodological Principles', p. 3.

[9] Gustafson, 'The Changing Use of the Bible', pp. 142–145.

[10] J. M. Gustafson, 'Christian Ethics', in P. Ramsay (ed.), *Religion* (New Jersey: Prentice-Hall, 1965), pp. 309–316.

[11] Hartin, 'Methodological Principles', p. 4.

[12] W. A. Beardslee, 'Ethics and Hermeneutics', in T. W. Jennings (ed.), *Text and Logos. The Humanistic Interpretation of the New Testament* (Atlanta: Scholars Press, 1990), pp. 15–32.

[13] Ibid., pp. 16–25.

[14] R. Lundin, A. C. Thiselton and C. Walhout, *The Responsibility of Hermeneutics* (Grand Rapids: Eerdmans, 1985), p. 107.

[15] Ibid., p. 113.

[16] J. H. Miller, *The Ethics of Reading* (New York: Columbia University Press, 1987), p. 4.

[17] Carroll, *Wolf in the Sheepfold*, p. 5.

[18] E. Schüssler Fiorenza, 'The Ethics of Interpretation: De-centering Biblical Scholarship', *Journal of Biblical Literature*, 107:1 (1988), pp. 3–17.

Select Bibliography

Beardslee, W. A. 'Ethics and Hermeneutics', in T. W. Jennings (ed.), *Text and Logos. The Humanistic Interpretation of the New Testament*. Atlanta: Scholars Press, 1990

Carroll, R. *Wolf in the Sheepfold. The Bible as Problem for Christianity*. London: SPCK, 1991

Curran, C. E. and S. J. McCormick (eds), *The Use of Scripture in Moral Theology*. New York: Paulist Press, 1984

Gustafson, J. M. 'Christian Ethics', in P. Ramsey (ed.), *Religion*. Englewood Cliffs: Prentice-Hall

Gustafson, J. M. 'The Changing Use of the Bible in Christian Ethics', in C. E. Curran and S. J. McCormick (eds), *The Use of Scripture in Moral Theology*

Hartin, P. J. 'New Testament Ethics: Some Trends in More Recent Research'. *Journal of Theology for Southern Africa*, 59 (1987), pp. 35–42

Hartin, P. J. 'Methodological Principles in Interpreting the Relevance of the New Testament in South Africa'. *Scriptura*, 37 (1991), pp. 1–16

Longenecker, R. N. *New Testament Social Ethics for Today*. Grand Rapids: Eerdmans, 1984

Lundin, R., Thiselton, A. C. and Walhout, C. *The Responsibility of Hermeneutics*. Grand Rapids: Eerdmans, 1985

Malherbe, A. J. *Moral Exhortation: A Greco-Roman Sourcebook*. Philadelphia: Westminster, 1986

Meeks, W. A. 'Understanding Early Christian Ethics'. *Journal of Biblical Literature*, 105:1 (1985), pp. 3–11

Miller, J. H. *The Ethics of Reading*. New York: Columbia University Press, 1987

Ogletree, T. W. *The Use of the Bible in Christian Ethics. A Constructive Essay*. Philadelphia: Fortress, 1983

Smit, D. J. 'Responsible Hermeneutics: A Systematic Theologian's Response to the Readings and Readers of Luke 12:35–48'. *Neotestamentica*, 22 (1988), pp. 441–484

Smit, D. J. 'The Ethics of Interpretation – New Voices from the U.S.A.' *Scriptura*, 33 (1990), pp. 16–28

Smit, D. J. 'The Ethics of Interpretation – and South Africa'. *Scriptura*, 33 (1990), pp. 29–43

Smit, D. J. 'The Bible and Ethos in a New South Africa'. *Scriptura*, 37 (1991), pp. 51–67

Spohn, W. C. *What Are They Saying About Scripture and Ethics?* New York: Paulist Press, 1984

Verhey, A. *The Great Reversal. Ethics and the New Testament*. Grand Rapids: Eerdmans, 1984

PART TWO
Ethical Theories

4

Natural Law Ethics

N. BARNEY PITYANA

Veritatis Splendor[1] was published amidst controversy in September 1993. Pope John Paul II authorised this encyclical on the church's moral teaching in order to stem the drift towards realitivity in a social environment in which he was convinced that moral standards were declining. As the Pope put it, the purpose of the encyclical was 'to state that some trends of theological thinking and certain philosophical affirmations are incompatible with revealed truths'. John Paul II wished to reaffirm the moral teaching of the church, assert the pastoral authority of the bishops, and strengthen the authority of the Roman magisterium. It is clear that the encyclical is designed to address the 'problem' of dissident theologians in the Roman Catholic Church and to unite the church under the central authority of the Pope in Rome.

Controversy about the encyclical revolves around its mere assertion of conservative values, its authoritarian tone, and the fact that it undermines dialogue and debate about moral questions within the church. The proponents of the document, on the other hand, wish it to be seen as bringing about clarity and certainty to an area of the church's teaching which is under threat from the dominant mores in society. In order to do this, one commentator has asserted, *Veritatis Splendor* proceeds by a 'systematisation of revealed truths and a defence of natural law in the strictest Thomist tradition'.[2] In this view natural law theory is considered to be outdated and conservative. Another critic calls the encyclical fundamentalist because 'it is inspired by a desire to turn the clock back to the halcyon days before the Second Vatican Council when liberal Roman Catholics let the corrosive mores of the secular world into the citadel of faith'.[3] According to this critic, Roman Catholic moral teaching is still based on the universalising concepts of medieval ecclesiology even though much has changed and is changing in the world; the church no longer has the same authority over the lives of the faithful that it once had; and the environment in which the church now has to operate is distinctly multi-cultural and ecumenical.

Arguments against the papal encyclical can be said to be of the same kind as those against natural law in ethics. The moral principles underlying *Veritatis Splendor* are drawn from the golden age of natural law. What the debate suggests further is that the wheel is turning once again to a discussion of the relevance of natural law in ethical discourse today. Natural law can no longer be considered irrelevant in moral philosophy and ethics.

This chapter will sketch the history and content of natural law and its application in moral theory. It will then consider the relationship between law and morality, and finally will analyse natural law in the constitutional developments now taking place in South Africa.

Elements of Natural Law [4]

Natural law or *ius naturale* is a system of legal discourse advanced during the late Middle Ages as a basis and test for the lawfulness of authority. It deduces rules of human behaviour from the rational observation of natural phenomena.[5] These rules are constant and predictable; they can be observed, and proved or falsified empirically.

But *ius naturale* is not an invention of the medieval Schoolmen. Geoffrey Koziol[6] demonstrates that natural law concepts can be found in early Christian theology and in antique jurisprudence. It was not, however, till the twelfth century that natural law became a common method of moral and theological explication. Koziol explains that this must have had something to do with a new intellectual movement, the Twelfth-Century Renaissance, that saw the need to limit the absolute power of kings. The absolute discretion and authority of kings had led to injustice and arbitrariness.[7] In the hands of the medieval Scholastics natural law became a radical movement for justice and fairness in the administration of law. To them, law was something constant and not subject to the vicissitudes of human psychology. The law had to be rational and transcend human finitude. Natural law, therefore, gave the Schoolmen a way of anchoring human laws in universal principles which they believed were fixed and constant.[8]

Thomas Aquinas was the most articulate exponent of natural law among the medieval Schoolmen. He wove this theory into his philosophical and theological system and popularised it in the intellectual life of his time. It was theological because it formed an essential part of Aquinas's understanding of the divine nature as being eternal reason. The law of God was eternal *ex parte Dei*, as Frederick Copleston explains it. Copleston goes on to say that 'this eternal law, existing in God, is the origin and fount of the natural law, which is a participation of the eternal law'.[9] To this extent, Thomist theology could be understood as natural theology. Aquinas saw no discord between faith and reason, between what God has commanded and the deep desires of human nature. Humanity is in tune with nature. Nature is made for grace; grace does not ignore nature but perfects it.

On this understanding Aquinas built his philosophical and moral system. His epistemology asserted that the reality of the nature of being does not depend on human perception. This knowledge of reality comes from God and is part of the nature of God. God, the creator, is the source of all true and certain phenomena. If it is part of the divine nature, then humanity, which was created by God 'to be like himself' (Gen. 1:27), is endowed with that same capacity and those same gifts. Human reason and intelligence are dependent on the divine nature. Because it is so dependent, the reality of human nature is 'an ultimate and constant concept beneath all individual differences'.[10] This 'being' of a thing, its 'form' or 'final cause', as its maximum perfection or the goal of its becoming, is what anchored Thomist epistemology. Because of this perceived constancy, natural law provides an objective foundation for morality.

Thomist moral theory was based on natural law. Aquinas's system presupposed a 'natural morality', meaning that humanity, created beings, were endowed with the power to use reason to exercise their freewill. It is reason that provides human beings with the capacity for discernment, in order to evaluate moral obligations and make moral judgements. For Aquinas, the practical object of practical reason is the supreme good, *summum bonum*, which is the end of all human conduct: *bonum est faciendum et prosequendum, et malum vitandum.*[11] But the good for humanity is that which benefits human nature, that which is the natural inclination for humanity as rational beings.

Natural law, on this understanding, forms the rational and objective basis for morality. This system of morality is rational and natural in the sense that it is not arbitrary or capricious but derives its force from nature. Natural law, according to Aquinas, satisfies the essential conditions of justice — reliability and predictability — in that they are entirely unchangeable 'since their fulfilment is absolutely necessary for the good of humankind'.[12] Because they derive from a rational basis, therefore, they are plain and understandable to the ordinary citizen and can be applied fairly and justly. K. McDonnel holds that the natural law precepts are self-evidently natural principles (in that they are so inextricably part of human nature); to deny them would be a contradiction. One cannot deny what one already is.[13]

McDonnel also makes a distinction between two uses of the word 'reason'. In one, reason is a ground, a principle or a proposition. It is presented to explain or justify human actions. In another use, reason is the adverb which, as the *Oxford Dictionary* glosses it, expresses a relation of place, time or circumstance and qualifies the procedures or operations of reasoning. Johannes Messner explains that 'reason' is insight into the mental and physical impulses of human nature which are necessary for one to be fully human. On another reckoning, 'reason' is insight into the moral principles which are implicit in all human nature.[14] However, there is a third view which questions this idea of reason as insight into reality. But Messner insists that insight into moral principles and insight into reality are indissolubly linked at root.[15] The problem of 'reason' becoming a mere intellectual abstraction does not arise. It is important that the principle of natural law should not be arbitrary or whimsical. McDonnel argues that there is a place for reason, properly understood, in moral theory. He goes on to express the hope that the 'contemporary exploration of ethical problems might be enhanced by attempting to discriminate the basic from the derived principles of practical reason, and the principles from their applications'.[16]

In a further exploration of the idea, R. A. Duff states that the 'rationality' of legal enactments must be justified to the citizens whom they are meant to bind. It is important to do so if law is not to become just a coercive exercise and if it is to be based on the recognition of the rational nature of humanity. Law must not be a vindictive instrument in the hands of a brutal dictator. 'Law involves, not just manipulating or controlling the citizens' behaviour towards some morally approved goal but subjecting them, as rational agents, to the requirements of rules which impose obligations on them'.[17] On this understanding, therefore, natural-law moral principles are conceived of as practical rather than abstract, concrete rather than formal, objective rather than subjective.

Law and Morality

What moved the late medieval Scholastics to structure a new system of natural law was an attempt to set law within a mode of justice which was constant and consistent as well as fair. As already indicated, the aim was to address the problem of arbitrariness in the use of power, to set human law within a moral setting which might regulate it. Valid human law, for Aquinas, had to uphold justice and the divine will.

In order to understand the nature of legal obligation, Barry C. Hoffmaster suggests that three criteria must first be fulfilled. Firstly, it must explain the nature and source of the obligation. Why do we obey some laws and are disinclined to obey others? Secondly, what makes the obligation to obey a law a distinctly legal obligation rather than a mere preference? For example, how does one choose between a legal obligation and a moral obligation? Thirdly, it must explain whether every valid human law has a legal obligation attached to it or not.[18]

What Aquinas thought essential to assert is not that a law which fails the exclusionary test is invalid, but that there is no moral obligation to obey it. 'That which is not just seems to be no law at all: wherefore the force of a law depends on the extent of its justice.'[19] The critical distinction here must be observed. It is not what makes a law a law that matters but that it is necessary to make the connection between legal and moral obligation. Aquinas argued that the purpose of human law was to lead humanity to virtue. The link between law and virtue was, for him, the engine driving humanity towards the common good.[20]

Critique of Classical Natural Law Theory

Natural law theory has been subjected to much criticism since the time of Aquinas. J. Philip Wogaman argues that while the natural law approach to ethics is right in so far as it locates moral issues in the context of the natural order, it is wrong, he says, 'in so far as it considers nature itself to be the source of good'.[21] With the advances in the natural sciences, it has become much more debatable whether natural phenomena are as constant as the Scholastics made them out to be, nor does the fact that they are subject to empirical observation and interpretation entitle them, by that fact alone, to constitute the basis for valid or reliable truth-claims. Further, where natural law ethics has been applied rigorously it has often led to insensitivity, conservatism and the violation of human rights. This is definitely the charge made against much Vatican moral theology, from *Humanae Vitae* to *Vertitatis Splendor*.[22]

R. A. Duff refines this criticism somewhat. He argues that the natural-law attempt to define the essence of law on the basis of certain moral obligations fails on two accounts. Firstly, these principles have no foundation in ordinary practice. Society does live with laws which have no moral value. Secondly, the natural law premise fails to make the distinction between 'fact' and 'value', which was the essence of the positivist critique of natural law. Natural law theory does not take sufficient account of human sin. It is, after all, just as much a part of being human to be disobedient and to have the propensity for evil. A moral system based on this cannot claim consistency and reliability. There is a difference between law as it is and law as it ought to be; between the descriptive concepts of law, like validity, obligation and authority, for example, and the moral concepts and standards by which law may be assessed.[23]

In a criticism of Kantian metaphysics, John Kemp argues that one cannot assert that nature is purposive. One cannot understand nature unless one has investigated it. He goes on to argue that 'no moral conclusions can validly be drawn from an "as if" proposition of the kind' that Immanuel Kant makes in the *Critique of Judgement*.[24] Ernest Gellner summarises the moral philosophy of Immanuel Kant as one 'concerned with preserving minimum humanity, namely freewill, moral responsibility and autonomous cognition, but, for the rest, [he] accepted that part of the price for the advancement of knowledge is that [human beings] too become objects of knowledge'.[25]

As a result of this criticism, various attempts have been made to modify or reconstruct natural law theory. Karl Rahner, for example, centres his theological—ethical reasoning on the fact of human existence in order to discover what guides human freedom. He charts a middle course between supernaturalising nature and defining nature as pure substance, which leads to dualism. One observes that the essence of 'nature', for Rahner, has shifted from the cosmos or physical phenomena to person-centredness. Josef Fuchs also continues this anthropological emphasis. For him, natural law ethics simply guides one towards the moral imperative to live and act humanely. Fuchs understands the search for the human as a gift of grace illumined by the gospel and not simply a process of rational enquiry.[26]

Contemporary Debates in Jurisprudence

It has been necessary to outline Aquinas's natural law theory of morality, which John Finnis refers to as a 'paradigm for natural law theorists',[27] and to take note of the reaction to this Thomist system, especially in respect of the debate on law and morality, before we can begin to address the controversy which all this has generated in modern jurisprudence. The debate flows in at least two streams: there are those who are committed to natural law theory but recognise a need to recast it in order to meet some of the objections advanced against its classical expression; and there are also legal positivists who are hostile to any linking of law and morality. The debate is best captured in the dialogue between Lon Fuller, a Harvard Law School scholar of jurisprudence who advances a refined natural law theory, and H. L. A. Hart of Oxford, a positivist philosopher.[28]

Professor Hart believes that legal obligations are imposed by primary legal rules. Secondary rules are those which define and authorise the activities of officials in creating and administering the law. One might call these administrative rules, as distinct from adjectival law, which sets out procedures for law enforcement. It is worth noting that a law may be valid and impose obligations even if its effect is undermined by lack of acceptance by the citizenry. People may obey a statute, but that in itself does not signify acceptance. However, for a law to have authority, the voluntary co-operation of all citizens is required. Such 'voluntary co-operation' need not in itself arise out of a moral obligation. It may be simply expedient to obey in certain circumstances. Should circumstances change, such co-operation may be withdrawn. Duff puts it this way: 'A legal system could logically exist, imposing legal obligations, even though *no one* within it ascribes it any moral worth: for the practical or moral criticisms we may make of such a system have no bearing on its legal status.'[29]

While Professor Hart accepts, to some degree, a place for shared values in law, he argues that lack of moral values in themselves does not nullify the legal nature of legislation. What makes it law is not its moral content but the rules which have been followed in order to bring it into being, 'the fundamental accepted rules specifying the essential lawmaking procedures'.[30] For the essence of law, according to Hart, is not derived from what may be regarded as its moral content or the justice or otherwise of the procedures. The agreed processes simply need to be obeyed.

Hart's is a morality of 'universal values', observes Basil Mitchell, which are, *ex hypothesi*, respected . . . in any society'.[31] The law, according to this positivist principle, and especially criminal law, should not be used to enforce morality. In criticising Hart's system of rules, Duff notes that, as formulated, the idea of 'self-interest' need not translate into justice. It is not a moral category. He believes that essential questions like the following can be asked: Are such attitudes to the law appropriate or not? Are they proper or defective? In other words, a value judgement still needs to be made. Lawmaking procedures, in themselves, are not self-legitimating.

Professor Lon Fuller, on the other hand, appears to attach some significance to the notion of value in the content of law. Law is not morally neutral and cannot be abstracted from the validity or otherwise of the procedures which went towards making it. Locating himself firmly in the natural law tradition, Fuller claims that the purpose internal to the law generates certain moral constraints which are essentially rather than contingently connected to the idea of law. He believes that law has more affinity with just and moral ends than with unjust and iniquitous ones. Respect for the principles of legality is a prerequisite of substantive justice. It coheres more readily with good rather than with evil. It incorporates the conception of humanity as autonomous, rational and responsible rather than oppressive and merely self-centred.[32] Fuller states the moral dilemma in a manner that shows that it is irresolvable: 'On the one hand, we have an amoral datum called law, which has the peculiar quality of creating a moral duty to obey it. On the other hand, we have a moral duty to do what we think is right and decent. When we are confronted by a statute we believe to be thoroughly evil, we have to choose between two duties.'

Fuller begs the question whether law as such does impose a moral obligation. Is it not the fact of one's participation in its process, even if it is by some democratic fiction, which imposes the burden? In such circumstances, a decision not to obey is a matter of conscience. One could only make the statement that 'laws have a peculiar quality of creating a moral duty to be obeyed' of laws passed in democratic constitutions. There was no moral duty to obey the laws of the Third Reich. By the same token, there was no moral duty to obey the laws of the apartheid regime in South Africa. They were obeyed by most people, even by the oppressed, because it was expedient to do so.

Duff's contribution to this debate is to say that law only has significance if it has value attached to it. This value is the common good which is the standard or yardstick according to which any legal principle may be evaluated or criticised. Duff argues, against some natural law interpretations, that there is not a fixed or determinate set of moral standards but a range of moral concepts, which are themselves susceptible to differing moral interpretations. Daniel Brudney notes that Fuller's system is based on the conception of human beings as morally responsible agents and that there are interlocking responsibilities between the citizenry and the organs of government. But Fuller's essential point is that no legal system could long endure if compliance relied solely on behavioural training or brute force. Laws are designed for and directed at beings with certain cognitive and volitional capacities.[33]

The problem for Fuller in this formulation is that it places no bar on the state enacting slave laws or an oppressive system. It only needs to develop a myth of the sub-humanity of the victims, 'so to dehumanise the oppressed that moral categories apply to them no more and often no less than to animals'.[34] Such an ideology was frequently promoted by the advocates of apartheid in South Africa. They undermined the humanity of the black population and, like the Aryan philosophy of Nazism, they created a myth about the superiority of white people. That is how racism, sexism and class oppression have been justified in history. But, throughout history, such regimes have not been able to sustain their moral legitimacy. Once that was eroded, they soon collapsed, because the system could no longer sustain its claims to moral legitimacy. Its officials or executors could no longer believe in the moral justification of their actions.

It is no longer enough to claim that the legal system of apartheid or Nazism was law in a positivist sense; nor does Fuller's natural law ethics make sense. Barry Hoffmaster concludes that 'human law *qua* human law has its own unique obligation, not merely a moral obligation derived from natural law'.[35] This may sound like a device to smooth over the cracks, but it brings out the fact that the compulsive or coercive aspect of law does not necessarily derive from its moral force. It may have none, but moral citizens would still feel bound to obey.

This writer takes his stand on the notion that there is a necessary, essential and intrinsic relationship between natural law and positivism. While one may understand the need to maintain the 'independence' of law from morality in a context where morality is subject to the uncertainties of differing and changing interpretations and values, one must also note that such distance does not divest law of all moral content. In his essay 'The Political Limitations of Natural Law', Edgar Scully argues that the dichotomy that has developed between natural and positive law is unnecessary. Positive law signifying a body of law *posited* or laid down by authority builds on the natural law fundamentals. Like natural law, it can only be founded on the common good and it will have to earn the acceptance of the people, otherwise it will not be morally enforceable. Scully declares that 'there is an unbroken continuity of law from eternal law in the divine mind through its participation in natural law up to and including the natural evolution of political society and state authority with its positive laws'.[36] Beyond the philosophical disputation, I would agree with Barry Hoffmaster that legal positivism and traditional natural law 'are much closer . . . than is generally allowed, at least with respect to the issues of legal validity and legal obligation'.[37]

Natural Law Ethics Beyond Apartheid

Since February 1990 South Africa has been undergoing a process of change: change from the constraints of oppressive rule under apartheid; change from the authoritarianism of repressive Calvinist morality; and change from a legal system which lacked legitimacy. In responding to years of pressure at all levels, the apartheid regime conceded that it could neither sustain any longer nor morally justify its maintenance of the system of apartheid. There are at least two consequences to these developments. One is the search for a more legitimate system of law, and the other is the need to take account of the diverse cultural roots and systems of the people of South Africa in such a manner that they can identify themselves with the evolving system. The idea is not to repeat the mistakes of the past. This concern has been dramatised in recent events. The multi-party negotiating forum at the World Trade Centre in Johannesburg has agreed on some principles for a Bill of Rights which are to be entrenched in a future constitution; its provisions will be justiciable.

Objections have been raised to some of the equity clauses, especially as regards the rights of women. Traditional African leaders are objecting that these clauses would effectively nullify traditional practices whereby women are not allowed to take part in certain traditional ceremonies. Further, what would these clauses mean for polygamy, which customary law allows but which often comes with inherent inequalities for women? There is reason to believe that a similar objection can be raised by the Muslim community in South Africa, which is a not insignificant minority. What form will a parallel legal system take in South Africa, involving both customary law and the law of the land, which is bound to be interpreted according to the Bill of Rights?

The second noteworthy aspect of the recent changes in the country has been the debate in favour of a secular state. White South African society has been inclined to assume that the country is Christian, and its values, therefore, should be drawn from Christian ethics. These views are now upheld by the white right-wing and by the religious right. There is now a recognition that the diversity of cultures and religious beliefs can best be provided for in a spirit of tolerance by a secular constitutional and legal system. Does this suggest that the proposed legal system should remain neutral in matters of morality? By what rule should the moral content of the law be interpreted?

The South Arican legal system bears the marks of the seesawing fortunes of the debate between natural law and positivism. Whereas natural law emerged in order to limit the excesses of feudal laws, positive law became the answer of liberalism from John Stuart Mill to H. L. A. Hart. The aim was to preserve the law from the moral laws imposed by the ecclesiastical system.

Positivism arose in the context of the British legal system where there is no written constitution or a formal Bill of Rights. British law is governed by conventions which developed out of the practice of British institutions: the constitutional monarchy, parliament, the judiciary and the established church. On the other hand, in the newly liberated colonies of the United States of America it became necessary to base the legal system on a written constitution and a Bill of Rights in order to protect the rights of the citizens against invasion by the institutions of government.

The South African legal and constitutional system has its origins in a combination of Roman-Dutch law, English law and other conventions which grew out of the peculiar circumstances of South Africa. Although one of the streams on which South African law feeds, namely Roman-Dutch law, was based on the higher ideal law or natural law, by early this century the current began to turn towards legal positivism. One reason for this development was the growth of English law in colonial South Africa, but more likely it was the result of the fact that natural law doctrine was declining even in Europe. By the end of the Second World War, however, it became evident world-wide that legal positivism had failed to ensure the propriety of law. Its servile obedience to the will of the sovereign, comments John Dugard, and the strict distinction it made between law and morals were exploited by Hitler and resulted in the debasement of the German legal system.[38]

In apartheid South Africa, this legal philosophy was consistent with an autocratic and unaccountable perversion of democracy which became the trademark of the South African legal system. Blackstone's dictum that parliament can 'do everything that is not naturally impossible' was exploited for unjust purposes by the white regime in South Africa.

Sovereignty of parliament meant that the South African parliament was 'absolute and without control'.[39] Ironically, this principle was modelled along the lines of the divine right of kings, which natural law theorists believed led to arbitrary and unjust application of the law. Positivism substituted dictatorship by parliament for the absolute rule of kings.

Alongside this dictatorship, the rule of the separation of powers was strictly upheld in South Africa. While the sovereignty of parliament was jealously guarded even in abuse, the judiciary guarded its neutrality and failed to intervene even when parliament was being manifestly unlawful, as was the case in the celebrated matter of the High Court of Parliament. For the purpose of removing Coloureds from the common voters' roll, the upper house of parliament was packed in order to overrule the Appellate Division of the Supreme Court.[40]

The influence of positivism has been all-pervasive. It can be detected in the principle of the sovereignty of parliament. This has meant that, as Professor D. V. Cowen puts it, 'the declared will of parliament cannot be challenged in the courts on the score of unreasonableness'.[41] The natural justice principle that unless there was a statutory provision to the contrary, statutes should be interpreted so as to avoid manifest injustice, was eroded in the relentless violation of the rule of law and human rights by the South African legislature. Where the executive and the legislative wings of government abdicated their responsibility to uphold justice in the lawmaking process, it was left to the judiciary to uphold a modicum of natural justice. That it consistently failed to do.

Professor Dugard notes that South African law has enshrined in its tradition a body of legal principles of natural justice and human rights like *audi alteram partem* and freedom of speech. These, however, do not have the force of law and, on the contrary, have been progressively curtailed by statute. Dugard suggests that these principles could have been utilised by South Africa's judges as guiding values and persuasive principles of judicial interpretation. But the judges were generally loth to uphold these values.[42]

In addition to the sovereignty of parliament, the South African legal system has been based on the independence of the judiciary and the positivist notion of the separation of law and morality. The result was that the tyranny of parliament was allowed to prevail for far too long and in the process served to discredit the judicial process in the country. It is not difficult to speculate why judges were so reticent to interfere or, indeed, to apply vigorously principles which were a part of South Africa's legal tradition. The irresistible answer is that the judges were all part of the dominant culture, the race oligarchy; appointed by the executive, they were drawn from the ruling white minority, and their interests were intertwined with the fortunes of the white minority regime.[43]

Apart from reform of the legal system, the second matter that is at present on the agenda in South Africa is how account should be taken of the claims of a multi-cultural and multi-religious society. The effect of legal positivism was to allow the exclusive dominance of legal principles derived from European law. These principles enabled a system of injustice to be entrenched in the country for too long. Natural law principles need not be confined solely to administrative law, as was the case in recent years.[44] Since South Africa will have to take account of parallel legal principles which some citizens consider valid and binding, customary law will have to be reviewed. I would agree with Edgar Scully that natural law is implicit in customary law. Thomas Aquinas developed the principle that custom is superior to statute and that the people's consent takes precedence over the ruler's authority.[45] This principle would, however, only cause uncertainty in law, which would be deleterious to order in society. But to the extent that customary laws are not in conflict with the express provisions of a Bill of Rights as interpreted according to customary law, they ought to be valid and obligatory legal provisions. One difficulty is that such laws should be universally applied or available to all citizens.[46] In principle all South Africans could have recourse to such customary law.

John Dugard, for his part, has proposed what he calls a 'realist-cum-value-oriented approach to the judicial process and civil liberty'. Such a principle would concentrate on 'revealing the true nature of the legal process and how its defects might be remedied by a purposeful application of the legal values of Western civilisation'.[47] But Western civilisation cannot be allowed to dominate South African moral culture nor does it deserve such a place of honour in a changing South Africa. In the name of Western civilisation, much injustice was perpetrated in South Africa. Charles Villa-Vicencio's criticism that John Dugard's suggestions fall far too short has some merit. He argues that Dugard fails to take note of the discontinuity of values which will be necessary for a new South Africa. A radical foundation for a new art of lawmaking needs to be laid down, drawn from the best of the cultural and intellectual traditions of South Africa. In large measure, however, Professor Dugard's proposals have been taken into account in the legal system now proposed for the new constitution of South Africa.

Conclusion

What Professor Dugard is seeking, however, is that there should be public debate about the first or fundamental principles and values for the constitutional and legal system of the new South Africa. Those values cannot simply be constructed from the negative experience of the system under apartheid, nor is it good enough to draw from the experience of oppression and exile. Some more fundamental moral principles are called for. Liberal democratic values are fine as far as they go but they still need to be etched in the moral consciousness and praxis of the people of South Africa.

One detects that the pendulum is swinging towards natural law ethics once again. For this to be a credible way forward, however, a reconstruction of natural law is indicated. This is recasting of the kind that liberation theologians have undertaken and one which John Cogley performs in uncovering the core principles of natural law. He suggests that natural law affirms the primacy of reason over the non-rational in nature. Secondly, he avers that natural law is not anti-progress for, he says, 'alongside the natural lawyer's insistence on stable standards is an insistence on giving due weight to the changing and changeable factors of human existence'.[48] On this basis, it can be said that ethics takes on a rational foundation. The ethical function becomes a matter of the intellect reflecting on experience. In South Africa we need to capture that moral universe which is essential for a proper ordering of society. My conclusion is one which I share with Daniel Brudney:

> It is sometimes said that law has a 'halo' of morality, an expression
> suggesting that law and morality are connected, but in a way which is
> difficult to pin down. Law's halo, such as it is, is probably not to be
> accounted for by a single link of law and morality. Perhaps there are a
> variety of such links even if no single one nor even all taken together can
> ensure that all legal systems are morally acceptable. . .[49]

[1] *Veritatis Splendor* (London: Catholic Truth Society, 1993).

[2] Henry Tincq in *Le Monde*, reprinted in *Weekly Mail and Guardian* (Johannesburg) 15–21 October 1993.

[3] 'The Not So Splendid Truth' in *Weekly Mail and Guardian*, 15–21 October 1993.

[4] I am indebted to an earlier draft of the chapter by Dr Augustine Shutte, 'Philosophical Ethics', in this volume for some insights into the evolution of natural law.

[5] D. V. Cowen, *The Foundations of Freedom with Special Reference to South Africa* (Cape Town: Oxford University Press, 1961), p. 209.

[6] 'Lord's Law and Natural Law' in Harold J. Johnson (ed.), *The Medieval Tradition of Natural Law* (Michigan: Medieval Institute Publications, 1987), pp. 103–117.

[7] J. Philip Wogaman, *A Christian Method of Moral Judgment* (London: SCM, 1976), p. 118, sets this shift within the realisation of human propensity for evil. He argues: 'Given the fall away from goodness, social policy could no longer be expected to function on the basis of a positive natural law alone. A remedial, relative natural law must now be employed to compensate for the effects of the fall and to maintain a tolerable degree of harmony with the pure law of nature.'

[8] Koziol, 'Lord's Law and Natural Law', p. 106.

[9] Frederick Copleston, *A History of Philosophy*, Vol. 2: *Medieval Philosophy* (London: Image Books, 1962), p. 129.

[10] Cowen, *Foundations of Freedom*, p. 213.

[11] 'Good is to be done and pursued and evil avoided'; see Copleston, *A History of Philosophy*, Vol. 2, p. 127.

[12] Ibid., p. 128.

[13] 'Nominalist Natural Law Theory Revisited' in Johnson (ed.), *Medieval Tradition of Natural Law*, p. 133.

[14] Johannes Messner, *Social Ethics: Natural Law in the Western World* (London: B. Herder, 1965), p. 29.

[15] Ibid., p. 31.

[16] 'Nominalist Natural Law Theory Revisited', p. 135.

[17] R. A. Duff, 'Legal Obligation and the Moral Nature of Law', *The Juridical Review* (1980), p. 80.

[18] 'Natural Law and Legal Obligations' in Johnson (ed.), *Medieval Tradition of Natural Law*, p. 67.

[19] *Summa Theologiae* I–II. 95.2

[20] *Summa Theologiae* I–II. 96.2; 94.3.

[21] Wogaman, *Christian Method of Moral Judgment*, p. 69.

[22] See Thomas L. Schubeck, 'The Reconstruction of Natural Law Reasoning: Liberation Theology as a Case Study', *Journal of Religious Ethics*, 20:1 (1992), pp. 149–178.

[23] Duff, 'Legal Obligation', p. 63.

[24] John Kemp, *The Philosophy of Kant* (Oxford: Oxford University Press, 1968), p. 83. 'When theology is applied to physics, we speak with perfect justice of the wisdom, the economy, the forethought, the beneficence of nature. But in so doing we do not convert nature into an intelligent being, for that would be absurd; but neither do we dare to think of placing another being, one that is intelligent, above nature as its architect, for that would be presumptuous. On the contrary our only intention is to designate in this way a kind of natural causality on an analogy with our own causality in the technical employment of reason, for the purpose of keeping in view the rule upon which certain natural products are to be investigated.'

[25] Bryan Magee (ed.), *Men of Ideas* (London: BBC, 1978).

[26] Summarised from Schubeck, 'Reconstruction of Natural Law Reasoning', pp. 151–152.

[27] John Finnis, *Natural Law and Natural Rights* (Oxford: Clarendon Press, 1980), p. 28.

[28] There is a useful summary of this debate in C. Villa-Vicencio: 'Theology, Law and State Illegitimacy: An Agenda for Theologians and Lawyers', *Journal of Law and Religion*, 5:2 (1987), pp. 244–246.

[29] Duff, 'Legal Obligation', p. 68.

[30] Quoted in Villa-Vicencio, 'Theology, Law and State Illegitimacy'.

[31] Basil Mitchell, *Law, Morality and Religion in a Secular Society* (Oxford: Oxford University Press, 1967), p. 25.

[32] See Duff, 'Legal Obligation', pp. 73ff; H. L. A. Hart, 'Positivism and the Separation of Law and Morals', *Harvard Law Review*, 71 (1957–8); H. L. A. Hart, *The Concept of Law* (Oxford: Oxford University Press, 1965); Lon Fuller, *The Morality of Law* (New Haven: Yale University Press, 1969). This debate may also be captured, as far as the British legal system is concerned, in Basil Mitchell, *Law, Morality and Secular Society*.

[33] Daniel Brudney, 'Two Links of Law and Morality', *Ethics: An International Journal of Social, Political and Legal Philosophy*, 103:2 (1993), pp. 284–285.

[34] Ibid., p. 286.

[35] In Johnson (ed.), *Medieval Tradition of Natural Law*, p. 73.

[36] Ibid., p. 155.

[37] Ibid., p. 73.

[38] John Dugard, 'The Judicial Process, Positivism and Civil Liberty', *South African Law Journal* (1971), p. 185. See also John Dugard, *Human Rights and the South African Legal Order* (Princeton: Princeton University Press, 1978); A. S. Mathews, *Law, Order and Liberty in South Africa* (Cape Town: Juta, 1971), and C. Villa-Vicencio, *A Theology of Reconstruction: Nation Building and Human Rights* (Cambridge: Cambridge University Press, 1992).

[39] Quoted in C. Villa-Vicencio: 'Whither South Africa? Constitutionalism and Law-making', *Emory Law Journal*, 40:1 (1991), p. 146.

[40] See reference to the background to this episode in ibid., p. 150.

[41] Cowen, *Foundations of Freedom*, p. 228.

[42] See Dugard, *Human Rights*, pp. 196–198; Mathews, *Law, Order and Liberty*, pp. 56–57.

[43] See my 'Revolution Within the Law?' in B. Pityana, M. Ramphela, M. Mpumlwana and L. Wilson (eds), *Bounds of Possibility: The Legacy of Black Consciousness and Steve Biko* (Cape Town: David Philip, 1991) and J. A. G. Griffith, *The Politics of the Judiciary* (London: Fontana, 1985).

[44] Cf. *Minister of Local Government* v. *Inkosinathi Property* 1992 (2) 236 (Tk) and *S.A. Geneeskundige* v. *Strauss* 1991 (3) 203 (A).

[45] E. Scully, 'The Political Limitations of Natural Law', in Johnson (ed.), *Medieval Tradition of Natural Law*, p. 152.

[46] Cf. Robin W. Lovin and Frank E. Reynolds, 'Ethical Naturalism and Indigenous Cultures: Introduction', *Religious Ethics*, 20:2 (1992), pp. 267–278. The authors are suggesting that indigenous ethics could transform the way in which natural law morals are understood, when they say: 'The study of indigenous ethics may . . . call our attention to details of the moral life that only come into focus when those questions about the transcendental circumstances of our lives are temporarily suspended. It may be that the particular roles and contingent choices that dominate the problems of indigenous ethics have moral significance only if the natural world of our experience does have the order and coherence about which modern accounts raise questions.'

[47] *Human Rights*, p. 401.

[48] John Cogley, *Natural Law and Modern Society* (Cleveland and New York: Meridian Books, 1966), p. 17.

[49] 'Two Links of Law and Morality', p. 301.

Select Bibliography

Duff, R. A. 'Legal Obligation and the Moral Nature of Law'. *The Juridical Review* (1980), pp. 61–87

Dugard, John. 'The Judicial Process, Positivism and Civil Liberty'. *South African Law Journal* (1971), pp. 181–200

Johnson, Harold. *The Medieval Tradition of Natural Law*. Michigan: Medieval Institute Publications, 1987

Schubeck, Thomas L. 'The Reconstruction of Natural Law Reasoning: Liberation Theology as a Case Study'. *Journal of Religious Ethics*, 20:1 (1992), pp. 149–178

Sturm, Douglas. 'Natural Law, Liberal Religion and Freedom of Association: James Luther Adam on the Problem of Jurisprudence'. *Journal of Religious Ethics*, 20:1 (1992), pp. 179–208

Villa-Vicencio, Charles. *A Theology of Reconstruction: Nation Building and Human Rights.* Cambridge: Cambridge University Press, 1992

5

Law and Grace

KLAUS NÜRNBERGER

Introduction

Together with the Trinitarian and the Christological doctrines, the dialectic between law and grace belongs to the few foundational statements in Christian theology. In fact these three statements are closely related. Whatever alternative one chooses — law or grace — will determine one's entire theological system, including Christian ethics.

Most fundamentally, the expression 'law and grace' refers to the dialectic between the gift and the expectation of a relationship. This dialectic does not occur only in theology. For children, for instance, parental care is a life-enhancing gift. But this gift goes along with certain expectations. The same is true for a marriage or a commercial contract. The critical question is whether the demand has to be fulfilled before the gift is granted, or whether the gift is granted freely but with the expectation that it will lead to a fulfilled relationship. In other words, is fulfilment of the expectation a condition or a consequence of the gift?

In the theological tradition the demand is called the 'law of God' and the gift is called the 'grace of God'. These terms stem from the New Testament, especially from the theology of Paul, but they have been interpreted further during the time of the Reformation. In Protestant theology the grace of God is specifically defined as God's redemption of the sinner in Christ and, for this reason, is simply called the 'gospel'. The law, on the other hand, acquired the specific meaning of the accusation, indictment, judgement and condemnation of the sinner. It is clear that when defined in this way the law cannot be 'good news'. In other traditions, the concept 'gospel' is defined much more broadly and the law is defined in much less negative terms.

Because of lack of space, we shall concentrate on the evolution of the dialectic between law and grace in biblical times, the basic alternatives formulated during the Reformation, and a few recent South African contributions. As we go, the relevance of the discussion for contemporary ethical issues will become apparent. The appended bibliography will lead the reader into further debates.

The Hebrew Background

The first decisive biblical formulation of the relation between God and humanity is the divine promise to the patriarchs of ancient Israel. Here God disclosed Godself as the Redeemer in a situation of need. Abraham, for instance, needed male progeny, otherwise his family would have died out, and God granted him a son (Gen. 15). While God would be faithful to God's side of the relationship, the expectation was that God's human partner would be equally faithful: Abraham was ready to sacrifice his God-given son, Isaac, when asked to do so (Gen. 22).

The mutual commitment of two partners to each other is called *zedaqah* in Hebrew. This word is usually translated as 'righteousness'. However, *zedaqah* refers primarily to unquestionable reliability in a covenant relationship rather than to the slavish fulfilment of a preformulated code of conduct. It is remarkable that the old patriarchal narratives do not contain specific moral commandments at all. It is simply taken for granted that the partners know what kind of attitude and action is appropriate under given circumstances.

This basic character of the divine—human relationship revealed itself again and again in the history of the biblical faith: God redeems Israel from Egyptian slavery, God grants Israel a land of its own, God guarantees the throne of the dynasty of King David, God leads the Jewish captives out of Babylonian exile, God will transform the human heart and the social order, God heals the sick through Jesus, God grants participation in the new life of Christ in the power of the Spirit.

In all these cases God redeems God's people in situations of need, in whatever dimension of life these needs occur. But God's human partners are immediately involved in the drama. In other words, God's initiative does not render human initiative superfluous, but calls for it. God's power does not make human beings impotent, but empowers them. God's action does not exclude human activity, but makes it possible. This insight is fundamental to the law—gospel dialectic.

We have not mentioned the law so far. It seems that there were at least two sources of the concept of law in ancient Israel, the idea of a 'cosmic order' in the ancient Near Eastern royal traditions, on the one hand,[1] and the Hebrew concept of a covenant between two unequal partners, on the other. The former assumes that the king is the representative and plenipotentiary of the Deity (Ps. 2). It is his task to guarantee the integrity of a divinely established cosmic order on earth and act as a channel of divine blessings (Ps. 72). The cosmic order includes the movement of the celestial bodies, the rhythms of nature, the social order and the moral law. To disobey the king is to disobey God; to disobey God is to endanger the blessings of God, in fact to shake the very foundations of the earth (cf. Ps. 82:5).

The Sinaitic covenant, on the other hand, bears the typical characteristics of nomadic contracts between a superior and a subordinate partner. There are clear stipulations which have to be followed by the parties concerned. Yahweh will be Israel's God, and will therefore faithfully protect them. Israel will be Yahweh's people, which means that it will witness to the justice of Yahweh by keeping the law. In this sense the Sinaitic covenant reflected the mutual commitment between two partners.

However, mounting political calamities began to bring the integrity of the covenant between Yahweh and Israel into question. The prophets issued warning after warning that, as covenant partner of Israel, Yahweh was not to be played with. Apostasy and injustice would have dire consequences. When the northern kingdom of Israel was eradicated by the Assyrians in 721 BC, the prophets interpreted the catastrophe as Yahweh's punishment of Israel for having broken the covenant. Deuteronomy reiterates their warning: if you keep the law, you will be blessed; if you transgress it, you will be cursed (Deut. 28, 30). Earlier promises were unconditional: you will be blessed, you will multiply, you will possess the land. In contrast, the Deuteronomic promise is conditional: Yahweh will grant comprehensive well-being (*shalom*) only if you are obedient.

The destruction of Jerusalem in 586 BC and the Babylonian exile seemed to bear out the prophetic reading of history. In spite of some protests against it (notably the Book of Job; cf. also Ps. 44), the correlation between obedience to the law and national well-being became standard Jewish orthodoxy. Yahweh would remain faithful to the covenant with the patriarchs and re-establish the glory of Israel, but only a remnant, those who were worthy of Yahweh's holiness, would benefit from the new dispensation. When the Persians allowed the Temple to be rebuilt and a Jewish religious satrapy to be established in Jerusalem under the leadership of a High Priest, the idea of the cosmic order again gained emphasis. The figure of Moses rather than the figure of David became prominent; the law became the central pillar of Jewish identity and hope; and keeping the law became the overriding preoccupation.

But the promises did not materialise as expected. The Jews remained an oppressed nation, while the pagan empires flourished. Those who faithfully kept the law were not better off than outright sinners. Both kinds of people simply died before justice was seen to have been done. Building on the prophetic promises, an apocalyptic vision pushed the future orientation of the biblical faith into extremes: the present world would be reconstructed, the dead would rise from the grave, a last judgement would take place, and the universal kingdom of God would be established. This vision absolutised the law as a condition of entry into the coming kingdom of God, and redemption increasingly acquired the meaning of survival in the last judgement.

The New Testament

Jesus and the early church shared the apocalyptic vision, but with a significant qualification. Jesus proclaimed the proximity of the kingdom God and called for repentance. But he interpreted God as a 'Father', that is as a God of mercy, not of mechanical justice. He granted fellowship and healing to those who were considered by the religious establishment to be under the wrath of God: public sinners, lepers, cripples, collaborators, harlots and so on. The intention of the law was to serve the well-being of humanity, not to enslave and cripple the people of God (Mark 2:27). But those who were served by God through the 'Son of Man' were, in their turn, expected to serve others in love (Matt. 20:25–28). The gracious acceptance of sinners into God's fellowship would change their lives. In other words, a new life was no longer the presupposition of acceptance into God's fellowship, but its consequence.

The clash of Jesus with the protectors of the law resulted in his crucifixion. But his disciples, convinced that God had vindicated Jesus as God's representative and plenipotentiary through his resurrection from the dead, upheld the message of God's infinite grace.

Paul, a fanatical proponent of the law as the only possible way to escape ultimate condemnation, swung to the opposite extreme when he encountered the living Christ (Phil. 3). His theology has provided us with the classical formulation of the dialectic between law and grace in the canon. God's judgement over sin is absolute and total: the sinner has to die. Because we are all sinners (Rom. 3:19ff), we shall all have to die. But Christ has already died to the old sinful 'flesh' and has risen into the new life of the Spirit in communion with God. By identifying with his death we anticipate our own death. By the gift of the Spirit we are able to participate in the new life of Christ. Both are appropriated in faith and enacted in baptism (Rom. 4:24f, 6:1ff). Those who are 'in Christ' or 'in the Spirit', and not 'according to the flesh', have been saved from the condemnation of the last judgement (Rom. 8). However, as long as we are still 'in the flesh' there is a continual struggle in which our sinful nature has to be overcome by the new life of Christ (Rom. 7:14ff; Phil. 3:12ff). Final liberation from sin can only be expected in the eschatological future.

Paul's proclamation of freedom from the law opened up another front. There were Hellenists who thought that 'everything was allowed' (1 Cor. 10:23ff). Paul's emphasis on freedom from the law (Gal. 3:23—4:7) seemed to underpin this idea. The letter of James (2:14—26) strongly protested, using the same biblical case, namely Abraham, for his argument in favour of works that Paul had used in favour of faith (Rom. 4). But that was a misunderstanding of Paul's intentions. The new life of Christ, in which we are allowed to participate through the power of the Spirit, is not unprincipled; it has its own 'law', the motivation of love. This motivation fulfils the intention of the law without being enslaved by its stipulations (Rom. 8:1ff, 13:8ff; Gal. 5:16ff).

The letter to the Ephesians, probably written by a disciple of Paul, found a tight and definitive formulation of the relation between 'faith and works'. Being 'dead' in sin as far as our own potential goes, we have been 'made alive' and empowered with Christ to share in his victorious heavenly reign. We are redeemed not by our moral achievements but by God's gift of grace in Christ, accepted in faith. In Christ, God reconstitutes us as new beings and prepares the new type of life in which we are to 'walk'. So, we are God's own workmanship, and it is this work of God which empowers us to do 'good works' (Eph. 2:4—10). In other words, the fulfilment of the expectation of God is a consequence of the gift of God, not its condition.

The beauty of this chapter lies in the fact that it immediately translates this crucial insight into community terms. In his grace God has suspended the law as condition of acceptance into his fellowship. And so it can also no longer divide us from each other. In Christ, the dividing wall of the law has been demolished, and

Jews and Gentiles are built up into the one new humanity, the 'Body of Christ' (Eph. 2:22). Its 'head', the risen Christ, has been enthroned above all the spiritual powers which tear us apart in this world (Eph. 1:20–23).

Moreover, by its very existence the community of believers is to make known to these cosmic powers that the intention of God, so far hidden but now revealed, is to reconcile the entire universe to Godself (Eph. 1:8–10, 3:10f). Thus salvation is not restricted to the individual believer or to the Christian community, but aims at the reconstruction of the universe. Yet these cosmic dimensions include, rather than exclude, a constant personal battle against evil in the power of the risen Christ (Eph. 6:10ff). In short, the gift of grace in Christ empowers us to realise the eschatological potential in personal, communal and cosmic terms.

John's gospel presents us with a similar picture. In its prologue the principle by which the cosmos is constructed according to Greek philosophy, the *logos*, is personalised and identified with Christ (John 1). Christ embodies the unique opportunity of entering into an authentic life where we have intimate fellowship with God and participate actively in God's redeeming love. The law is superseded by 'grace and truth' (John 1:14, 17). The last judgement takes place whenever we encounter Christ, who embodies our potential authenticity. We either reject it and condemn ourselves, or we accept it and thereby inherit 'eternal life' – that is, authentic existence (John 3:16ff, 5:24ff).

In both cases Christian ethics is not based upon the demand to fulfil a code of conduct in the strength of our own moral resources, but upon access to the power and the freedom of a life lived in the fellowship of God. In this fellowship we are meant to share God's creative authority, God's redemptive love and God's comprehensive vision for the world. We have become 'sons and daughters of God', and as such we are meant to be 'rulers', not slaves, but rulers who serve rather than lord it over the world.

This in turn has led to new formulations of the content of the will of God. According to the patriarchal family law in Exodus 21:2-11, for instance, a father had the right to sell even his own daughter into slavery; in Galatians 3:23–28, in contrast, there is neither slave nor free, male nor female in Christ – that is, in authentic humanity. God's unconditional grace is given equally to all people, irrespective of their social status. Similarly, according to Deuteronomy 7, Israel should have eradicated the Canaanite inhabitants of Palestine; according to Ephesians 2:11ff, Jews and Gentiles are destined to form a united new humanity in Christ.

Medieval Theology and the Reformation

It was the issue whether we are saved by fulfilling the law by our own moral achievement (called 'works'), or by the grace of God accepted in faith, that triggered the Reformation. The teaching of the late medieval church had concentrated on the last judgement and the prospect of eternal punishment in hell. At best, the souls of the departed would undergo a painful process of purification in purgatory – unless, of course, they had lived the life of saints on earth. All this is typical for the law; the gospel of grace had been lost.

Driven by fear of eternal condemnation, Martin Luther tortured himself mentally and physically, but without obtaining peace of mind. He realised that the law not only demanded fulfilment of a host of moral regulations, but more fundamentally it demanded love to God — a God whom Luther could only fear and hate because he seemed to be so cruel and vindictive. In his agony he discovered that the 'justice of God', mentioned by Paul in the letter to the Romans, does not refer to a quality of God but to the righteousness of Christ which the gospel imparts to the sinner as a free gift of grace.

When Luther proclaimed this newly found gospel, he rocked the ideological foundations of the power structure of the late medieval church to its roots and set off the avalanche of the Reformation with all its political, economic and social repercussions. Protestant theology has been built on the foundation of the doctrine of 'justification by grace accepted in faith' ever since, whether Lutheran, Reformed, Methodist, Evangelical or Pentecostal. So let us have a brief look at Luther's definition of the relation between law and gospel.

Luther distinguished between two functions of the law. The 'civil use of the law' (*usus civilis* or *usus politicus legis*) is meant to structure social institutions and offices, such as the state, the economy, the church and the family. This function operates in the outward sphere of the society, which Luther called 'the rule of God on the left'. The 'convicting use of the law' (*usus elenchticus* or *usus theologicus legis*) is meant to structure our consciences and expose our sins. This function operates within our hearts. Together with the gospel, it represents 'God's rule on the right'.

The sole task of the gospel is to reconcile us with God in Christ. Our sins are forgiven for Christ's sake, and the righteousness of Christ is imparted to us. However, the righteousness of Christ is an 'alien' righteousness (*iustitia aliena*), which is Christ's, not our own. It has to challenge and overcome our own sinful nature as long as we live in this world. So we are at the same time righteous in Christ and sinners in our own nature (*simul iustus et peccator*).

Where the gospel is in operation, the law ceases to function. That is, in as far as we are in Christ, Christ's own righteousness will bring forth good fruits in us. Living in fellowship with God, we need no law to know God's heart; we simply and joyfully share in his redemptive love. The specific contents of these good fruits will be determined by our motivation of love, our powers of observation and reason, and the vast pool of human experience at our disposal — whether found in Scripture or in other classical writings.

This does not mean that Luther could not spell out in concrete detail what the new life of Christ could entail under given circumstances. He did so, for instance, in his famous essay 'On Good Works'. But these concrete details are flexible guidelines. 'New decalogues' had to be written as situations changed.

It also does not mean that the law loses its function for the community of believers. In as far as we are still sinners and live in a sinful social context, the law in both its functions continues to be applicable. Moreover, although in Christ they are free, Christians know that the law is needed in this sinful world. They will continue to proclaim the demands of the law, they will take upon themselves the burdens of public office and administer the civil function of the law. So law and gospel form a dialectic, and both must at all times be preached.

Protestant Orthodoxy and the Council of Trent

John Calvin was a disciple of Luther's theology in most respects, including the doctrines of law and gospel and the two kingdoms, but he added a 'third use of the law' (*tertius usus legis*) to the scheme. This third use comes into operation after the gospel has granted us forgiveness of sins. Its function is to guide us into the will of God. Calvin described this function as the most important use of the law. Melanchthon, who was to put his stamp on Lutheranism after Luther's death, agreed with Calvin rather than Luther on this point. The model of the gospel and the three functions of the law (the political, theological and third use) became 'classical' during the consolidation of Protestant orthodoxy in the seventeenth century and still informs the debate today.

The consequences of Calvin's and Melanchthon's addition to Luther's scheme are far-reaching. In Luther's approach we are supposed to be free sons and daughters of God who share God's love. The law is only introduced as an emergency measure because of sin. Its task is to expose and contain evil. Once sin and evil are overcome, it has no place in our relation to God. In the approaches of Calvin and Melanchthon, by contrast, it is the law which forms the basis of our relationship with God and it is the gospel which only comes in as an emergency measure. To use a picture: the train of our lives is supposed to run along the rails of the law; owing to the accident of sin our lives are derailed; then the emergency team of the gospel comes in and sets us back on the rails of the law; after that, it is the rails again which guide our lives.

As a result, the Calvinist tradition has always placed great emphasis on strict moral discipline, sometimes reaching the extremes of Puritan legalism and fanaticism. Lutherans, by contrast, have been much more relaxed, often reaching the extremes of moral indifference and laxity.

It is interesting to note that the modern American debate between norm ethics (or deontology) and situation ethics (or teleology) unknowingly rehearses some of the alternatives formulated during the Reformation in this regard. Are Christians required to follow a preformulated code of conduct, or proceed by the infinitely flexible motivation of love, which adapts to any new situation?[2]

The Catholic Counter-Reformation represented a response to the Protestant challenge. The Council of Trent conceded that God's grace was paramount. But God's grace leads repentant sinners into a process of sanctification, which involves their own moral effort and which culminates in their justification. In other words, according to Trent sinners are made to be just and then found to be just.[3] According to Protestants, by contrast, sinners are proclaimed to be just (in so far as they have been accepted into the fellowship of Christ, where they draw from his righteousness), and this in turn leads them into a process of sanctification.

We see that the alternative between conditional and unconditional acceptance, between fulfilment of the law as a condition or a consequence of divine acceptance, again surfaces. Deep-going dialogue between representatives of the three traditions, Lutheran, Calvinist and Catholic, have largely removed the disagreements about grace and justification among theologians, but that does not mean that the traditional cleavages do not persist in the hearts and minds of the churches concerned.

Karl Barth and Neo-Lutheranism

The debate on the relation between law and gospel flared up again during the 'church struggle' in Nazi Germany between the Confessing Church and the German Christians. The details of the debate have been described by Forde and summarised by Nürnberger.[4] For lack of space we have to refer to these sources.

The main theological concern of Karl Barth, a leading voice in the debate, was the initiative of the sovereign God which, on the one hand, renders all human attempts futile and, on the other hand, graciously involves human action. The theological insight attained from this dialectical approach was that Christian ethics is not based on human effort to fulfil the divine will, but on the divine act which calls forth, empowers and directs the human act. Expressed in traditional terminology, the grace of God produces human works in those who accept God's grace in faith. This is a much more appropriate formulation than to say that we are saved by faith alone and not by works.

For Barth, the law could not simply be gleaned from the commandments found in Scripture, but must be deduced from God's revelation in Christ. For Barth, law is the 'form of the gospel'. This means that the law depicts the kind of human existence and the kind of social order which come into being when the grace of God in Christ incarnates itself in human reality. It is the gospel that determines our relationship with God; the law is a derived entity.

Existentialists and Liberation Theologians

The particular contribution to the debate of the existentialists, especially Rudolf Bultmann and his school, was their concentration on the decision we take here and now in response to a *kerygma* (message) which constantly challenges us to leave existing forms of security behind and depend on God's future. The law represents the futile attempt to achieve one's own authenticity by following the crowd; the gospel offers authenticity as the divine gift of self-determination. The problematic side of this formulation is that it reduces salvation to the solitary decision of the individual at a given moment in time.

In contrast, Jürgen Moltmann and other 'political theologians' translated the existentialist 'futuricity' of the gospel into the promise of a real future in time, the 'authenticity of human existence' into the legitimacy of the social order, and the challenge to take solitary decisions into a call for involvement in political transformations. Liberation theology, Black theology and feminist theology all began to redefine both law and gospel in historical and social-structural terms. The law of God was seen to expose structural evil and present a challenge to revolutionary action, while the gospel was heard as the promise of social and psychological liberation in a new political and economic dispensation.

The concern for personal salvation was not abandoned by liberation theology, but it was often overshadowed by the urgency of the political agenda, especially because the individual was perceived to be determined by social contexts. Moreover, the activist urge to achieve a better world tended to overemphasise the demand of the law and crowd out the gratuity of the gospel. The price which had to be paid was that when disillusionment and frustration set in among activists, because the social reconstruction did not materialise as envisaged, there was little comfort left in the Christian message. In recent times, therefore, a new quest for the spiritual dimensions of the Christian faith has begun to emerge in the liberation school.

Heinz Dehnke

Space does not permit us to describe the considerable contributions of South African theologians to the debate in detail. A few indications must suffice. Heinz Dehnke tried to make sense of the doctrine of justification in the context of traditional Tswana religion and came up with fascinating observations.[5] While Western Christianity brought a fairly superficial and moralistic concept of sin to Africa, Tswana traditional religion distinguished between *sebe* (filth, or sin in a moral sense), *boleo* (an act leading to guilt in relation to other human beings) and *bosula* (the chain reaction of evil which is set in motion by guilt, including disturbed communal relationships). *Bosula* in turn leads to specific forms of *dikgaba* or *madimabe* (instances of 'bad luck'). *Boleo* must be punished or forgiven, *bosula* must be exorcised. Such chain reactions of evil and their concrete manifestations can occur in any dimension of life: barrenness, conflict between the generations, unemployment, violence, drought and so on.

It is clear that what theology calls the 'law' is here perceived to be much more than a moral code of behaviour. It is a healthy set of relationships within a peaceful social and natural environment. To restore comprehensive peace and stop the chain reaction of evil, the grudge of the wronged party must be exorcised and the entire community, including the ancestors, must be reconciled to one other. In Christian terms, forgiveness of sin is not sufficient; there must be a healing which brings to an end the processes of evil set in motion by concrete misdeeds.

Simon Maimela

Maimela, a black Lutheran theologian, conducted his doctoral research on the law—gospel debate during the German church struggle. As a result he came up with a new formulation of the 'civil use of the law'. In the theological tradition this function of the law was often seen in static and negative terms: it was the emergency order of God which was meant to keep universal evil in check. In contrast, Maimela argued that the law is an expression of the 'dynamic and creative holy will of sovereign love', which bestows life on finite creatures.[6] This dynamic and open creativity points forward to the completion of creation rather than to the fire of eternal condemnation. Moreover, while sin cannot be removed from the world by human effort, God's creativity involves us in its dynamic, so that we engage in securing partial, provisional and relative victories over lovelessness, injustice, pain and suffering.

The law, which the tradition had always seen as a futile and frustrating incitement to fulfil God's will, is now defined as 'a profoundly disturbing' and 'transformative power', which functions as a 'mobilising challenge to action', as a 'denunciation of the existing order', as a 'utopian vision that produces revolutions'.[7] All this is the language of liberation theology, except that it is derived from a new and contextual interpretation of classical Protestant theology. The fact that the dialectic between law and gospel is maintained is of great importance in a revolutionary situation: it is typical of the law that it whips us into action but cannot sustain us in the hour of failure and frustration. The gospel declares that God's redemptive intentions infinitely transcend our possibilities, achievements and failures.

Klaus Nürnberger

Maimela concentrated on the social relevance of the law. The present author has attempted to show that the gospel itself, as defined by the Reformation, has decisive social—ethical implications for our situation. The legal concepts used by the Reformation (justification by grace, accepted in faith) can be translated into communal categories: God accepts the unacceptable and suffers their unacceptability to overcome what is unacceptable. The point is that those who are accepted unconditionally into God's fellowship cannot hurl conditions of acceptance against each other. Racist or sexist exclusiveness, for instance, is based not only on conditions of acceptance, but on conditions of acceptance which the other party cannot fulfil, however much it tries to make itself acceptable. This is not simply disobedience against the law of God; it is a denial of the gospel. Again for lack of space, we have to refer to the literature.[8]

Albert Nolan

Nolan is a Catholic religious who does not share the Protestant tradition about law and grace. Biblically, he is rooted more in the synoptic gospels than in Paul. As a result, his terminology is different from what we have discussed so far. Let us see how Nolan defines the 'gospel'.[9]

The gospel has no fixed content. Its specific content depends on the context. (Remarkably this had been said of the law by Luther!) But it does have a constant form. It is, as the word implies, always good news. But it is good news for the poor and, by definition, bad news for the rich and powerful. The gospel is not neutral; it takes sides.

Being contextual, the gospel is a prophetic message for a particular time. Essentially, the message of Jesus did not differ from the message of the prophets. The gospel always proclaims something new, yet it must be the gospel of Jesus Christ. It must reflect his mind.

Here Nolan does not refer to historical traditions or Christological doctrines but to the signs of the times — that is, 'what God is now doing in South Africa through the risen Christ'.[10] Nolan interprets actual events in this country in the light of God's liberating action in the world. It is the Spirit which shows us 'where God is' in the present situation of crisis and conflict — for instance, where the oppressed 'rebel, assert their humanity and become determined subjects of their own history and destiny'.[11] Against the backdrop of our discussion so far, this is surely a novel way of defining the gospel.

Nolan also deals with what we have called 'the law', without using the term in the traditional sense. He depicts the 'purity system' of the High Priest, the Sanhedrin and the Pharisees at the time of Jesus as a system designed to sanctify the structures of domination and to secure the privileges of the 'holy and pure ones' who have been able to conform to its dictates. Nolan says that Jesus rejected this system *in toto* and condemned the rich, the scribes and the Pharisees as the real sinners, while he made those who were officially classified as sinners his friends, namely the whole 'rabble' of the poor, sick and unclean.

Nolan then applies the biblical material to the South African situation. He speaks of the 'anger of God' directed against the injustices of the oppressive, exploitative and dehumanising system of 'racist capitalism'. While the 'struggle' is the manifestation of the gospel, the 'system' is the manifestation of the demonic power of evil in concrete South African terms.

A Protestant Response to Nolan

Nolan's book has challenged traditional Protestant theology very profoundly. I have argued that liberation theology renders Protestant theology the service of reformulating the structure-giving and sin-exposing functions of the law in terms of God's demand for equal dignity, social justice, economic equity, democratic rights and social–structural freedom.[12] All this is not only necessary but overdue. But in Protestant terms, all this belongs to the law, not the gospel.

The second problem is that Nolan defines, in straightforward political terms, who the saints and who the culprits are. He also mythologises good and evil as the 'struggle' on the one hand and the 'system' on the other. This neat distinction has at all times been the foundation for holy war and the crusade. Once you have found the devil outside your own camp, you can mobilise your people to root it out. This message is dangerous, especially at a time when a particular society is on the verge of an explosion.

Of course, I do not suggest that it was ever Nolan's intention to push our country into violent chaos. Far from it! But to become an instrument of justice and peace the church must stress that, although the concrete manifestations of sin differ vastly between rich and poor, and although the rich have more power to give effect to their sinful motives, human beings are all sinners and our respective failures must all be challenged and overcome. Similarly we all have received gifts for which we can praise God and with which we can serve one other. Of course, this in no way suggests neutrality between good and evil, nor a wrong kind of even-handedness in relation to the perpetrators and the victims of social–structural sin.

When we come to the gospel, it is the strength of Nolan's approach that it defines sin as whatever causes suffering, and the gospel as the affirmation of the right to liberty in social terms. Surely the right of existence of persons and groups is questioned when their life chances are impaired, and affirmed when space is provided for their flourishing. But the gospel is not simply the message that God opposes injustice and shall overcome it. There is indeed a difference between Old Testament prophets and Jesus Christ on this point. The gospel is the message that, in Christ, God has moved into solidarity with a humanity which has fallen helplessly into sin. God hates sin, but loves sinners. In grace God accepts the unacceptable and suffers their unacceptability — not to condone it, but to overcome it from within. That is the theological meaning of the Cross.

Political action should reduce evil and further good in social—structural terms as far as possible. It can also lead to considerable changes in collective consciousness. But human beings also need to be transformed in their very being if they are to be redeemed. This happens when sinners are granted the gift of fellowship with God and with each other, and begin to share God's creative authority, God's redemptive love and God's comprehensive vision for the suffering world. The struggle against evil must become 'democratic', which means that we must all become involved.[13]

Finally, we need to remember that the gospel goes beyond what can be achieved in this world. It postulates a new human being, a new community, a new earth, a new heaven. It aims at comprehensive well-being. Its target is every single deficiency in comprehensive well-being. By anticipating God's kingdom in word and deed we try to approximate comprehensive well-being as far as our powers reach in this world. But the gospel of God's absolute benevolence cannot simply be gleaned from those developments in history which seem to involve and benefit the suffering. On the contrary, the power of the gospel unfolds precisely where God's redemptive intentions are hidden under failures, atrocities and deteriorating conditions — even in death, which is the most complete catastrophe experienced by human beings.

[1] H. H. Schmid, 'Creation, Righteousness and Salvation: "Creation Theology" as the Broad Horizon of Biblical Theology', in B. Anderson (ed.), *Creation in the Old Testament* (Philadelphia: Fortress, 1984).

[2] See eg. C. J. MacFadden, *Medical Ethics* (Philadelphia: Davis, 1967), pp. 11ff and J. Fletcher, *Situation Ethics* (London: SCM, 1966), pp. 69ff.

[3] J. Neuner and J. Dupuis, *The Christian Faith in the Doctrinal Documents of the Catholic Church* (London: Collins, 1983), pp. 554ff.

[4] G. O. Forde, *The Law–Gospel Debate* (Minneapolis: Augsburg, 1969) and K. Nürnberger, 'The Law–Gospel Debate as a Possible Basis for a Theological Ethic', *Theologia Evangelica*, XIV (1981), pp. 25–47.

[5] H. Dehnke, 'The Proclamation of Justification in the Context of the Tswana Traditional Religion and Tswana Syncretism'. Written in 1968.

[6] S. Maimela, *God's Creative Activity Through the Law* (Pretoria: Unisa, 1984), p. 218.

[7] Ibid., pp. 222f.

[8] K. Nürnberger, 'By Grace Alone. The Significance of the Core Doctrine of the Reformation for the Present Crisis in South Africa', in K. Nürnberger and J. Tooke (eds), *The Cost of Reconciliation in South Africa* (Cape Town: Methodist Publishing House, 1988), pp. 181–198; K. Nürnberger, 'Socio-Political Ideologies and Church Unity', *Missionalia*, 10 (1983), pp. 42–53 and *JTSA*, 44 (1983), pp. 47–57; K. Nürnberger, 'Martin Luther's Political Ethics Against the Background of His Theological Approach', *Theologia Evangelica*, XVIII (1985), pp. 44–65; K. Nürnberger, 'Subscribing to Confessional Documents Today', *JTSA*, 75 (June 1991), pp. 37–47.

[9] Albert Nolan, *God in South Africa: The Challenge of the Gospel* (Cape Town: David Philip, 1988), pp. 5ff.

[10] Ibid., p. 18.

[11] Ibid., p. 144.

[12] Nürnberger, 'Subscribing to Confessional Documents Today', p. 40.
[13] Ibid., pp. 38–45.

Select Bibliography

Brakemeier, Gottfried. 'Justification by Grace and Liberation Theology: A Comparison'. *Ecumenical Review,* 40 (1988), pp. 215–222

Dehnke, H. 'The Proclamation of Justification in the Context of the Tswana Traditional Religion and Tswana Syncretism'. Unpublished essay

Fletcher, J. *Situation Ethics.* London: SCM, 1966

Forde, G. O. *The Law–Gospel Debate.* Minneapolis: Augsburg, 1969

Küng, Hans. *Justification: The Doctrine of Karl Barth and a Catholic Reflection.* London: Burns and Oates, 1964

MacFadden, C. J. *Medical Ethics.* Philadelphia: Davis, 1967

McGrath, Allister. 'Justification: The New Ecumenical Debate'. *Themelios,* 13 (1988), pp. 43–48

Maimela, S. *God's Creative Activity Through the Law.* Pretoria: Unisa, 1984

Mendenhall, George E. 'Law and Covenant in Israel and the Ancient Near East'. *The Biblical Archaeologist,* XVII: 2 (1954)

Neuner, J. and Dupuis, J. *The Christian Faith in the Doctrinal Documents of the Catholic Church.* London: Collins, 1983

Nolan, Albert. *God in South Africa: The Challenge of the Gospel.* Cape Town: David Philip, 1988

Nürnberger, K. 'By Grace Alone. The Significance of the Core Doctrine of the Reformation for the Present Crisis in South Africa', in K. Nürnberger and J. Tooke (eds), *The Cost of Reconciliation in South Africa.* Cape Town: Methodist Publishing House, 1986

Nürnberger, K. 'The Law-Gospel Debate as a Possible Basis for a Theological Ethic'. *Theologia Evangelica,* XIV (1981) pp. 25–47

Nürnberger, K. 'Socio-Political Ideologies and Church Unity'. Missionalia, 10 (1983) pp. 42–53 and *JTSA,* 44 (1983) pp. 47–57

Nürnberger, K. 'Martin Luther's Political Ethics Against the Background of His Theological Approach'. *Theologia Evangelica,* XVIII (1985) pp. 44–65

Nürnberger, K. 'Subscribing to Confessional Documents Today'. *JTSA,* 75 (1991), pp. 37–47

Räisänen, Heikki. 'Paul's Conversion and the Development of His View on the Law'. *New Testament Studies,* 33 (1987), pp. 404–419

Schmid, H. H. 'Creation, Righteousness and Salvation: "Creation Theology" as the Broad Horizon of Biblical Theology', in B. Anderson (ed.), *Creation in the Old Testament.* Philadelphia: Fortress, 1984

Sedgewick, Peter. 'Justification by Faith: One Doctrine, Many Debates?' *Theology,* 93 (1990), pp. 5–13

6

Ethics of Responsibility

CHARLES VILLA-VICENCIO

Situations, Exceptions and Flexibility

There is nothing particularly revolutionary or new in the argument that ethics is obliged to take each situation seriously, accepting that abstract claims about what is right or wrong do not always adequately address the complexities of life. The ability to adapt, to show flexibility and to be thoughtful in ethical decisions is surely a commendable feature in any moral agent.

Although taking many different forms, what characterises this model of ethical decision-making (over against legalism) is the explicit promotion of the belief that ethics is more than the application of ethical rules in some bookish or casuistic manner. At the same time it acknowledges (over against antinomianism)[1] that ethical principles are formative, though not prescriptive, elements in decision-making. An ethic of responsibility accepts that the demands of the actual situation or context are as important as the ethical norms on which one draws in deciding on what is morally right.

To the extent that a decision is taken from a Christian perspective, God's revelatory and redemptive work in Christ is a formative ingredient of an ethic of responsibility. For central to the Judaeo-Christian drama is the 'awful' obligation of believers to share in God's redemptive work. It is 'awful' in that it recognises that God's supreme redemptive work involved Jesus in taking the sin of others onto himself. In a different way, an ethic of responsibility recognises that ethical behaviour sometimes involves us in doing what is normally regarded as the 'wrong' or 'sinful' thing – for the 'right' reason, which is the love of neighbour and the promotion of justice in the world.

A popularised version of this kind of ethic is Joseph Fletcher's *Situation Ethics*. His book bearing that title as well as his subsequent writings immediately caught the public imagination on publication. There is nothing quite like an idea whose time has come. We give consideration to his work in what follows, comparing it to a book written three years earlier by Paul Lehmann. Attention is then given to two other models of an ethic of responsibility, which predate both Fletcher and Lehmann. The models are those of Karl Barth and Dietrich Bonhoeffer, both of whom wrote from within the ethical crisis of Nazi Germany. Drawing on these discussions, the chapter makes an attempt to identify the theological parameters of a Christian ethic of responsibility.

Situation Ethics

Joseph Fletcher's ethic is an attempt to expound the proposition that situations sometimes demand that one put aside one's moral principles and ethical rules, in order to do the right thing. His ethic of the 'right thing' recognises only one absolute, which is the act of self-giving love for the benefit of one's neighbour. 'Hence it follows that in Christian situational ethics nothing is worth anything in and of itself. It gains or acquires value only because it happens to help persons (thus being good) or to hurt persons (thus being bad).'[2] The nature of the loving act, Fletcher argues, can only be determined within the context of a particular situation. It is impossible to determine the nature of love in advance. In brief, his ethic is pre-eminently contextual.

Fletcher summarises his position in six propositions. Firstly, only one thing is ultimately good, namely love. Secondly, the ultimate norm for Christian decision-making is love. Thirdly, love and justice are the same, for justice is love distributed. Fourthly, love wills our neighbours' good whether we like them or not. Fifthly, only the end justifies the means. Sixthly, decisions ought to be made situationally and not prescriptively. Fletcher proposes that these principles provide an ethical method which steers a middle course between legalism and antinomianism.

In proposing his 'love only' ethic — 'only one thing is intrinsically good, namely love: nothing else at all'[3] — Fletcher is not rejecting all other ethical norms, but is rather relegating them to the status of general principles or rules of thumb, which indicate the direction in which a loving decision is likely to go. Ready to learn from the collective ethical wisdom of the ages, Fletcher is not a complete relativist. He regards traditional ethical 'principles or maxims or general rules [as] *illuminators*. But not as *directors*.'[4] They are not absolute, and need to be violated when in conflict with the absolute norm of love.

This kind of ethic is appealing for a number of reasons. From a Christian standpoint it seems to give expression to the New Testament command that teaches that the sum of all ethical commands is the love of God and of one's neighbour. It takes circumstances and people seriously, avoiding the dangers of legalism. It recognises the complexity of ethical decision-making, particularly in the case of ethical dilemmas. Its major difficulty is that it fails to explain precisely what one ought to do in a given situation — although few (if any) ethical systems achieve this in complex situations. Few Christians would deny that one's actions ought to be motivated by love. The question is, What constitutes love in a given situation?

Fletcher illustrates his ethic with a number of examples which demonstrate love in action in particular contexts. He refers, for example, to Scott's expedition to the Antarctic, during which the party decided not to abandon an injured member. The result of this decision was that the whole party died. While it can (and must) be acknowledged that this action was motivated by love, it is impossible to observe *how* love afforded the moral insight into exactly what to do. One could argue further that a very different and equally loving decision could have been made in that situation, depending on who was seen as the object of love. What, for example, about the families of the team members who elected to die? The injured person in the Scott expedition, as defined by Fletcher, was seen to be the object of love and the rest of the party the collective subject. If, however, the injured person was seen as the subject of love and the rest of the party the collective object of love, the loving thing (it could be argued) would have been for the injured man to insist that he be left to die alone, for the sake of the rest of the party.

Fletcher's ethic highlights the complexity of ethical decision-making — emphasising how difficult it is to apply specific ethical rules to all situations. It does not abandon all ethical rules, but it does make them secondary to the only absolute, which is love. Further, it leaves one asking to what extent the moral rules of the New Testament are in fact important. To what extent does Fletcher's ethic fail to give sufficient attention to these? Ought these rules not to be more explicitly included in the struggle to do the loving or right thing, than what his ethic seems to suggest?

Does Fletcher overstate his case? Ethical norms and principles, it could be argued, ought to be related to situations, or even suspended (as Kierkegaard suggested) in certain situations, rather than overridden by the loving demands of a given situation. The language used in giving expression to situational ethics is important. Before we turn to alternative solutions to the dilemma (suggested by Barth and Bonhoeffer), which take prescriptive ethics more seriously than Fletcher, and without becoming legalistic, it is helpful to compare Fletcher's model of situational ethics with Paul Lehmann's *Ethics in a Christian Context*, published three years before Fletcher's work.

Lehmann's approach stresses the theological basis from which the Christian moral agent engages in decision-making in a manner that Fletcher does not. Lehmann allows for the dynamism of situationalism, while showing a sensitivity to the need to define the place of ethical rules in the decision-making process. He does so by arguing that New Testament ethical rules are normative in the shaping of the Christian ethos or culture within which the Christian resides and in relation to which he or she makes an ethical decision — while not regarding them as prescriptive for actual behaviour. There is a sense in which he regards them as being part of the spirituality that nurtures those renewed by Christ and that inspires Christian *community*, within which Christians find their personal identity. He insists at the same time that Christians have the responsibility to decide what God requires of them in each new situation (rather than simply reading and applying a set of ethical rules).

Lehmann, in other words, rejects any notion of a legalistic or prescriptive ethic. The question of what we are to do is ultimately, for Lehmann, decided by who we are. Our *doing* (ethics) is a consequence of our *being*. Lehmann's ethic, in this regard, is quite straightforward: the duty of the Christian is to obey the will of God. 'Doing the will of God is (however) doing what I am.'[5] It is acting in accordance with the spirit and values that become part of my being, as a result of the transforming and humanising work of Christ. My task is to share in God's work, which is 'to make and keep human life fully human in the world'.[6] Without suggesting that the Christian has some special insight into what this humanising work involves, Lehmann insists that it is to be discerned within the context of the Christian community (*koinonia*). In so doing, the Christian realises that there is ultimately only one ethical absolute, namely the will of God, and that this may require a person to act in violation of what is commonly regarded as normative Christian behaviour.

Lehmann concedes that 'such an ethic will be puzzling, even ridiculous, to those who have no eyes to see the signs of the times, who do not know what belongs to their peace. Such knowledge comes by insight, not by calculation. It is the gift of faith available to those who are willing to take seriously what faith knows about the doing of God's will in the world.'[7] Leaving the difficulties of this confessional line of reasoning aside, Lehmann recognises that the responsibility of the ethical agent goes beyond simply applying 'the rules'. For him, the moral insight of the agent, to the extent that he or she affirms the Christian faith, is to be shaped and honed within the tradition and mores of the Christian community. Thereby he locates the place of Christian ethical teaching and community at the centre of the ethical decision-making process. To this extent Lehmann's ethic, as expressed in *Ethics in a Christian Context,* is self-consciously Christocentric, grounded in the salvific and transformimg demands of the New Testament.

There are obviously others who wrestle with the problem of the relationship between ethical rules and situational demands in different ways. In each case, however, to the extent that the proposed solutions are situational in orientation, they prepare the ethical agent to violate any rules (important as they may be as accumulated ethical wisdom) when the dictates of love may so require. Fletcher's ethic emphasises the uniqueness of each particular ethical act. Bruno Schüller, a Roman Catholic theologian, on the other hand emphasises the continuity between normative ethics and the challenge of each new ethical situation. He makes a distinction between what he calls the goal and the realisation of moral behaviour. His contention is that unqualified obedience to the norm 'Thou shalt not kill' could result in more deaths than the violation of the norm if, for example, it prevented one from killing a tyrant or a gun-wielding person in a supermarket. In essence, he argues that even the most normative ethicist is obliged in certain (extenuating) situations to violate the rules for the sake of the intention of the rule.[8]

An Ethic of Exception

We turn now to two further models of an ethic of responsibility. They provide a systematic development of the kind of insight which both Lehmann and Schüller suggest, though predating their models, having been formulated in the crucible of Nazi tyranny earlier this century. These are the *Grenzfall* ethics of Karl Barth and Dietrich Bonhoeffer. More particularly in the case of Bonhoeffer, it is what has been called an ethic of 'free responsibility'.[9]

Karl Barth

Karl Barth's ethics, like the rest of his theology, must be seen within the context of the times within which he lived. Central to the development of Barth's theology was his growing disillusionment with the anthropocentric liberal theology of the nineteenth century. This arose partly out of his experience as pastor in Safenwil (in Switzerland) where he became frustrated with the doctrinaire and over-confident socialism of left-wing workers, although he remained committed to the socialist ideal for the rest of his life. The support given by his former theology teachers at the beginning of the First World War to the war policy of Kaiser Wilhelm II further alienated him from their theology. The result was the emergence of his characteristically radical theocentric theology and ethics, which affirmed a qualitative difference between God and humanity. His subsequent move to Germany brought him into direct conflict with Nazi attempts to integrate Christianity into their National Socialist vision. Barth's refusal to compromise led to his dismissal from his teaching post at the University of Bonn and his return to Switzerland. Here Barth continued in his opposition to Hitler and in his support for those who were struggling against Nazi tyranny. His ethics was thus developed within this context of conflict, where ethical decisions had immense consequences.

Barth's theocentric ethic persuaded him that ethical good is not to be found in human insight or any code of morality. It is located in the command of God, as revealed in Jesus Christ as the Word of God — a revelation that at once says no to all human effort (we cannot save ourselves) and yes to humanity (God's grace is freely given). God's yes to humanity at the same time means that humanity is placed under God's command, which requires obedience. Because God's command is an expression of God's sovereignty and freedom, human decision-making must always be made in obedience to the *free* command of God. As such, God's command is never a statement of general principles. It is definite, concrete and personal. If it were less than that, human beings would have to decide how to interpret and apply it. In that case, they would cease to be responsible before God and to God, becoming autonomous agents. (The difference between Barth's ethic and that of Fletcher is obvious.) Because, however, God's command is specific and concrete, the human response is confined to deciding whether to obey or disobey. In affirming this position, Barth saw the biblical commandments, such as the Ten Commandments or the Sermon on the Mount, not as general principles but as specific contextual commands. They function as tried and tested examples of what God's command usually involves, and are thus to be obeyed in most situations. There is, however, only one theological—ethical absolute, which is the command of God to which all other biblical commands are relative. God cannot be bound by any ethical system, because God is free and God is the only absolute.

In this regard Barth makes a helpful distinction between 'ethics' and 'ethos'. Theological ethics may not arrogate to itself the task of telling someone how he or she ought to act in a particular situation. To attempt to do so would be idolatrous. It would be to assume God's prerogative to issue commands. 'Ethics' is thus the discipline which reflects on the decision that has already been made, seeking to evaluate it in the light of God's command in Jesus Christ. As such it is distinguished from 'ethos', which (in Barthian language) is the moment of decision, made in response to the command of God.

Barth's understanding of the command of God is not simply a revelation of God from above, although his language sometimes suggests it might be. He refers, for example, to 'the definiteness of the divine decision'.[10] Barth's concern that we analyse each situation, in order to rationally discern what God's Word (Christ) requires, is enough to counter any suggestion that he is speaking of a mystical revelation of some form of superhuman information. The command of God, for Barth, is 'heard' as the Christian stands before the challenge of a particular problem, seeking to gain the fullest possible understanding of all that is involved. It is a decision that is made prayerfully, in dialogue with others, in faith, in community and as a result of the fullest application of an intelligent mind to a vexing problem. Barth's notion of 'command' is not vastly different from the 'emergent coherence' that occurs when, Walter Muelder suggests, the different social science disciplines are brought to bear on a particular problem.[11] For Barth the decision is, however, explicitly theological. It occurs within the community of faith and in obedience to God's declared Word, as revealed in Jesus Christ. (The similarity between Barth and Lehmann is obvious at this point.)

An important category in Barth's ethic is the notion of *Grenzfall*.[12] This German word means the 'limiting' case, the 'extreme' case or the 'borderline' situation. The concept is best expressed as the 'exceptional' case. It is the exceptional case in which God commands something contrary to what is normally considered as 'right' or 'good'. It is a case in which there is a contradiction or apparent contradiction between what God has commanded in the past (in the biblical record) and what God is now commanding. This, suggests Barth, is not a common occurrence and by definition will only take place in an extreme or exceptional situation. What is good is defined by God's command alone and not by any human standard. The *Grenzfall* ethic is ultimately, therefore, an instance of God's sovereignty and freedom. It safeguards human responsibility, as no one can take refuge in a rule book or moral code (not even the Ten Commandments). It emphasises the finitude of all values and norms.

Questions abound. How does the Christian come to a conviction which (Lehmann and Barth would argue) contains a dimension beyond human scrutiny or explanation? Is this a legitimate theological stance to adopt? To what extent ought all ethical theory to be publicly and rationally defensible? Is the defence of an action as being in response to an inscrutable 'divine command' any more than theological talk for intuitional thinking? By what criteria does Barth allow for deviation from ethical norms? The debate on these questions continues, propelled by a strong dialectic in Barth's ethic between what is a spiritual existential moment of conviction and a rational decision which draws on all the human and scientific resources available to make a thoughtful decision that is rationally defensible. To emphasise the sense of personal address, which illuminates vacillation and hesitancy once the decision has been made (and Barth criticised Bonhoeffer for precisely this, a failure of nerve, in the plot against Hitler),[13] at the expense of the rational dimension of Barth's ethic, is to underestimate the complexity of his

Grenzfall ethic. Certainly in his illustrations of his ethic in relation to abortion, war, capital punishment and other issues, one can say that it is rationally executed, taking full cognisance of the consequences. It constitutes more than a moment of subjective insight. To return to Barth's distinction between 'ethics' and 'ethos', it is (in addition to all else) rational reflection on a decision that has been made in response to the command of God. It is also reflection prior to the event. Ethics, thus defined, includes an *ante mortem* as well as a *post mortem* (or rationally) reflective dimension.

What do we then conclude about Barth's ethic? It involves three interrelated dimensions. It includes, firstly, an analytical interpretation of the event in question. Secondly, in facing the situation, the Christian is addressed by the declared Word of God spoken in Jesus Christ, as recorded in the Bible. Thirdly, the decision as to how one should act, taking the situation and the recorded Word of God into account, is a deeply personal matter taken within the Christian community, in response to the Word of God.

Barth's own application of his ethic to certain specific issues illustrates the point. He argues, for example, that the protection of life is a norm but not an absolute.[14] To absolutise the norm would be to turn it into an idol. No human being may, on the other hand, decide when it is right to take another's life; to do so is to commit murder. There are, however, cases in the Bible where God commands the taking of someone's life, and if obedience to God's command alone is the good (the only absolute) it follows that in certain circumstances the good requires that one takes someone else's life. This is, for Barth, a situation which can only be entered with extreme vigilance and great hesitancy, under the command of God.

Barth considers a number of situations in which the ethical norms of the Bible need to be violated: suicide, abortion, euthanasia, self-defence, the death penalty and war.[15]

Suicide. While no human being has sovereignity over his or her own life and thus no one may bring it to an end, there are circumstances, Barth argues, in which God might command suicide. In these cases suicide would be an act of self-sacrifice. Examples could include martyrdom and the act of a person who commits suicide in order to avoid betraying others when being subjected to torture.

Abortion. It is God's will to preserve life, and therefore abortion can never be the norm. Yet there are circumstances, Barth suggests, where it might be possible to make a case for an exception. An example of this would be when a continued pregnancy endangers the life of the mother. Even here the situation must be carefully evaluated, and a decision taken before God and in the knowledge of God's forgiveness.

Self-Defence. The New Testament injunctions on self-sacrificial love led Barth to argue that non-resistance is the norm for the Christian. As such, it is best (Barth argues) for Christians to err on the side of pacifism. Despite the general right of self-defence, Barth argues that a person who kills someone in self-defence becomes the aggressor and is thus claiming sovereignty over someone else's life, although here too in certain extreme circumstances God might command the taking of life in self-defence. Barth suggests that killing as a consequence of defending someone else may well be an example of this kind of exception commanded by God.

The Death Penalty. In general, Barth rejected capital punishment as part of the normal action of the state, and regretted that the church had failed to oppose capital punishment while in some cases actually advocating it. Yet there might be certain extreme cases, he allowed, in which the death penalty is commanded by God: certain cases of treason or tyranny, for instance.

War. Barth came closest to an absolute no in the case of war. He sought to 'deconstruct' modern warfare, pointing out the realities that lie behind the political myths used to justify it. War, he argued, usually involves two communities seeking to destroy one another; in most cases both are motivated by what he regarded as little more than some form of ethically unjustifiable patriotic zeal. Having come close to a categorical rejection of war, he proposed that it is possible that God might command war in an exceptional case. He believed that the defence of Switzerland (a neutral country – and his home!) was such a case.

In brief, Barth's ethics involves a methodology which attempts to safeguard the reality of norms and yet make allowance for the exception. In terms of a general ethic it may be questioned whether Barth solved the problem of knowing what the right thing is to do. He does not tell us how to recognise God's command. He would argue, however, that to do this would be to provide a set of prescriptive rules that would deny the freedom of God, the responsibility of the human agent and the dynamic of history. For Barth, one can only dare to act in faith and then evaluate one's decision in the light of God's revelation in Christ. The evaluation process may show that the decision was in fact wrong, requiring one to repent. It will invariably provide ethical insight which ought to be taken into account in future decision-making situations.

The complexity of ethical decision-making is seen nowhere more clearly than in Barth's *Grenzfall* ethic. Barth speaks at the same time of certainty in such an ethic. It is this very dimension of his ethic that has evoked the charge that it does not give sufficient attention to the possibility of self-delusion. This is particularly true in situations of war, where the general populace is the victim of large-scale propaganda. The South African experience of 'total onslaught' ideology and the suspension of civil liberties (limited as they were) during the time of the states of emergency in the mid-1980s demonstrated how the state can use, not the norm, but the exception to justify tyranny in the name of defending freedom and order. The problem, it could be argued, is intensified when the exception is given the tone of a command.

John Howard Yoder's criticism of Barth is particularly telling in this regard. He suggests that Barth's notion of *Grenzfall* is

> simply the label Barth has seen fit to attach to the fact that in some
> situations, he considers himself obliged to make a choice which runs
> against what all the formal concepts of his ethics would seem to

require... He has simply found a name for the fact that in certain contexts he is convinced of the necessity of not acting according to the way God seems to have spoken in Christ.[16]

While Yoder's criticism is perhaps an overstatement which reflects his own Anabaptist presuppositions (which allow no deviation from biblical norms), it does identify Barth's *Grenzfall* ethic for precisely what it is – an exception to an otherwise fairly 'normative' ethical approach.

Dietrich Bonhoeffer

Dietrich Bonhoeffer faced the same kinds of issues as Barth. His theology, like that of Barth, emerged within the context of Nazi tyranny. His first attempt to articulate an ethic in this situation was in *The Cost of Discipleship*, where he called Christians to single-minded discipleship and absolute obedience to the details of the New Testament ethic. Then, as the tyranny of Nazism intensified, Bonhoeffer became involved in a very different kind of opposition to Nazism. Opposed to Hitler, he joined the *Abwehr* (the German military intelligence) in order to avoid conscription into the army. Ironically, the *Abwehr* was the centre of resistance against Hitler. Supposedly gathering intelligence to further the war effort, Bonhoeffer advanced the cause of this resistance conspiracy. This inevitably involved him in lying and deceit, as he became engaged in plans to murder Hitler – behaviour that violated the simple ethic of *The Cost of Discipleship*. He adopted an appearance of support for Nazism in order to overthrow it. The plot failed and he was executed on a charge of treason on 9 April 1945.[17]

Debate continues about the extent to which Bonhoeffer's later ethical teaching constitutes a complete break with his earlier teaching. He had previously insisted: 'To renounce rebellion and revolution is the most appropriate way of expressing our conviction that the Christian hope is not set on this world...'[18] There is at the same time no evidence to suggest that 'exception' was not always part of his earlier theology, the exception which declares that while obedience to the state is required of Christians, such 'obedience is binding on [the Christian] until government directly compels him [or her] to offend against the divine command, that is to say, until the government openly denies its divine commission and thereby forfeits its claim'.[19]

His 1932 address 'Dein Reich komme' also provides evidence of continuity between his (later) more radical period and his earlier writings. In this important address he observed that it is the task of the church to limit the state just as the state limits the church. And in 'The Church and the Jewish Question' he suggested that direct political action by the church is necessary in extreme situations because 'the existence of the state, and with it its own existence, is threatened'.[20] The debate about continuity aside, Bonhoeffer's ethics did take on a new kind of responsibility for the world in his later writings. To quote Rasmussen, the shift was 'from single-minded obedience in the *Cost of Discipleship* to responsible freedom in *Ethics*'.[21]

Bonhoeffer provides no detailed theological explanation of his decision to share in the plot against Hitler, although his fragmentary notes in *Ethics* offers some insight into an ethic of 'free responsibility'.[22] Written during the time of his involvement in the conspiracy, these notes throw light on his thinking, without providing a fully coherent account of the thought that must have gone into his decision to become involved in the assassination plot. The notes are, however, sufficient to locate his ethic at the cutting edge of theological and political responsibility.

Driven by the contextual question which required him to address the concrete problems that challenged society at the time, he asked: 'Who is Jesus Christ for us today?' Presented in these terms, Bonhoeffer's ethics is inherently theological and radically Christocentric. 'The problem of Christian ethics', he argued, 'is the realization among God's creatures of the revelational reality of God in Christ, just as the problem of dogmatics is the truth of revelational reality of God in Christ.'[23] In facing this challenge, Bonhoeffer draws on three related aspects of theology: Christology, justification by faith, and the law—gospel debate. A brief comment on each must suffice.

Christology. The incarnation stands central in Bonhoeffer's thought. It is here that God and reality become one. From an ethical perspective Bonhoeffer realised that 'reality' (the prevailing situation in Germany) was such that normative theological-ethical teachings were inadequate as a basis for doing the right thing, which was to end the tyranny. At the same time he saw traditional ethical systems breaking down in the face of the evil reality of Nazi Germany. These systems produced answers that contributed to the survival of Nazism. A valid ethic, he insisted, must enable one to look at both God and the world simultaneously, to become responsible to the demands of both.

God became human in order to reconcile the world to Godself, which means that ethics is not primarily about principles, motives or concepts. It is about the realisation of Christ's form or presence in the world, a form that is concrete and specific. The ethical implications of the incarnation require us to be like Christ, to be Christ's deputies in the world — conforming to the image of Christ as the incarnate, crucified and risen Lord.[24]

Justification by Faith. Bonhoeffer emphasised that in the incarnation Christ took the sin of humanity on himself. Not clinging to his innocence, as the 'Man for Others' he became guilty for humanity's sake. The ethical implications of this are clear: to the extent that we view Christ as our ethical norm, we too must be prepared to become sinners in being people for others. We do so, however, in the sure knowledge that our salvation is not earned by our moral behaviour, but is a gift of God. It is here that the doctrine of justification by faith becomes central to Bonhoeffer's thought.

Bonhoeffer introduces the notions of ultimacy and penultimacy in life in relation to this doctrine. Justification is the ultimate act, God's final declaration with regard to a human being. All else that happens in life is penultimate and of no direct soteriological significance. Justification is by grace alone, through faith. Bonhoeffer suggests, however, that penultimate acts do have significance at another level. They prepare the way for the ultimate. In engaging in these acts, struggling to do what is right and in seeking to live responsible lives, not only are we realising our potential as persons by being morally responsible, but we also come to understand that whatever we do is insufficient and inadequate in terms of our responsibility to God and to others.

Translated into soteriological language, this means we cannot save ourselves. Bonhoeffer himself realised that he could not have avoided guilt by not sharing in the plot. He could not claim non-responsibility by allowing Hitler to continue in his ways. The ultimate and the penultimate are related, although (so Bonhoeffer stresses) God's grace is never wholly dependent on what is penultimate.

Law and Gospel. Bonhoeffer further explains his ethic in terms of law and gospel. Thereby he affirms his own Lutheran roots, while going beyond Luther's understanding of the relationship between the two. His major shift from the Lutheran position[25] occurred in *The Cost of Discipleship*, where he stressed the need to link faith and obedience. Grace without discipleship, he argued, is cheap grace, which he rejected in favour of costly grace. In *Ethics* he goes a step further. Here, although the law remains an important teacher of what is right for the Christian, it is not the final consideration. Christ alone is Lord, and at times we are required to break the law in order for Christ's form to be realised in the world and for us to become Christ's deputies.

What, then, is Bonhoeffer's ethic of responsibility? In brief, driven by a realisation that traditional ethics were of little value in the 'real' world of Nazi Germany, his ethic (much like Barth's) addressed the need to act responsibly in exceptional situations. Bonhoeffer's ethic speaks to a situation where the choice is between good and good or one evil and another — which is precisely where most of our difficult decisions are located. In such situations, he realised, the absolute good is sometimes the enemy of the next best thing. In an ideal situation no one should be assassinated or killed. But in his own situation he thought that if Hitler were killed, the lives of millions of people could be saved. Benhoeffer understood responsible action as demanding ethical behaviour that violated the ideal ethical norms of society.

For Bonhoeffer the responsible person is one who shares in the transforming work of Christ in the world, without seeking to protect his or her innocence. In acting responsibly, a person is required to assess the situation in the most careful and precise way possible, and to act according to what would best further the purposes of Christ in the world. Thereafter, believers are to commit these actions and themselves to God's grace, realising that it is by God's grace alone that ultimate good will be realised in the world, and that it is by God's grace alone that they will be justified. In taking on themselves the guilt involved, no attempt is made to justify or legitimate the violation of the ethical norms of the Christian tradition.

In brief, from Bonhoeffer's perspective, the person who acts in free responsibility acts as a guilty person. 'Before other men, the man of free responsibility is justified by necessity; before himself he is acquitted by his conscience but before God he hopes only for mercy.'[26] As such, acts of free responsibility can only flow out of an understanding of justification by grace through faith.

Like any ethic of exception, Bonhoeffer's ethic is open to abuse. But its strong Christological form and emphasis on acting in a manner that resolutely promotes the good of humanity protect it against some obvious dangers. The most striking feature of Bonhoeffer's ethic is perhaps that it involves the assumption of guilt. This militates against triumphalism, and calls for careful (and fearful) decision-making. The problem with his ethic (for some people) is that it renders a person guilty for doing the right thing. This strongly contrasts with Barth's emphasis that implies acceptance, if not the blessing of God, in a *Grenzfall* situation which may require a violation of normative ethics.

An Ethic of Responsibility

Comprehensive theological ethics is obliged to take the quest for an ethic of responsibility and exception seriously. In the modern world we are obliged almost daily to make difficult choices for which the traditional norms do not provide straightforward or adequate answers.

Obviously there are dangers involved. The primary one is perhaps that of the exception becoming the norm. It is easy for norms to begin to be undermined, because most ethical decisions involve one or other exceptional (extenuating) circumstance. This is the concern that some people have with Joseph Fletcher's situational ethics. Karl Barth and Dietrich Bonhoeffer, on the other hand, allow for flexibility in ethics, while affirming the importance of ethical norms.

Three closing observations must suffice. First, the Christian tradition requires a Christological understanding of God's redemptive purpose for creation. The exceptional action should not be seen as an arbitrary action or a simple act of human ingenuity. In order to be self-consciously Christian, an ethic of responsibility should arise out of the same theological basis that governs 'normal' actions – a will to share in God's creative and redeeming activity in the world.

Secondly, an ethic of responsibility involves a hierarchy of values and norms. The exceptional act is thus not taken without regard to values, but recognises that we are constantly required to seek to be obedient to higher values at the expense of what, in a given situation, may be regarded as lower values. Here again the danger of arbitrary action and the misuse of 'responsible' action require a mechanism for testing, weighing and assessing our behaviour, even if after the event. This involves both the kind of dialogical community of which Lehmann speaks and the theological framework which Bonhoeffer articulates. An ethic of responsibility can never be allowed to be an excuse to do as we like.

Finally, it must take full recognition of human rationalisations and the inclination to self-justification. In moving into an exceptional situation, one needs to recognise that there is a tremendous danger that the action we take might be the wrong decision, promoting evil rather than good.

An ethic of responsibility asks us to act responsibly. It requires us to be human beings who are ready to risk ourselves in the service of others. As fearful as this is, we have no real alternative other than to reduce our function in life to seeking to implement a set of rules which we, for one or other reason, regard as absolutely applicable in all situations of life. The problem is that these rules do not always fit — they do not always address the changing demands of life. They do not always promote *responsible* action.

[1] Antinomianism contends that the moral law is not binding on Christians.

[2] Joseph Fletcher, *Situation Ethics* (London: SCM, 1969), p. 59.

[3] Ibid., p. 68.

[4] Ibid., p. 31.

[5] Paul Lehmann, *Ethics in a Christian Context* (New York: Harper and Row, 1963), p. 159.

[6] Ibid., p. 85. For a full exposition of Lehmann's ethics see Nancy Duff, *Humanization and the Politics of God: The Koinonia Ethics of Paul Lehmann* (Grand Rapids: Eerdmans, 1992).

[7] Lehmann, *Ethics in a Christian Context*, p. 141.

[8] See discussion in R. A. McCormick, 'Current Theology 1977: The Church in Dispute', *Theological Studies*, 39:1 (March 1978), pp. 76–138.

[9] See J. W. de Gruchy, *Dietrich Bonhoeffer: Witness to Jesus Christ* (London: Collins, 1988), pp. 30–35.

[10] Karl Barth, *Church Dogmatics* II/2, edited by G. W. Bromiley and T. F. Torrance (Edinburgh: T. and T. Clarke, 1957), p. 661.

[11] Walter Muelder, *Moral Law in Christian Social Ethics* (Richmond: John Knox Press, 1966), pp. 152–156.

[12] Barth, *Church Dogmatics*, III/4, Section 55 (1961).

[13] Ibid., p. 449.

[14] Ibid., pp. 397f.

[15] Ibid., pp. 401f.

[16] J. H. Yoder, *Karl Barth and the Problem of War* (Nashville: Abingdon, 1970), pp. 73–74.

[17] Eberhard Bethge, Dietrich Bonhoeffer: *A Biography* (London: Collins, 1977).

[18] Dietrich Bonhoeffer, *The Cost of Discipleship*, translated by R. H. Fuller (London: SCM, 1959), p. 234.

[19] D. Bonhoeffer, *Ethics*, translated by N. H. Smith and edited by E. Bethge (London: Collins, 1964), p. 342.

[20] Dietrich Bonhoeffer, *No Rusty Swords, Lectures and Notes, 1928–1936*, edited by E. H. Robertson, translated by E. H. Robertson and J. Bouden (New York: Harper and Row, 1965).

[21] Larry L. Rasmussen, *Dietrich Bonhoeffer: Reality and Resistance* (Nashville: Abingdon, 1972), p. 15.

[22] Bonhoeffer, *Ethics*, pp. 224–254.

[23] Ibid., p. 190.

[24] Ibid., pp. 64–88.

[25] Luther argued that the law points us to Christ in the sense that we realise that we are not able to fulfil its demands. It also controls human sinfulness by means of the operations of the state. The Christian, however, who is saved by grace, has no need of it as a teaching mechanism.

[26] Ibid., p. 248.

Select Bibliography

Barth, Karl. *Church Dogmatics* III/4, edited by G. W. Bromiley and T. F. Torrance. Edinburgh: T. and T. Clarke, 1961

Bonhoeffer, Dietrich. *Ethics*, translated by N. H. Smith and edited by E. Bethge. London: Collins, 1964

Duff, Nancy. *Humanization and the Politics of God: The Koinonia Ethics of Paul Lehmann*. Grand Rapids: Eerdmans, 1992

Fletcher, J. *Situation Ethics*. London: SCM, 1969

Lehmann, Paul. *Ethics in a Christian Context*. New York: Harper and Row, 1963

Rasmussen, Larry L. *Moral Fragments and Moral Community*. Minneapolis: Fortress Press, 1993

Wogaman, J. Philip. *A Christian Method of Moral Judgment*. London: SCM Press, 1976.

7

Ethics of Character and Community

NEVILLE RICHARDSON

By the middle of this century the study of ethics in the English-speaking world had become uninteresting. It was as though ethics had forgotten what had always been its main task, that of providing guidance for the moral life, and concentrated solely on analysing the theories and language of morality. A counter-movement has now gathered momentum. Its first positive move is to look in another direction for a more adequate understanding of morality, not least in the matter of relating theory to practice. The direction in which it looks and to which it points is that of character.

My intention is to introduce this counter-movement by dealing first with its emphasis on character, and then to show how character ethics goes hand in hand with a new focus on community. This will lead to a brief account of the Christian communal ethics of Stanley Hauerwas, probably the most developed statement of the new ethics of character and community in modern theology. Finally, some critical issues will be considered, arising mainly from a South African context.

The Reinstatement of Character

One of the nice things about the rediscovery of character as a vital moral concept is that books on ethics have again started to focus on the lives of people, both real and fictional – a lively and refreshing change from the interminable reflection on moral theories, which alone used to hold centre stage in ethics. As the spotlight swings onto people's lives, questions of the moral quality of those lives become central. Two examples spring to mind.

James Gustafson tells of an incident in a Manhattan bar in which he was personally involved.[1] Gustafson himself is a relatively minor player in the brief drama. The focus is on his colleague who seemed to know instinctively and instantaneously all the right things to do when a drunken soldier was shortchanged by the bartender. Through a few decisive actions initiated by the colleague, the bartender confessed his 'mistake', the correct change was given, the bartender was faced with the prospect of explaining the incident to his employers, a taxi was arranged in such a way that the helpless soldier would be taken safely home, and contacts were set up so that communication on the entire episode could be maintained retrospectively.

The incident takes on the role of a parable or governing illustration. Gustafson refers back to it at various stages in his argument in order to make key points. According to him this relatively minor incident illustrates the complexity of moral behaviour. It can be viewed from many perspectives — among others, those of principles, values, rules and consequences. But for Gustafson, the central consideration is the character of the people involved. The bartender showed himself to be the kind of person who would cheat a customer if he thought he could get away with it. Gustafson's colleague was the sort of person who realised that some kind of active response was required and somehow knew precisely the kinds of action that were appropriate. How did the colleague know all this? His sources of moral knowledge were not easily accessible. There was not even any recourse to religious convictions, for the colleague was 'not a religious man in any traditional sense'.[2] It is in terms of his character that Gustafson finds the most adequate explanation of his moral ability.

The effect of the incident on Gustafson himself was also mainly at the level of moral character. He considers it to have been an experience through which his own character was developed by his involvement in assisting 'an experienced artist of moral action'.

The second example of character as a central moral consideration is from Stanley Hauerwas.[3] Here an air traveller on a flight home is approached by a stewardess who proposes 'that they might enjoy one another's company for a while'. The traveller, reflecting later on his rejection of her proposal, realises that his first thought in response had not been in terms of any rules such as 'Thou shalt not commit adultery', but rather the practical consideration that he would have had to lie to his wife about why he was late. Neither the lie nor the casual affair may have been of any great significance at one level, but at another level they were of deep moral significance — they would have changed the kind of person he was. Hauerwas explains:

> In refusing the stewardess he did not feel as if he had made a 'decision'; the decision had already been made by the kind of person he was and the kind of life he had with his family. Indeed, all the 'decision' did was make him aware of what he already was, since he really did not know that he had developed the habit of faithfulness. I expect that many of our decisions are of this sort. We tend to think of them as 'decisions' when in fact they are but confirmation of what we have become without realizing it.[4]

The similarity in moral reflection in these two examples is clear. In neither is the focus on such normal moral references as principles, values or rules, although these may well have been influential factors in the moral development of those concerned. Nor are consequences the primary consideration, although the likely consequences of the various possible courses of action almost certainly were in the minds of the key players in each case. The focus is on the respective characters of the moral agents. They act according to who they are and, in so doing, facilitate the ongoing shaping of their moral character.

For a number of reasons character, as a moral concept, had until recently become unfashionable and outmoded in modern Western thinking. It seemed to call up the ghosts of strict, starchy Victorian schoolmasters insisting that their young pupils 'be of good character'. From a theological perspective it suggested salvation by works as people engaged scrupulously in the business of developing their moral character. From a psychological perspective it smacked of an unhealthy preoccupation with the individual self.

In moral philosophy, the displacement of character from centre stage was one of the effects of the eighteenth-century Enlightenment. Strangely, almost paradoxically, occupation of the centre stage was taken over as never before by the thinking, questioning human individual, but more the human critical faculty than the whole, historical, living person. The moral concepts with which that individual operated were no longer those concerned primarily with character. Consideration of 'the person I am' gave way to judgements which were either deontological (what is my duty, what are the rules that apply?) or teleological (what are the likely consequences of my proposed action?). Typifying deontological ethics was Immanuel Kant, and typifying teleological ethics was Jeremy Bentham, the father of utilitarianism.

In their common emphasis on character, Gustafson and Hauerwas are embarking on an approach to and an understanding of ethics which is at once both new and very old. It is new because it arises in the context of a critique of the ethics springing out of the Enlightenment, sometimes referred to as 'modern ethics'. It is old because it locates its ancestry as far back as the fourth century BC in the ethics of Aristotle. Many of those who are critical of the general state of modern ethics and who point to character as a concept with potential for a richer, more adequate account of the moral life look to Aristotle as a father figure. That is not to say that they seek to reinstate the Aristotelian metaphysics which was dispelled once and for all with the coming of the age of science. Nor is it their desire to call back Aristotle's static and hierarchically arranged social system. Their common conviction is that Arisotle's ethics and the entire ethical tradition at the head of which it stands were wrongly dismissed when the rest of Aristotle's thinking was dismissed.

One of the fundamental points of dissatisfaction with modern ethics is the impression it gives that ethics is an activity to be brought into play only when problems of a particular kind emerge and when decisions of a particular kind need to be made. For the rest of life, apart from isolated moral episodes, ethics is something kept in the drawer, like a nutcracker! In the face of this fashionable 'quandary ethics' a plea is made for the reinstatement of the dispositional element, for a serious consideration of the dimension of continuity in the moral self, as a necessary and central feature of moral reasoning.

It is not enough to ask the general moral question 'What is right?' We must ask more specifically, 'What is right *for me*?' The latter question requires that a careful consideration be made of the personal identity of the moral agent not only as an interesting moral adjunct, but as central to ethics itself. Edmund Pincoffs points out that the Enlightenment's governing metaphor in ethics was that of law, whether scientific or legal. He pleads that this impersonal metaphor, which has the effect of driving ethics and the moral self apart, be replaced with the essentially personal one of character. Pincoffs urges: 'what I have to take into account as well as the situation is the question what is *worthy of me*: what may I permit myself to do or to suffer in the light of the conception I have of my own so far formed, and still forming, *moral character*.'[5]

So far, the role of character in ethics has been discussed, but no attempt has been made to explain the precise meaning of character. It is a complex concept and it has a number of meanings. For example, it can refer to a trait which a person has 'by nature'. This is a passive sense of the term and means something like temperament. While the actions to which character in this sense gives rise may be open to moral praise or blame, it is not itself open to moral evaluation, for it is inborn and not chosen. But there is another sense in which character is indeed chosen by the moral agent. This is the active sense of the term which entails the freedom of the moral agent to choose to be a certain kind of person. It is this active sense of character that is not only open to moral evaluation, but is at the heart of the ethics under discussion.

Hauerwas's understanding of character is clearly of the latter kind. He defines character as follows:

> Character is thus the qualification of our self-agency, formed by our
> having certain intentions (and beliefs) rather than others. Character is not
> mere public appearance that leaves a more fundamental self hidden: it is
> the very reality of who we are as self-determining agents. Our character
> is not determined by a particular society, environment, or psychological
> traits; these become part of our character, to be sure, but only as they are
> received and interpreted in the descriptions which we embody in our
> intentional action. Our character is our deliberate disposition to use a
> certain range of reasons for our actions rather than others (such a range is
> usually what is meant by moral vision), for it is by having reasons and
> forming our actions accordingly that our character is at once revealed and
> molded.[6]

Lurking behind this definition, of course, is the freedom versus determinism debate. Obviously the kind of character which is of central moral significance for Hauerwas requires the freedom of the moral agent, because it is character which the moral agent chooses, character in its active sense. Yet, although the active sense always takes precedence over the passive, the passive sense is not lost. The very choices we make, especially in terms of our convictions, locate us socially, thereby limiting and directing our choices, and our social experience in turn shapes the people we are. The two senses of character are not mutually exclusive or, in practice, even separable. This is because of a fundamental understanding of persons not as isolated individuals, but as essentially persons-in-community.

The Centrality of Community

Those who call character back to centre stage and who look to Aristotle's ethics as seminal recognise that for Aristotle ethics is a branch of politics. As such, it presupposes a particular community as the social ground for its norms. It is significant that the goal of Aristotelian ethics is the good person rather than the good action. It is also significant that for Aristotle there can be no way of judging the goodness or otherwise of the person without reference to the particular community in which the person belongs. That is to imply that the good is socially relative, for what is regarded as morally commendable in one community is not necessarily regarded in the same light in other communities. That which is good must be understood, and the moral decision must be calculated, according to the describable nature of each community. The description of each community therefore takes on a morally normative dimension and function.

The membership of moral agents in a community is, for Aristotle as well as his modern followers, the decisive factor in morality. Such membership is the key to recognising, learning and accounting for what is morally good. This by no means promotes moral conformity. On the contrary, diversity of opinion is to be encouraged as a mark of strong and healthy community. It is desirable that there be vigorous moral discussion and argument among fellow-citizens as to their precise moral proposals and even as to their respective descriptions of their own community. In terms of ethical method, then, the agent's particular community is the meeting point between description and moral evaluation, between what is the case and what ought to be the case. The community shapes my character and, reciprocally, my character contributes to the kind of community of which I am a member. Therefore, to say that Aristotle's community is indispensable to his ethics is something of an understatement.

Stanley Hauerwas is among those modern Christian theologians who take their direction from the Aristotelian tradition in ethics. The goal of his ethics is the person as Christian rather than the deed or rule as Christian, and the Christian person in his view cannot be conceived of, let alone shaped, without the Christian community. That is to say, there can be no Christian ethics as understood by Hauerwas without Christian community. While Aristotle's community was the ancient Greek *polis* or city-state, Hauerwas's equivalent is the Christian community. While the Christian moral self is at the centre of the stage in his account of the Christian moral life, there is no script and no theatre without the Christian community. The community as institution is therefore prior to the characters of its members in the logical, chronological and practical senses, and is always more than the sum of its individual members.

For Hauerwas, the church, as a community of interacting Christian people, is as central and essential to Christian ethics as the *polis* is to Aristotle. But unlike Aristotle, who seems to have been able to think only in terms of one kind of social arrangement in the city-state, Hauerwas does not lay down one historical form of the church as normative. Were he to do that, he would be in danger of becoming a church politician in the narrow sense of party politics. Instead, he refers to his ecclesial eclecticism, describing himself lightheartedly as 'a high-church Mennonite',[7] and seeks rather to put forward a vital, more general point about church politics.

Whatever the historical form of the church, and Hauerwas is interested only in its concrete expressions, not in spiritual abstractions, it is in those concrete expressions of its communal life that Christians must together start their ethical thinking. The ongoing struggle to be the true and faithful church in particular historical situations moulds not only the character of the church but also the characters of those who make it up. In this way, character and community are inextricably intertwined, each reciprocally shaping the other. The precise nature of the Christian community as understood by Hauerwas, his concept of the church, is obviously of vital significance to his entire ethical scheme. It is to that concept that we must now turn.

An Ethic of Christian Community

Hauerwas's concept of the church is complex and multifaceted. Justice cannot possibly be done to it in this chapter. A few points must suffice to indicate the kind of community he envisages as being a school for the shaping and developing of Christian character.

Borrowing from narrative theology, Hauerwas sees the church as constituted by a particular narrative or 'story'. Christianity, for him, is a radically historical religion. It is a way of life which springs out of particular events in history. The most important of these events is the life of Jesus of Nazareth. Stated at its simplest, the church is a socially identifiable community of people with a collective memory of that history. That memory is the basis of the church's continuing existence. That is why he describes the church as 'a story-formed community'.[8] The Christian Scriptures are seen as the major vehicle of its narratives. The Bible is the resource book of the church in that 'this book provides the resources necessary for the church to be a community sufficiently truthful so that our conversation with each other and God can continue across generations'.[9]

Far from being a biblical inerrantist, and accepting that the Bible is not without error, he sees truth in the relationship between the particular community and the narratives which it takes to be its fundamental authority. The first task of the church is to be faithful to those narratives, and faithfulness consists in being the kind of community capable of remembering the narratives and living in a manner appropriate to that remembering. The entry of individuals into church membership can be described as the joining of our individual stories to the ongoing story of God and his people.

Clearly such a community is going to be unlike other communities which are formed by other narratives, be they of other religions or secular. Distinctiveness is a hallmark of Hauerwas's ecclesiology. It is also the hallmark of his ethics. This is not to say that Christians must disagree on every point with those who do not share their narrative. Indeed, Christians should collaborate positively and vigorously with all social causes which they judge to be commensurate with their own convictions. Underpinning this ethic of social engagement is the theological conviction that God's purposes are being worked out in the world and not only in the church. Nevertheless, it is the church's task to be the kind of community that is able to read the signs of the times and to recognise God at work in the world. 'As the church we have no right to determine the boundaries of God's kingdom, for it is our happy task to acknowledge God's power to make his kingdom present in the most surprising places and ways.'[10] But in that task the church is distinctive. Any other group claiming to do the same is in effect claiming to be the church too! The church, then, is a distinctive community, shaping the moral characters of its members in a distinctive way, according to a distinctive story.

In speaking of the ethics of the church, Hauerwas makes the point that the church does not so much have a social ethic, as though that ethic were a set of principles or rules somehow detachable from the life of the Christian community. Rather, he says, 'The church is a social ethic.'[11] In a statement which runs counter to much modern Christian social ethics, Hauerwas denies that the distinctiveness of Christian ethics should be downplayed and that Christians should merely seek to work with all people of goodwill for a more peaceful and just world.

> Yet that is exactly what I am suggesting we should not do. I am in fact
> challenging the very idea that Christian social ethics is primarily an
> attempt to make the world more peaceable or just. Put starkly, the first
> social ethical task of the church is to be the church — the servant
> community. Such a claim may well sound self-serving until we remember
> that what makes the church the church is its faithful manifestation of the
> peaceable kingdom in the world. As such the church does not have a
> social ethic; the church is a social ethic.[12]

To say that the church is a social ethic is not to imply that active, critical moral reasoning no longer takes place and that casuistry is no longer appropriate. The church does not magically or automatically know what is right in any given circumstance. It is a historical fact that the church is as fallible as other human institutions and is often guilty of self-deception and errors of moral judgement. That is why communal self-examination and listening to the voices both of outsiders and of dissidents within are such important ongoing challenges. The task of making decisions about difficult cases is part of what it means to be the church. But for Hauerwas the focus is not on the decisions that have to be made. Rather, as seen in the first two sections of this chapter, the focus is on the *character* of the people making the decisions and on the quality of the *community* of which they are part. The casuistry of the church is primarily that of constantly working out and testing 'the implications of the story of God, known through Israel and Jesus Christ, for its common life as well as for the life of the world'.[13]

While not promoting any particular Christian denomination as normative, Hauerwas has clear criteria for what qualifies as 'church'. Instead of the four traditional marks of the church — unity, holiness, catholicity and apostolicity — he lays more emphasis on concrete expressions and actions. For Hauerwas, the sacraments of baptism and eucharist are crucial because they are the institutional means which make it possible for people to become part of the story of Jesus Christ and to be shaped as his peaceable people in the world. He explains:

These rites, baptism and eucharist, are not just 'religious things' that
Christian people do. They are the essential rituals of our politics.
Through them we learn who we are. Instead of being motives or causes
for effective social work on the part of Christian people, these liturgies
are our effective social work. For if the church is, rather than has, a
social ethic, these actions are our most important social witness. It is in
baptism and eucharist that we see most clearly the marks of God's
kingdom in the world. They set our standard as we try to bring every
aspect of our lives under their sway.[14]

Preaching is also vital. In his understanding of the church, Hauerwas sees
preaching not only as instructional and envisioning to the existing members, but
also as proclamatory, reaching out to strangers. 'Stranger' is a technical term in
Hauerwas's ethics. It echoes the law of the Old Testament and refers primarily to
those not only unknown, but different and therefore threatening. A characteristic
of Christian community should be its welcome to and caring for strangers. He sees
the mentally handicapped as prime cases of strangers in his society.

A third characteristic is to be expected in a community concerned about its
own nature and witness — that of disciplined discipleship. A democratic form of
community discipline is envisaged, a kind of 'tough love' by which members are
constantly being shaped into a 'holy people'. The effect of this process is two-
way — inwardly on the vigour of the internal relationships, and outwardly on the
wider society in which such an explicitly Christian community must be a
challenging presence.

It should be added that in addition to these marks of the church, Hauerwas
looks for certain characteristic communal virtues.

The virtues of patience, hope and charity must reign if the community is
to sustain its existence. For without patience the church may be tempted
to apocalyptic fantasy; without courage the church would fail to hold fast
to the traditions from which it draws its life; without hope the church
risks losing sight of its tasks; and without charity the church would not
manifest the kind of life made possible by God. Each of these virtues, and
there are others equally important, draws its meaning and form from the
biblical narrative, and each is necessary if we are to continue to
remember and to live faithful to that narrative.[15]

The other 'equally important' virtues include forgiveness (the readiness to be
forgiven as well as to forgive), non-violence in a world so characterised by
coercion and violence, and the hospitality to strangers noted in the previous
point.

Questions and Comments from a South African Context

Before any specific issues are raised, it should be noted that the approach to
ethics we have outlined has a context of its own in the history of ethics and
theology. At the motivational level it is to a large extent an ethics of protest against
the perceived inadequacy of modern Western ethics. Stated positively, it is put

forward as a therapeutic alternative to modern ethics. It is put forward against the trend in Christian ethics to become bland, over-accommodating and almost indistinguishable from the generally held ethics of the day.

The same can be said about the emphasis on community. In modern urban existence in the Western world there is a widespread sense of the loss of community and belonging. The individualism that has infected society and philosophy has also infected theology and church life. Voices like that of Hauerwas are now raised against this undesirable and unhappy state of affairs in the interests of establishing a more adequate theology and Christian ethics.

The first group of comments we shall now make relates to social and political issues.

Most of those who advocate the broad ethical approach I have been outlining are strongly aware of their social context and its effect on their thinking. The question is whether their thinking applies unproblematically to social contexts other than their own. The thinking of Hauerwas, born in the United States, perhaps takes on a somewhat different significance in a country like South Africa from what he would wish. The degree of poverty, suffering and oppression here may require a different theological note to be sounded. Perhaps a different kind of church is called for from that which he envisages for his American context. According to the categories of the *Kairos Document*, Hauerwas would be located within 'Church Theology', which is heavily criticised for the inadequacy of its involvement in the struggle against the oppression of apartheid. My view, in Hauerwasian terms, is that the Christian community in South Africa can and should be deeply and sacrificially involved in the struggle against oppression. But that involvement should not be *primarily* the following of some secular political agenda. The social involvement of Christians should be primarily the working out of their role in the ongoing story of Jesus Christ and the expression of their belonging to the church as Christ's serving community in the world.

The Christian virtue of non-violence is another case in which Hauerwas is found to be at odds with the *Kairos Document*, which locates itself within the just war and just revolution tradition. Would he perhaps have seen things differently if his theological development had taken place in a revolutionary, rather than a post-revolutionary, society? Two points should be made here. First, there can be no doubt that for all his admirable theology of non-violence, Hauerwas and his fellow United States citizens live in the beneficent wake of an eighteenth-century war which secured freedom from colonialism. Secondly, in a political context so thoroughly violent as that of present-day South Africa, one must be very sensitive to such questions as: Who is now calling for non-violence? To whom is the call for non-violence directed? Who stands to benefit from it? Again, there can be no doubt that white people in South Africa have benefited vastly from a violent system, and those who have thus benefited should examine their moral right to demand non-violence from those who have suffered. Nevertheless, the response in the light of the ethics we are considering must be in terms of the distinctive Christian community, which should be made up of both oppressor and oppressed, thus dissolving one of the *Kairos Document*'s main ecclesiological distinctions, a community which is capable of embodying and witnessing to a different and much-needed way of life within the present 'culture of violence'.

The charge of sectarian withdrawal from the 'real world' has often been made against the kind of church and theological ethics we are considering. Doubtless this tendency is an ever-present danger, but it arises from a misunderstanding of the approach rather than from its substance. The misunderstanding is almost inevitable given the Constantinian framework within which most thinking about the church is done. In this arrangement, the church either collaborates to the point of merging with the secular power, or stands in criticism, but still in acknowledgement of that power as central. Since the secular power is now so all-powerful and omnipresent in most Western countries, any community which declares itself to be outside that arrangement must appear to be withdrawing with a vengeance! Furthermore, what is not often realised is that the current mode of social thought recognises very little communal reality between the individual and the state. Alasdair MacIntyre is among those who wish to place the focus in social ethics on neither of those two poles, but rather on the many small 'interim communities' which, when we stop to think, are indeed central to our social experience. While for secular thinkers those communities would include towns and cities, schools and clubs, for Hauerwas the social ethical focus is on the church, and the first task of theological ethics lies there before it busies itself with trying to create nations that are 'more Christian'. Perhaps a less contentious way of stating the point would be to say that Christian ethics must first engage itself in the creation of a more Christian church *in order that* simultaneously it might be an effective catalyst in the development of a national life more in keeping with the gospel.

Where are concrete examples of the kind of Christian community envisaged by this approach? Balcomb agrees that the 'existence of such a visible community could indeed be a powerful political witness in society',[16] but he makes the telling point that if a distinctively Christian community wishes to be such a witness it must exist in concrete form. He observes that claims for this community are usually made from a theoretical rather than a concrete position, and adds: 'The fact that there are no demonstrable models of the alternative community means inevitably that if any use is to be made of the alternative community motif it has to be on the level of abstract theory rather than empirical reality.'

Balcomb is correct, and his point illustrates the frustration of so many with this approach. It seems to promise so much, but if no concrete examples can be presented, then it is indeed the proverbial oasis in a burning desert that turns out to be nothing but a mirage. I have argued elsewhere[17] that this approach generates 'a double-edged normativity'. That is to say, as well as witnessing to and challenging society, it faces its advocates with 'a profound and searching challenge' to work to develop precisely such a church! Perhaps the most fruitful starting point in South Africa's diverse society would be the practice of 'hospitality to the stranger' — of actively opening our communities to those who are different from us and threatening to our security.

It might be argued, as Hauerwas seems to in places, that the church indicated in his concept of Christian community is indeed an empirical reality. 'There is no ideal church, no invisible church, no mystically existing universal church more real than the concrete church with parking lots and potluck dinners.'[18]

In order to make this claim, however, he exposes himself to the danger of theological relativism, a case of 'any old church will do'. This is, indeed, a danger in the context of South African history. Over the issue of apartheid, rival groups both claiming to represent the Christian church have been in bitter opposition to the extent of the apartheid-supporting churches being declared heretical by those opposing apartheid. Even now, as apartheid is being officially dismantled, the racially defined reality of the church of the oppressor and the church of the oppressed still stands as clearly as when it was highlighted in the *Kairos Document.* Which is the church? It cannot be both. In such a socially and culturally divided country as South Africa, unguarded theological relativism simply cannot be entertained. But if relativism is to be avoided, are we not back in the difficult position of having no empirical church as concrete model? As in the previous point, the challenge facing advocates of our model seems to lie in the direction of developing concrete instances of the Christian community they envisage.

My second group of comments relates primarily to ethics.

Much of the ethical guidance of the past encouraged a moral minimalism. That is to say, there was a tendency to look for the least one had to do in order to be moral. Natural law morality carries the assumption that the basis of our moral sense is our common humanity. Therefore our morality is founded on the very slender base of what is likely to be agreed to by all human beings in their widely disparate cultures. All rule-based ethics carry the temptation of a morality of 'Whatever I can get away with is good!' In contrast to this, the ethics we have been considering invites a moral maximalism. Where is the end of the growth of moral character in the Christian community? This is not only the development of the moral virtuoso, but the growth of the saints, and its limit is in the perfection of our Father in heaven (Matt. 5:48). It is also the working out in life of the often forgotten or spiritualised doctrine of sanctification.

Ethics according to Hauerwas is thoroughly and distinctively Christian. It has already been explained that this does not mean that it requires disagreement with everyone who does not profess Christianity. There may well be a large measure of agreement and collaboration, but on a wholly distinctive basis. The church as envisioned by him is a distinctive community. In South African society it would be striking in its distinctiveness, for it would be welcoming to our many 'strangers', therefore non-racial; and it would be egalitarian in its communal life and democratic in its decision-making structures and practices. As such it would be a powerful moral presence and a model to those seeking to fashion the communal life of the future South Africa.

One of the most valuable contributions of this approach to theological ethics is that it bridges the gap between worship and practical morality. Worship is recognised as having a powerfully community-creating function, and therefore is also a force for moral formation. As noted earlier, the sacraments become the primary means to belonging, participating and witnessing, and preaching is a channel of expression and outreach. The moral force of the rich and varied worship of the churches in South Africa could be extremely powerful. It carries the potential to break down the cultural and political walls that presently divide our society.

Ethics of character offers a way to bridge the theory-practice gap that has become a yawning chasm in modern ethics. The incident recounted earlier between the air traveller and the stewardess is a good example of the way character-casuistry operates. In that case of sexual ethics at work, a moral reference point prior to any consideration of rules or consequences is 'the person I am'. This may seem close to a loose intuitionism, but character ethics provides a much sounder moral base than mere intuition. Other cases of sexual ethics can be similarly handled. The question of abortion, for instance, is notoriously difficult to answer satisfactorily from the point of view of either rules or consequences. Character ethics suggests that the key to a correct decision lies in the question 'What kind of person do we wish or ought to be?'[19] In the same way the church should rethink its understanding of abortion in the light of the kind of community it ought to be. The method can be taken further and applied to national questions. When framing legislation, law-makers should ask what kind of national community they wish to create by the powerful means at their disposal.

Conclusion

Ethics of character and community certainly offers a powerful and attractive alternative, given the state of modern ethics in general. The potential of this approach in theology is enormous and wide-ranging, promising to meet many of the pressing needs of modern theology and practical Christian life. In a radically divided and revolutionary society such as South Africa, a church which demonstrates in its communal life its unequivocal commitment to the story of Jesus Christ will undoubtedly have an impact. But Christianity in South Africa has still to find its own identity distinct from both its colonial form imported by the European missionaries and its oppressive form developed by the apartheid churches.

Finding that identity will be a long, probably painful journey. Whether the end result is faithful or not to the story of Jesus will depend on the faithfulness of the characters of Christians along the way. Their faithfulness, in turn, will depend on whether or not there is an actual Christian community to sustain them.

[1] J. M. Gustafson, *Can Ethics Be Christian?* (Chicago: University of Chicago Press, 1975), pp. 1–2.

[2] Ibid., p. 22.

[3] S. Hauerwas, *The Peaceable Kingdom: A Primer in Christian Ethics* (Notre Dame: University of Notre Dame Press, 1983).

[4] Ibid., p. 130.

[5] E. Pincoffs, 'Quandary Ethics', *Mind*, 80 (1971), p. 561 (my emphasis).

[6] S. Hauerwas, *Vision and Virtue: Essays in Christian Ethical Reflection* (Notre Dame: University of Notre Dame Press, 1974), p. 59.

[7] S. Hauerwas, *A Community of Character: Toward a Constructive Christian Social Ethic* (Notre Dame: University of Notre Dame Press, 1981), p. 6.

[8] Ibid., p. 9.

[9] Ibid., p. 64.

[10] Hauerwas, *The Peaceable Kingdom,* p. 101.

[11] Ibid., p. 99 (my italics).

[12] Ibid., p. 99.

[13] Ibid., p. 132.

[14] Ibid., p. 108.

[15] Hauerwas, *A Community of Character,* p. 68.

[16] A. Balcomb, *Third Way Theology* (Pietermaritzburg: Cluster Publications, 1993), p. 187.

[17] N. Richardson, 'Why Medicine Needs the Church: Reflections on Christianity and Medicine in South Africa', *Koers,* 56:3 (1991), p. 469.

[18] Hauerwas, *The Peaceable Kingdom,* p. 107.

[19] Hauerwas, *Vision and Virtue,* p. 155.

Select Bibliography

Balcomb, A. *Third Way Theology*. Pietermaritzburg: Cluster Publications, 1993

Gustafson, J. M. *Can Ethics Be Christian?* Chicago: University of Chicago Press, 1975

Hauerwas, S. *A Community of Character: Toward a Constructive Christian Social Ethic*. Notre Dame: University of Notre Dame Press, 1981

Hauerwas, S. *The Peaceable Kingdom: A Primer in Christian Ethics*. Notre Dame: University of Notre Dame Press, 1983.

MacIntyre, A. *After Virtue*, 2nd ed. Notre Dame: University of Notre Dame Press, 1984

Pincoffs, E. 'Quandary Ethics'. *Mind*, 80 (1971), pp. 552–571.

8

Marx and Beyond

ROBIN PETERSEN

There is no doubt that one of the most significant yet ambiguous features of the twentieth century is the heritage of Karl Marx (1818–1883). The social theory associated with his name has inspired the struggles of millions of oppressed people around the world. They have found in him one of the few thinkers who claim to provide an analytical and systematic account of the contradiction between the Western, liberal and Enlightenment rhetoric of equality, democracy and liberty, and the stark reality of poverty, dispossession, domination, colonisation and alienation experienced by those on the 'underside'. They have also found in his social thought the hope-inspiring idea that the current system of domination can be transcended, and that — despite the claims of many — work, leisure and quality of life do not necessarily have to have the alienating form that they currently do.

And yet no one can fail to ask critical questions about the current status of Marx's thought and practice. It is no longer possible to avoid facing up to the undemocratic, repressive and alienating reality of the social systems constructed in his name. What is more, it has become clear from the failure of all 'actually existing socialist' countries[1] that their collapse was due not only to the unpopularity of their undemocratic and repressive political systems, but also to their profound economic failure. In this respect, the capitalist nations — with all their faults and inequities — have seemingly demonstrated an ability to create and sustain economic growth and development, despite periodic crises and slumps and a radical inequality of distribution.

Coming to terms with this ambiguous heritage of Marxism is not simply an academic exercise. For as South Africa moves towards a period of social and political reconstruction, it confronts us as a critical ethical issue. The question whether the Marxian vision is still able to embody the emancipatory hopes of a new society free from racial, political and economic domination is crucial. If it is, how? If not, what are the alternatives? This chapter will not provide any easy answers to these questions. It will, however, outline the terms of the current debate on this heritage.

Modernity and Post-Modernity

Before we proceed with an account of Marxian ethics, the criticisms levelled at it, and the various attempts to reformulate it in the light of some of these criticisms, it is necessary to situate the discussion in another theoretical context: the debate between 'modernity' and 'post-modernity'.

'Modernity' is the term used to describe the philosophical, social and political ideas of rationality, objectivity, truth, equality, freedom and the overcoming of the domination of tradition. These ideas came to birth in the philosophical revolution of the Enlightenment. They found their political expression in democratic revolutions (from the French and American revolutions of the eighteenth century to many of the twentieth-century anti-colonial revolutions); their social expression in bureaucratic rationalism, in rational architecture and town planning (for example the destruction of the 'slums' of District Six, Cape Town, and Sophiatown, Johannesburg, and the creation of 'garden suburbs' and 'townships'); their cultural expression in modern art, music and dance; their religious expression in the great tradition of liberal scholarship (Schleiermacher, Ritschl, Troeltsch and others); and their moral expression in the idea of human progress towards equality and tolerance under the guidance of reason (represented supremely in the work of Kant).

The traumatic events of the twentieth century — the two world wars, the Nazi holocaust, the continuing domination and impoverishment of millions around the world — have radically shaken Western confidence in the project of modernity.[2] The question of the relation of these crises to this project has been raised with great urgency. Are they simply profound failures to fully implement this heritage, or have the Enlightenment forms and ideals themselves given rise, even indirectly, to them? Is the contemporary social, ethical and political task therefore to recover this Enlightenment heritage in a new way and so complete the project of modernity (as argued, for instance, by Habermas),[3] or is the whole project to be abandoned as fundamentally flawed and oppressive from the start? This latter position, in its multitude of forms, has come to be known as 'post-modernity'.[4]

It is very difficult to define exactly what post-modernity is. This is partly because post-modernism avoids any fixed or firm 'objective' definition of anything, including itself. It is also, however, because of the immense proliferation of often competing interpretations of the phenomenon. A number of common threads can be identified: a stress on radical pluralism, a celebration of difference, a resistance to single or fixed definitions, and an emphasis on the local and particular in contrast to the universal and global. It is, in the words of Jean-François Lyotard, a 'war on totality'[5] — on any hope to gain a total picture, a universal point of view, an encyclopaedic philosophical or scientific account of the 'whole'. It is also an attack on the Enlightenment notion of 'the self' as an autonomous, centred, rational subject, capable of clear and decisive action.[6]

As Robert Young has pointed out, post-modernism can above all be defined as 'European culture's awareness that it is no longer the unquestioned and dominant centre of the world'.[7] It therefore implies a 'de-centering' of Western history, philosophy and humanism, tied in its origins to a resistance to the intellectual and political colonisation of 'the Other' by the West.

Marxism, Modernity and Post-Modernity

This discussion on modernity and post-modernity has direct consequences for the contested evaluation of Marx's legacy. For both the criticisms and rejections of Marx, and the attempts at recovering Marxism from its 'captivity' to undemocratic and repressive forms, often have as their starting point the question whether Marxism is to be evaluated as part of the project of modernity, or whether it provides the basis for a fundamental critique of modernity. The decision about which way to read Marx has major implications, as I will attempt to demonstrate.

Marx the Modernist

One way (a very prominent way) of reading Marx is to see him as providing a critique of capitalism from the perspective of modernity itself. In this account, it is argued that what Marx does is to expose how the moral ideals of modernity (equality, freedom, democracy, etc.), its rational and scientific methods, and its forces of production, are 'fettered', or hindered, by the property relations (class structure) and system of distribution (the market) of capitalism. Thus, while the ruling class proclaims the virtues of freedom, democracy and equality, this is 'ideological' because it masks or hides the reality that these values cannot be fully attained by everyone under capitalist class relations. Overcoming capitalism, therefore, entails overcoming these capitalist class relations by means of the victory of the proletariat, the class which produces all the wealth but does not share in it. Only with this victory will the project of modernity, and those values associated with it, be realised. Only then, therefore, will the social conditions for the realisation of freedom, democracy and equality be established.

Marx, in this account, is the 'modernist' *par excellence*. The critical power of his philosophy, it is argued, lies in his notion of history as the teleological development of freedom through the mechanism of class struggle; in his demonstration that ideas are situated within a social structure and are distorted in favour of the interests of the ruling classes; and in his criticism of the philosophers of modernity (Kant and especially Hegel) as 'idealists' — that is, as people who think that the way to change the world is to get people to change their ideas through rational thought or criticism. Marx shows that it is impossible to fully change thought without changing the social structures that produce thought. Hence, in this account, the ethical ideals of modernity will never be realised unless and until the social structures themselves are transformed. The task of philosophy, therefore, is not (in the famous eleventh thesis on Feuerbach)[8] to interpret (or even to criticise) the world, but to change it.

A further distinction can be drawn within this modernist account of Marx between those who stress the 'scientific' dimension of Marxism and those who stress its humanism. Although these two interpretations of Marx are usually seen to be diametrically opposed, they are, in fact, united in their commitment to different aspects of the heritage of modernity.

Scientific Marxism. Beginning with Marx's collaborator and friend, Friedrich Engels, and continuing through many thinkers and political forces, one interpretation of Marx has stressed the 'scientific' nature of his theory, which is opposed to 'bourgeois' and hence 'ideological' thought.[9] In this reading, Marx's social theory has been seen to provide a 'real', 'scientific' and 'non-ideological' account of both the structures of contemporary society and the development of history itself. Marx's philosophy of history, it is argued, shows how all history is actually the history of class struggle, and that the religious, political and social forms in which this struggle is played out are not what is ultimately at stake. This is because, at root, society is constituted by its economic structures, and these determine, to varying degrees, the social, political, religious and cultural forms of society and history. The 'scientific' task of Marxist thought and practice is thus to expose this distorted history and, through practice, seek to overcome the distortions that the class structure of society imposes.

Along with this claim to 'scientificity' goes, to varying degrees, an evolutionary account of history which, in its crudest form (Engels's dialectical materialism), sees the development of history towards socialism as inevitable and necessary. To be scientific, therefore, is to 'side' with this historical development. Socialism, in this account, is not a moral ideal or an ethical demand, it is simply the result of abstract economic and historical forces which find their embodiment in the social class that is the historical bearer of this process: the proletariat.

The ethical consequences of this position are, ultimately, a denigration of human practice and a dismissal of ethics itself. Ethics must give way to 'science', to an acknowledgement of this historical process and the inevitability of its victory. Since this victory is assured, it is 'reactionary' and 'bourgeois' to hold the proletariat to an ethical standard, or to stand in the way of its coming to power by 'any means necessary'.

The consequences of this position are vividly demonstrated in the many legitimations advanced in the name of Marx and 'science' for the undemocratic and repressive practices of the various Communist parties and governments of Eastern Europe, both by these governments themselves and by their supporters in the West and South. Thus, for instance, Stalin's destruction of the independent Soviet peasantry and the process of forced collectivisation, the elimination and imprisonment of ideological opponents in all Communist regimes (including the most progressive like Cuba), and various other forms of repression and terror, are legitimated and excused as 'unfortunate' but 'necessary' consequences of the imposition of 'scientific socialism'.

Humanistic Marxism. In reaction to this 'scientific' Marxism, a new reading of Marx emerged in the second half of the twentieth century. Spurred by the publication of the works of the early Marx, especially the *Economic and Political Manuscripts* of 1844, a 'humanist' Marx was recovered and presented as the key to understanding the mature, more 'scientific' Marx of *Das Kapital*. There is no doubt that these early works reveal the deeply humanist concerns and ethical commitments of the young Marx as he begins to develop his social theory.[10] It is in them, for instance, that one finds his famous account of the alienated form that labour takes under capitalism, a deep ethical commitment to human emancipation, and his argument that the basis of the critique of capitalism derives from the way it alienates the human essence (the 'species being') of the worker and the capitalist alike.

This ethical Marx is seemingly a far cry from the 'scientific' Marx of Engels and Lenin. But, as post-modern critics are quick to point out, humanism and rationality are two sides of the same Enlightenment coin. Both are central to the project of modernity, although they often seem to be in tension. This post-modern critique will be developed more fully at a later point. But first it is necessary to briefly outline attempts to rethink and recover Marxism in the twentieth century.

Lukács, Gramsci and the Frankfurt School

By the mid-1920s it was clear that the Communist revolution was not going to spread beyond Russia. There was soon also a growing criticism of the repressive and coercive turn that had been taken in Russia under Stalin. In this context a variety of thinkers, including Lukács[11] in Hungary, Gramsci[12] in Italy, and the members of the Frankfurt School of social thought in Germany, set out to rethink the philosophical and practical bases of Marxism. They were all concerned to provide answers to three related questions: why the working class in the West did not develop a revolutionary consciousness; the related question as to how capitalist democracies were able to perpetuate their rule in a seemingly non-coercive fashion; and the role of the intellectual in the development of critical theory and critical consciousness.

In their respective reconstructions, all these thinkers attacked any determinism of history which ignored the role of human practice in making history. They all sought, therefore, to rethink the role of human action and consciousness in the struggle for socialism. This signalled a decisive turn in neo-Marxism away from the detailed economic analyses that characterised the mature Marx to a concern with ideology, history and consciousness.

The decline of revolutionary impulses in the working class of Western Europe thus came to be analysed by means of various accounts of how capitalism affects the consciousness of people, leading to an understanding of the ability of capitalism to perpetuate its rule without necessarily resorting to overt coercion.

The key category Lukács developed to account for this is that of reification. 'Reification' means treating human practices and social relations as things. As capitalism becomes dominant, Lukács argued, it systematically reduces human relations and interactions to relations between things, between objects. Reification takes hold of consciousness in such a way that a reified society seems to be normal and natural.

Gramsci's important notion of hegemony plays a similar explanatory role to that of reification. Hegemony, broadly speaking, means 'leadership', but Gramsci uses it to describe the ability of the ruling class to rule without overt coercion, by gaining the seeming, or hegemonic, 'consent' of the ruled. Ruling-class domination, therefore, is not simply crude and coercive, but continually seeks to 'naturalise' itself, to make it seem normal and inevitable — a product of reality itself — rather than a socially constructed form of systematic domination.

Theorists of the Frankfurt School (including Horkheimer, Adorno, Fromm, Marcuse and Pollock) gave a different account of the same phenomena.[13] Using Weber's notion of the 'iron cage' of reason, they argued that the problem in both capitalist and Communist states lay in the development of the growing power and domination of instrumental rationality over all of social life. In increasingly pessimistic tones, these theorists confronted the fact that the two sites of emancipation heralded by traditional Marxism – the rationality of the Enlightenment and the revolutionary potential of the proletariat – led in fact to increasing social domination, not emancipation. Capitalist society had become increasingly 'one-dimensional'[14] and fundamental change seemed impossible. Furthermore, Horkheimer and Adorno articulated a growing belief that Enlightenment rationality itself lay at the root of the forms of domination of modernity.[15]

This pessimism was challenged by Jürgen Habermas,[16] who, although the primary inheritor of the legacy of the Frankfurt School, sought to recover the emancipatory roots of critical theory. He challenged this pessimism on two fronts. On the one hand he argued that capitalist society is not one-dimensional – that it is still subject to contradiction – and that the possibility of a critical theory therefore still exists.

The contradiction he analysed is that between two forms of rationality, each of which has a base in society and in the constitution of what it means to be human. Human beings are not constituted by their labour alone (as Marx had supposedly argued), but by communication and symbolic interaction as well. This dual constitution of what it means to be human is the source of two forms of rationality, related to two 'realms' of social life. The first realm is that of the 'system' – the basic structuring principles of economy and technology related to labour. The 'system' gives rise to instrumental rationality. In its place within the 'system', this rationality is perfectly appropriate and necessary for human flourishing. The problem emerges when it comes to 'colonise the life-world', or the second realm of human social life characterised by communication and symbolic interaction under the guidance of emancipatory reason. The task of critical theory is therefore to contest this 'colonisation of the life-world' and to regain the emancipatory and critical resources of communicative action. This has led, in Habermas's thought, to a restatement of the possibility and the necessity of a normative and ethical dimension of human life.[17]

A major set of problems arises from all these reworkings of Marxism and critical theory. If Western capitalist societies are fundamentally reified, if the ruling class exercise their rule hegemonically, and if society is one-dimensional, then how is it possible even to develop a criticism of this society, let alone seek to change it?

For all of these theorists, the answer lay in a turn to human consciousness and the possibility and necessity of transforming it. For Lukács, it was the 'standpoint of the proletariat' and the work of the critical philosopher that provided the objective and subjective possibility of overcoming the system that produces reification. For Gramsci, it was the necessity of exposing hegemony through ideological struggle waged by the working class and the 'organic intellectual'. For Habermas, it is emancipatory reason made possible by communicative action. All, therefore, in different ways, indicate why the thrust of neo-Marxist thought has been away from detailed economic analyses and towards issues of culture, aesthetics, philosophy, ethics and even religion. If changing consciousness is an essential part of overcoming domination, then ideological struggle and the role of the intellectual become crucial.

The Post-Modern Critique

For the majority of post-modern critics, Marxism, even in these reconstructed forms, is just one more 'totalizing meta-narrative',[18] that is, a comprehensive theory that seeks to explain 'the whole'. As such, it is a position which ignores difference and pluralism, and leads inevitably to repressive and authoritarian practices. For these critics, all these accounts still seek some 'archimedean point' from which they can move the whole. Whether it be the scientific rationality of the 'scientific Marx', the abstract human essence of the 'humanist Marx', a notion of History and its development (for Lukács), or even the pragmatically reconstructed notion of critical rationality of Habermas, all remain bound to the Enlightenment notions of reason, history and the subject.

Equally as significant, they criticise Marxism for privileging only one form of social domination — that of class. Against this, it is argued that other forms of domination — those based on race, gender, sexual orientation, etc. — are equally important but ignored by Marx and many Marxist theorists.[19]

This critique has proved to be extremely powerful in its effects. What has made it more so is the fact that the primary theorists of post-modernity (Lyotard, Foucault, Derrida) all were formerly Marxists. Their abandonment of Marx cannot therefore be easily dismissed. What is also significant, especially in our own context, is the turn to post-modernism by theorists of race, gender and colonialism.[20]

To this post-modern critique, some Marxists have simply restated their own position and attempted to argue that post-modernism is a form of neo-conservatism.[21] The basis of the criticism is that with the post-modern de-centering of the subject, the emphasis on difference and 'play', and the suspicion of any 'master-narrative', the possibilities of effecting fundamental change in the system of domination are dismissed. Resistance in post-modernism is reduced to a kind of 'guerrilla warfare' with no possibility of success; all that remains is to snipe at the system in a radically localised fashion, to make limited gains in limited struggles, and to recognise that one's own actions of resistance are implicated in the same system of power relations. While this critique of post-modernism is valid, it does not, as is claimed by Marxist critics, emerge from a conservatism, but from a position that argues that the paradigm of traditional Marxism is fundamentally compromised, both in theory and in practice.

It is possible to see post-modernism, therefore, as accepting the analysis of the one-dimensionality or the reification of capitalist society advanced by Western Marxism, but disallowing the consolation of assuming that there is still the possibility of escape by means of the 'standpoint of the proletariat' or a reconstructed 'emancipatory reason'.

There have, however, been a few attempts to develop a Marxism which takes account of the post-modern critique, some by attempting to show that the respective critiques complement rather than contradict each other,[22] others, like

Cornel West, attempting to reclaim an ethical Marxism that avoids major philosophical accounts of history or consciousness.[23] One of the most significant reworkings of Marx's mature critical theory, that of Moishe Postone,[24] does not attempt to bring together these two forms of critique, but shows rather how Marx's account of the abstract forms of social domination produced by commodity production under capitalism provides an analytic basis to account for the systems of power and the rise of new social movements analysed by Foucault and other post-modern thinkers.

'Marx and Beyond:' Key Ethical Issues

From our discussion, it is clear that both Marxism and post-modernity offer significant contributions and major problems for ethical practice. In this closing section, these contributions and problems will be outlined.

Key Ethical Issues in Marxism

Structural Injustice and Oppression. Marxist thought emphasises that social domination and oppression are not simply the result of wrong attitudes, or of evil intentions. They are, rather, structural evils which arise from the system of production and distribution in capitalism. It is inadequate, therefore, to pass moralistic judgements on the evils of capitalism or individual capitalists. For whatever the intention of individual capitalists, whether good, bad or indifferent, they are constrained by the system itself to maximise profits by exploiting labour. Even a worker-owned company operating in a capitalist economy would be compelled to act in a similar way. If it did not, it would simply go out of business.

This has two consequences for ethics: firstly, it points to the necessity of changing the system of domination itself if the alienation of labour and of the capitalist alike is to be overcome; and secondly, that a moral critique of capitalism is simply inadequate.

The Role of Ideology. A notion of ideology or hegemony means that any ethical position which claims to base itself on 'reality' must be treated with suspicion, for it is precisely 'reality' that is ideological or hegemonic. Remember that the effect of hegemony is to make itself seem 'natural', 'the way things are'. Any appeal, therefore, to 'the facts' will be treated with suspicion by a Marxist ethics.

The Critique of Religion. Marx's critique of religion is well known. This is not the place for an analysis or evaluation of that critique. What it means for a theological ethics, however, is that it keeps in the foreground the reality of the ambiguity of religion. In other words, it reminds us in a powerful way that religion is not necessarily liberating, but is often caught up in the ideological web of the domination of capital. It also alerts us to the danger of overestimating the power of religious language or practices to effect fundamental social change.

Key Problems Within the Marxist Paradigm

Race and Gender. Despite the work of socialist feminists and Marxist theorists of race, the fact that traditional Marxist theory privileges class domination and class struggle over all other forms of domination and struggle remains a significant problem. Those who argue for the equality or even primacy of other forms of oppression have therefore increasingly turned to other ethical and theoretical sources.

Marxism and Democracy. As has been argued in this chapter, the heritage of 'actually existing socialism' has been fundamentally undemocratic. It is also clear that there are ideas in Marx (the dictatorship of the proletariat, etc.) that have been used to justify this. It remains a significant challenge for any Marxist political ethics to show how democracy and a socialist order can co-exist.

Historical Determinism. It has also been argued that any theory of historical determinism raises serious philosophical and ethical problems, as it leads to a justification of oppression and domination under socialism as 'historically necessary', and also undermines the ground for ethical critique.

Key Ethical Issues in Post-Modernism

The 'Other', the Marginal, the Excluded. Rather than the working class, post-modernism privileges the marginalised, excluded 'Others' of society. For Foucault, for instance, it is the mad and the prisoner that are not only the true victims of the disciplinary regimes of the Enlightenment and the West, but the source of opposition and struggle against the system as well.

This stress on the ethical importance of 'the Other' results in a politics of difference and pluralism, which cannot be reduced to one struggle or organisational base. At best, one can talk of politics of coalition and solidarity between marginalised groups.

Race, Gender and Difference. This stress on multiple sites of resistance is tied to an emphasis on race, gender, sexual orientation, minority status and so on, as the primary social base for political movements. It allows for a plurality of political options and struggles not controlled by the Party or by a common ideological line. It therefore stresses radical democracy.

The 'Micrologics' of Power. Foucault's analysis of how power circulates through society not only or even primarily by means of the traditional institutions of power (the state, the bureaucracy, the military), but as it is inscribed in the practices of everyday life, means that no one escapes complicity in the exercise and abuse of power. There is, therefore, no 'pure' struggle. Moreover, attacks on the central institutions of power are hopelessly inadequate.

Key Problems Within the Post-Modern Paradigm

Inability to Act Decisively. As has already been indicated, the key critique of post-modernism made by Marxist theory is that the notions of the de-centred subject, the dispersal of power, the suspicion of large-scale political projects, all have the effect of calling into question the possibility of any responsible ethical action. In this account, therefore, the struggles waged by the liberation movements in South Africa would be viewed with intense suspicion, and their chances of effecting fundamental change would be viewed pessimistically.

Pessimism and Despair. This analysis does have the consequence of producing cynicism and despair, as it sees no fundamental way out of the situation of domination. The only struggles possible are those on the margins, where the power of the centre is not so strong, and where the cracks in the otherwise smooth surface of domination can be exposed and attacked in a limited way.

[1] It seems to be somewhat of an act of romantic desperation to continue to argue for the viability of 'actually existing socialism' based on the claim that Cuba remains an example of a possible historical option. It is highly unlikely that Cuba will survive in its current form for many years longer. It is also unfortunate that the closer it comes to economic collapse, the more undemocratic its political formation becomes.

[2] It is clear that for those countries and peoples colonised at the very time of the constitution of these ideals, modernity has always been embodied in repressive forms. This was the point first developed with great force by Frantz Fanon in *The Wretched of the Earth* (Harmondsworth: Penguin, 1967).

[3] See his essay, 'Modernity: An Unfinished Project' in C. Jencks, *The Post-Modern Reader* (London: Academy Editions, 1992).

[4] Key theorists of the 'post-modern' include Michel Foucault, Jean-François Lyotard, Jacques Derrida, Emmanuel Levinas, Gayatri Spivak and Homi Bhabha. Robert Young's book, *White Mythologies: Writing History and the West* (London: Routledge, 1990), provides a good account of some of these thinkers.

[5] The full quotation situates this aphorism in an ethical context: 'We have paid a high enough price for the nostalgia of the whole and the one, for the reconciliation of the concept and the sensible, of the transparent and the communicable experience. Under the general demand for slackening and for appeasement, we can hear the mutterings of the desire for a return of terror, for the realization of the fantasy to seize reality. The answer is: Let us wage war on totality; let us be witnesses to the unpresentable; let us activate the differences and save the honor of the name.' See *The Postmodern Condition: A Report on Knowledge* (Minneapolis: University of Minnesota Press, 1984), p. 82.

[6] Here see, especially, the works of Michel Foucault. A good collection of his writings is found in Paul Rabinow (ed.), *The Foucault Reader* (New York: Pantheon Books, 1984).

[7] *White Mythologies: Writing History and the West* (London: Routledge, 1990), p. 19.

[8] See Robert Tucker, *The Marx–Engels Reader* (New York: W. W. Norton, 1978), pp. 143–6.

[9] The most influential recent representative of this tradition is Louis Althusser. See especially *For Marx* and *Reading Capital* (London: Verso, 1979).

[10] The difference in tone between them is so marked that the relation between the early and the mature Marx has become a major point of contestation in Marxist scholarship. For Althusser, the distinction between the two is so great that he posits a fundamental break between the two 'Marx's', and regards the mature Marx as presenting a 'scientific' account of Marxism that fundamentally contradicts his early humanism and philosophical account.

[11] Georg Lukács, *History and Class Consciousness: Studies in Marxist Dialectics* (London: Merlin Press, 1971).

[12] *The Prison Notebooks* (London: Lawrence and Wishart, 1971).

[13] See the excellent overview of the Frankfurt School and Habermas in David Held, *Introduction to Critical Theory: Horkheimer to Habermas* (London: Hutchinson, 1980).

[14] See H. Marcuse, *The One Dimensional Man* (Boston: Beacon Press, 1964).

[15] *The Dialectic of Enlightenment* (New York: Herder and Herder, 1972).

[16] Habermas's work is voluminous. His most important work is the two-volume *The Theory of Communicative Action* (Boston: Beacon Press, 1984).

[17] See his work on ethics, *Moral Consciousness and Communicative Action* (Cambridge, Mass.: MIT Press, 1990).

[18] See Young, *White Mythologies*, p. 3.

[19] Ibid., p. 4. Nancy Fraser's *Unruly Practices: Power, Discourse and Gender in Contemporary Social Theory* (Minneapolis: University of Minnesota Press, 1989) provides a good example of an attempt to bring together these new forms of social movements within a reconstructed version of Marxism.

[20] Here see Henry Louis Gates, *'Race', Writing and Difference* (Chicago: University of Chicago Press, 1985); Fraser, *Unruly Practices*; and Edward Said, *Orientalism* (New York: Vintage Books, 1978) respectively.

[21] A good example of this response is the work by the expatriate South African, Alex Callinicos, *Is There a Future for Marxism?* (London: Macmillan Press, 1982). His answer, of course, is 'yes', but his continual appeal to the traditional role of the working class as the revolutionary agent ignores the reality of the situation of working-class politics, and seems particularly dated in the aftermath of the collapse of the Eastern bloc. Habermas, too, has labelled Derrida a neo-conservative.

[22] Fraser, *Unruly Practices*; Michael Ryan, *Marxism and Deconstruction: A Critical Articulation* (Baltimore: Johns Hopkins University Press, 1982).

[23] Cornel West, *The Ethical Dimensions of Marxist Thought* (New York: Monthly Review Press, 1991).

[24] *Time, Labor, and Social Domination: A Reinterpretation of Marx's Critical Theory* (Cambridge: University Press, 1993).

Select Bibliography

C. Jencks. *The Post-Modern Reader.* London: Academy Editions, 1992

M. Postone (ed.) *Time, Labor and Social Domination: A Reinterpretation of Marx's Critical Theory.* Cambridge: Cambridge University Press, 1993

R. Tucker. *The Marx-Engels Reader.* New York: W. W. Norton, 1978

R. Young. *White Mythologies: Writing History and the West.* New York: Routledge, 1990

PART THREE
Ethics in Context

9

Ethics in Liberation Theology[1]

ZOLANI MGWANE

Liberation theology takes the historical praxis of the church as a major point of departure in doing theology. For this reason, we begin by examining the category of 'church' – in South Africa and in other post-colonial contexts. But in so doing, we immediately discover the ambiguity of the institution. Throughout its history it has functioned as a vehicle which promotes oppressive social structures, yet it has also functioned as an agent of liberation. It is imperative that this double role be kept in mind in seeking to understand the function of ethics in liberation theology.

Essentially, liberation theology engages in two kinds of critique. Firstly, it provides an external ethical critique of Christian theology and church, from the perspective of the oppressed, and challenges the dominant approach of ethics in Christian theology. It does this by identifying 'the other', which it defines as the oppressed, as a key ethical category for assessing all ethical behaviour. Put differently, liberation theology engages in ethical debate from the perspective of the poor and oppressed, arguing that in the process it exercises an epistemological privilege in ethical enquiry – a notion to which we shall return.

Secondly, liberation theology engages in internal self-criticism. In its commitment to the promotion of the concerns of the oppressed, it subjects its own reflection and praxis to critique. Only that within its own reflection and praxis which promotes the interests of the poor is judged to be theologically legitimate.

Christianity, Colonialism and Church

Let us start with the historical emergence of the church and its own self-perceived mission: 'Go therefore and make disciples of all nations, baptizing them in the name of the Father and of the Son and of the Holy Spirit, teaching them all that I have commanded you; and lo, I am with you always, to the close of the age.'[2]

For many missionaries this commission marked the dawn of an era of co-creation in which the church came to play a major role in the formation of character. It also pointed to an eschatological moment. In this co-creative venture the church saw itself as called to participate in God's salvific project, giving birth to a new humanity. In South Africa and other colonial situations, conversion and rebirth resulted for converts in a change of social and cultural identity, which included the assumption of new names and clothes. It often involved a change of location (relocation to the mission station) and entrance into a highly stratified society. In brief, it constituted the Westernisation of African people. Secondly, as an eschatological vision, the commission pointed to a future utopia, the final consummation of Jesus' work. This, too, was seen from a colonial perspective.

These two poles of beginning and end, or inauguration and consummation, were, and still are, separated by the 'scandal of the Cross'. It is the community of those within the early church who were scandalised – a small community of believers who suffered persecution and other abuses – that attracts the attention of liberation theologians.[3] The poor in contemporary situations, who are the subject of liberation theology, readily identify with this early church community.

The peripheral location of the early church was not, however, to last long. The establishment of Christianity as the official religion of the Roman Empire (by the Edict of Milan, AD 312) placed the church in a privileged position. The universalising vocabulary of Christianity ('not Jew, nor Gentile,' 'not man, nor woman,' 'not slave, nor master') was used to explode cultural and geographical boundaries, providing an ideology of unity and cohesion in the service of empire. In the process, the identity of Rome was elevated into an ontological order under the mark of *Pax Romana*.[4] This discourse of unity (the 'brotherhood of man') was to conceal, although it never quite erased, all class, race and gender differences in the formation of the self-identity of the Western European person. It is this vocabulary which has reached us in a curious combination of Albert Schweitzer's dictum, 'The African is indeed my brother, but my junior brother',[5] and Archbishop Tutu's controversial statement in the 1980s, 'P. W. Botha is my brother whether he likes it or not.' Within words like these the inner contradictions of Christianity are often obscured and lost.

As Europe encountered and colonised 'other worlds',[6] this 'European person'[7] became globalised. Civilisation and proselytisation became a means of incorporating alien people and lands into the economy of European cultural and political systems.[8] In a colonial context, the encounter between the European person with his or her civilised sensibilities and the exotic 'other' with her or his dark legacy of ritual killings, polygamy and cannibalism takes on a highly ambiguous form. The Rev. R. Shepherd of Lovedale, in his evaluation of the 'place of the native under the sun', provides an example of this ambivalence:

> A liar? Very often; but also in certain circumstances evincing a gratitude touching in the extreme. Low in morals? Yet how wonderfully vital, as his persistence in the face of the European inrush displays. . . Proud? True, often foolishly proud. And yet bearing a sense of inferiority that darkens his life.[9]

Shepherd's text is an instance of the kind of discourse on cultural imposition (also called economic developmentalism, which often tries to ignore culture) that has not received much attention from liberation theologians, primarily because of their concentration on economic liberation and development.[10] Shepherd's text is an example of how the discourse of cultural imposition (which appears to distance itself from the negative images by use of the question mark) implies that European cultural and ethical standards are those against which the native is to be evaluated. Yet because this is not explicitly stated, European culture acquires an absolute and universal norm. This kind of discourse promotes the project of the church and other civilising agencies as the burden of the white man, which is a mission to help the natives emerge from their dark past to a new (European) freedom. Another example of this missionary self-perception emerges also in the Cottesloe Statement of 1961, wherein concern is expressed about 'the revival of heathen tribal customs' among Africans.[11]

Suffice it to say, the above illustrations show the extent to which the church failed in its cultural mission to recreate African people in the image of Christian Europe. Missionary activity simply resulted in the emergence of native gentlemen and ladies, trapped in the expediency of 'mimicry'.[12] In the words of Rev. Francis Wrangham:

> In a single interview
> they listen, hesitate, believe:
> they depart, they forget.[13]

Beneath an outer 'European' appearance, African identity has remained. Black Christians often wear Western designer clothes while the traditional ritualistic scars on their bodies are there for all to see. Church includes my African grandmother, who always inserted a few words of Latin in her prayers, and my aunt, whose own prayers included spraying the walls with treated water while mumbling the names of the ancestors. Church, in its essence, loses itself in this diversity. This ecclesial diversity is at the same time the only church that we have.

Is the church a mere tool of conquest in the hands of the dominant power? Is the perception of the church as 'London in Africa' justified? It is also important, on the other hand, to recall the solidarity which some missionaries showed with African people. Dr Johannes van der Kemp is but one example. David Livingstone lost his library to the fires of Boer farmers because of his apparent bias towards the natives, and Bartolomé de Las Casas (the Apostle to the Indians) opposed many colonial practices in Latin America. We cannot, however, merely point to the divergence of interests and practices of various missionary agents. This kind of response ignores the agency of Christian natives themselves. After their conversion African proselytes were soon directly involved in the process of understanding, interpreting and reinterpreting the church in African societies. If we approach the question from their perspective, we begin to see the category of the 'church' as a highly contested symbolic field. Despite the appropriation of missionary-imposed identities, some within the church heard and recalled the radical message of the gospel, which contradicts the colonising message of the church.

The poor have always sought to redefine and recreate the church. It is partly in response to this situation that liberation theology has emerged. In other words, liberation theology did not inaugurate the church of the poor. Liberation theology did not even coincide with the moment of the church's involvement in people's struggles. It located itself within the already existing praxis of the poor. Like the early church, the contemporary church of the poor seeks to radically reappropriate the Great Commission in a manner that the colonial church perhaps never understood. In so doing, liberation theology emerges as a new missionary voice within the church.

Liberation Theology and the End of Ethics

If Christian ethics is to be understood as a total, systematic and scientific discourse which considers questions of right and wrong, and if liberation theology announces the return of the poor to the centre of the church, there is a sense in which liberation theology also announces the end of Christian ethics as we know it now. At the very least, it radically relativises normative Christian ethics, constituting a new way of doing ethics. Ethics within liberation theology speaks at the place of traditional ethical silence and pause. It is Christian reflection and discourse executed with the aid of critical social and human scientific tools. Moreover, it does so from the perspective, not of the colonial order or the church, but of the poor, whose interests liberation theology seeks to serve.

Armed with this 'clear-eyed'[14] analysis and commitment to the liberation of the poor, liberation theology emerges with a two-pronged agenda: denunciation and annunciation. On the one hand, it denounces the hypocrisy of the church, which teaches equality, charity and love while showing neither solidarity with nor serious commitment to the cause of the oppressed. It also denounces the morality of the state, whose rhetoric of 'law and order' serves as an ideological legitimation of the interests of the rich over the poor. On the other hand, liberation theology announces the good news of God's work through the poor in their struggle for liberation. It points beyond social and historical reality to an eschatological dimension that is total salvation — in which the poor shall inherit the earth. In this sense, liberation theology locates itself within the liberation project.

The Poor as Ethical Category

Liberation theologians view the poor as embodying the experience, location and practice which provide the only valid site for transformative action. As such, the category of 'the poor' comprises a key hermeneutical space within which the ethics of liberation theology emerges. Poverty is also seen as more than an unfortunate mistake of history. It is defined in structural terms as a social category.[15] The poor are seen as 'a by-product of the system under which we live and for which we are responsible'.[16] Dussel argues that the poor are a 'correlative of sin' — they are the 'fruit of sin . . . for no-one is poor unless there are rich.'[17] Poverty is a 'scandalous condition',[18] a 'symptom of alienation',[19] and an 'effect of repression by sin'.[20] The scandal of poverty is thus likened to that of the Cross, which was also 'an instrument of execution . . . death . . . torture and punishment'.[21] In brief, the condition of the poor is identified with the suffering of Jesus Christ.

The poor are at the same time a category outside of the repressive structures of society. The lives of the poor are a cry against those who benefit at their expense. In this sense, ethics is not a set of systematic standards for the judgement of rightful behaviour. It is a form of praxis, life and commitment.

Another way of conceiving of the poor as the hermeneutic of ethical praxis is to invoke the notion of the 'other'. The poor as the 'other' challenge the vision of Christian anthropology. In liberation theology, the 'other' is that which stands beyond the church, pointing to the absolute transcendence of the reign of God. 'The poor are the nothing, the nonbeing, of "this world" and it is in virtue of their not having been stained in "this world" that they are "subjects" of the reign of God.'[22] As eschatological subjects, the poor emerge with a voice of their own. Gutiérrez speaks of the poor as 'making their voice heard, . . . discovering themselves, . . . speaking for themselves and not through intermediaries. They want to be subjects of their own history and to forge a radically different society.'[23]

In short, 'the poor' as an ethical principle occupy an outside position which relativises any attempt to view everyone else as an extension of myself. The poor question, rebuke and transform the anthropological and ethical presuppositions of the dominant church. The poor, as outsider, fill a position whose very brokenness and pain are a judgement on the comfort and contentment of the rich. The praxis of the poor, their liberation struggle, becomes an intervention in the dominant Christian self-understanding. Liberation theology announces and celebrates this intervention, this tearing down of the comfortable world of the dominant church and colonial Christianity. The presence of the poor is a mocking counter-gaze to any fantastic ecclesial notion of wholeness.

Sin and the Ethics of Responsibility

According to Dussel, 'The praxis of sin is institutionalised by way of political, ideological, religious and economic structures.'[24] 'The place we occupy in the social texture determines (although not absolutely) our being.'[25] It is upon this foundation that 'we construct our life'. This position does not take away individual responsibility, because every one of us 'consciously assumes — in the light and shade of her/his biography . . . and to a greater and lesser degree — the meaning of his or her "place" in the institutional structure of sin'.[26]

Although we are indeed influenced, and our moral world is shaped, by the institutions we are born into, we also shape and construct these institutions in the likeness of our moral world. Sin is, therefore, related to the quality of our praxis.

The poor are not, of course, without sin. Hard pressed by the violence of political regimes and the need for survival and self-preservation, they develop alternative modes of surveillance and cohesion in order to guard against infiltration by repressive forces. These are sometimes harsh and violent. There are also oppressive social practices among the poor, notably sexism, which need to be criticised and challenged. For the poor (like everyone else), the praxis of liberation forms a site of ethical learning and transformation. Here the poor discover other poor, as well as their own role in reproducing their own oppressive condition — and their potential power in the struggle for liberation.[27] In their collective involvement in the struggle for liberation, the poor are the inaugurators of transformation and agents of the salvific work of God. The liberation of the poor is the standard against which the praxis of the poor and liberation theology itself must be measured.

Conversion and the Ethics of Location

The poor as 'other' are always located beyond the liberation theologian and the church. As such, the poor are always calling us to conversion. Gutiérrez suggests that this requires us in a concrete way to 'opt for the poor – for one class over another'.[28] Conversion, he insists, means a 'break with our mental categories, our cultural milieu, our social class'.[29]

In this way, conversion leads to solidarity, which entails a break with our 'normal' course of life, and a decision to embark on a new path. Conversion is thus a development that grows with our participation and involvement in the world of the 'other.' Solidarity is, in turn, the new way of life that results from conversion and forgiveness. Conversion in this sense is 'not possible without an integration into their world'. It has no meaning apart from bonds of real friendship with those who suffer despoliation and injustice.[30]

Conversion means commitment as an act of 'entering, and in some cases, remaining in [the poor's] universe with a much clearer awareness, making it a place of residence and not simply of work'.[31] More than that, conversion means risking my body by depriving it of its 'normal' comforts of a healthy environment, good diet, pleasure and familiar surroundings. Conversion to the 'other' involves the risk of becoming a stranger to my own body.

Put differently, location is an important mediating factor in our lives. Location influences the extent to which we may be able to risk ourselves for others, to see ourselves as implicated in the poverty of others. Because we cannot ultimately speak for others as if we had recourse or access to their own experiences, location also requires us to be conscious of our own finitude and of the limitations imposed on us by such mediatory factors as class, gender, race, culture and language.[32]

The ethics of location is an ethic of relativism, an ethical reminder of our inability to extend the 'self' to cover the space of the 'other'. It is in relation to this that criticisms in South Africa are sometimes levelled against white theologians who write liberation theology. The criticism needs, however, to be broadened, because the ethics of location raises the question of the place of most social critics and most liberation theologians. If we cannot assume that liberation theologians (who are invariably not themselves totally poor) are transparent transmitters of the experiences of the poor, then what are their roles? This is a question that stands central to the contemporary debate in liberation theology.

Human Dignity and the Ethics of Identity

Casting the poor as the 'other' poses another ethical challenge: How are we to view human dignity and identity? Where traditionally we would assume human dignity to be an innate, natural endowment, given in our creation 'in the image of God', liberation theology has shown that this endowment is in practice denied to the poor. We have also seen with the 'return of the other' – the poor – that this dignity can be reclaimed.

To invoke human dignity as an absolute ethical principle is not necessarily idealistic. Its affirmation provides an opportunity for opposition and transformation. Liberatory praxis is a dignifying activity. Through participation in the liberation struggle we become dignified, realising our God-given potential. We become dignified by becoming co-creators with God. To invoke human dignity through struggle is at the same time to deny to the oppressor the possibility of total hegemony. It is to claim liberation, which is always more than asking for charity.

Liberation Theology as an Internal Criticism

The point should by now be clear: liberation theology is in addition to all else an internal criticism, not only because it bases itself on the Christian faith, but also because it takes the expression of that faith — in favour of the poor — very seriously. In Latin America, for instance, liberation theologians cite papal documents, the Second Vatican Council, pastoral letters and resolutions from bishops' conferences as a basis for their work.[33] In South Africa the various ecumenical statements — Cottesloe, *The Message to the People of South Africa* and, more recently, the *Kairos Document* — are almost unfailingly cited as evidence of the church's witness to liberation.[34] This approach points to a space within the church where transformation is possible. Besides this ecclesial tradition, liberation theology uses Scripture as a key source. The Exodus and New Testament are seen as paradigmatic to the liberation struggles of the present. In these contemporary struggles we read God's will and God's manifestation in history — a reading that is authorised and witnessed to by the biblical record itself.

Liberation theology, in short, is 'not a new theology but a new way of *doing* theology'.[35] 'It states that it attempts to make Christianity more self-critical and therefore more radical.'[36]

One History, One Salvation

As a result of the global march of capitalism, the development of communications networks and the global transmigration of human labour, we can no longer conceive of boundaries and divisions in traditional terms. We all live within one system in which our lives interact and intersect, forming hierarchical relations. This history does not only underline the extent of the political, economic and cultural colonial conquest by Europe; it also points to the internalisation of this 'one world' by colonial and post-colonial subjects, in their appropriation of Western civilisation.

We are *all* part of this history. There is no space outside of it by which to judge and fully comprehend the whole. There are, however, communities of practice that are constantly opening up spaces for themselves by celebrating the diversity and pluralism of history — in the quest for alternatives to the dominant society. The church cannot claim a position outside of history by which to judge society. Its very being is situated in the world. In showing solidarity with the poor, the church is at the same time able to see things a little differently. Reference is often made to the 'epistemological privilege' of the poor. In essence this means that the poor see things differently. Their view of reality is largely from outside of the social contract worked out by the dominant classes. By identifying with the poor, liberation theologians seek to expose those (both within and without the church) who deny the poor to the challenge of the poor — which is the challenge of the 'other'.

The industrialised and wealthy European countries can no longer define themselves in isolation from the poverty of the third-world countries where they extract raw material and open markets. In South Africa, try as they may, it would be hard for whites to account for their lives and history apart from the presence of blacks.

Liberation theology is the voice within the Christian church which pleads for the expansion of the space occupied by the poor. The poor do not announce a different salvation, they do not convene a different church. They seek to salvage, through the affirmation of a different perspective, the same church. In this sense, the poor announce the unity of history.[37] Liberation theology seeks to persuade the broken church to recognise this unity.

Solidarity and the Ethics of Eschatological Reserve

It can, of course, be argued that liberation theology has succeeded in its task. There is a sense in which it no longer needs to emphasise the intervention of the 'other' — the entry of the outsider. Most Christians have come to accept that the poor are part of the church. The question is, however, whether the church has the capacity to hear the call of the poor as the 'other' and to respond in solidarity. This involves a willingness to participate in the dissolution of the divide between the poor and rich as the basis for the creation of true community.[38]

For the church to be complete, it needs the poor. It is at the same time insufficient for the poor to be theologically or ethically complacent. The poor also need to become a true community. If liberation theology, done from the perspective of the poor, were merely an uncritical discourse of the poor, it would risk reducing itself to a 'Christian ideology of revolution' whose role is simply to 'baptise the revolution'. The revolution of the poor needs also to be exposed to the critique of liberation.[39]

Miguez Bonino expresses concern at what he calls the 'monist' tendency of liberation theology. He sees this occurring when love of God is collapsed without remainder into love of neighbour. When this happens, he suggests, it becomes very difficult to differentiate between the full theological implications of salvation and the more limited (but theologically important) understanding of political liberation. To use Miguez Bonino's words, this occurs when 'reference to the history of divine revelation is secondary, merely exemplary, or even dispensable'. 'If we carry that tendency', he continues, 'to its ultimate conclusion, we will end up wittingly deifying history or humanity itself. . . There can be no doubt that contemporary Latin American theology has no such intention. But we must ask ourselves whether the formulations we have worked out so far do enough to rule out that possibility.'[40]

As a self-critical space within the church, liberation theology facilitates the construction of a 'Christian ethics of revolution, a community ethics of liberation, an ethics capable of justifying the struggle for social justice'.[41] Liberation ethics, as

Christian ethics, will 'always maintain a certain critical . . . an eschatological reserve',[42] which will afford any new society an openness to God, an openness to its own finitude. As such, it will be self-critical.[43]

Liberation Theology as an Ethical Conversation with the Poor

As an internal critique, liberation theology constitutes a conversation in which the voice of the poor meets the ears of those prepared to hear and participate. Liberation theology differs from classical models of dialogue in that it does not hide its 'preferential option for the poor'. On the one hand, this position strengthens liberation theology by preventing it from falling into the trap of 'objectivism' and 'neutrality' or the kind of neutrality which Gutiérrez says 'comes down to non-commitment'.[44]

But what does a 'preferential option for the poor' actually mean? Two questions must suffice. Firstly, what is the real position and role of the actual poor in this conversation? Gutiérrez puts the dilemma more succinctly. 'The fact is that so far this critical reflection of liberation praxis has come from sectors in which the popular classes are not present in important or decisive numbers. . .'[45] He goes still further: 'The native peoples and cultures of Latin America are not sufficiently taken into account in our present efforts at theological reflection.'[46]

To be poor is to suffer more than economic deprivation. It often involves cultural deprivation. In South Africa as well as the Americas, it often involves being at the receiving end of racism. Moreover, in more recent years liberation theology has also been criticised for its insensitivity to gender.[47]

A second (and related) question concerns the identity of liberation theologians themselves? It has often been assumed that they exercise the role of what Gramsci calls 'organic intellectuals' — seeking to articulate the values and perspectives of the poor, while allowing their theology to be shaped by the demands and expectations of the poor. Perhaps the major challenge facing liberation theologians is not so much whether they spend their lives in the shacks with the poor — although this would have direct implications for their theology. It is, rather, how critically conscious they are of the various factors that mediate their own engagement with the poor.

In brief, ethics in liberation theology is an ethic of empowerment. It seeks to empower the poor. As such it gives expression to values that emerge from within the struggle of the poor — a struggle in dialogue with the gospel as understood by the poor.

[1] See also C. Villa-Vicencio, 'Liberation Theology' in the first volume of *Theology and Praxis* (Maryknoll: Orbis Books and Cape Town: David Philip, 1994).

[2] Matt. 28:19–20.

[3] See Paul Keresztes, *Imperial Rome and the Christians: From Herod the Great to About 200 AD*, Vol. 1 (Lanham: University Press of America, 1989).

[4] See Erwin R. Goodenough, *The Church in the Roman Empire* (New York: Cooper Square Publishers, 1970).

[5] Quoted in Chinua Achebe, *Hopes and Impediments* (New York: Doubleday, 1989), p. 69.

6 For the various ways in which this expansion and its motives have been theorised, see especially I. Wallerstein, *The Modern World-System* (San Diego: Academic Press, 1974), and S. Greenblatt, *Marvelous Possessions: The Wonder of The New World* (Chicago: University of Chicago Press, 1991).

7 Mary Louise Pratt, *Imperial Eyes: Travel Writing and Transculturation* (Chicago: University of Chicago Press, 1991).

8 On Columbus's 'taking possession' of alien lands see R. H. Major (ed.), *Christopher Columbus: Four Voyages to the New World in His Own Words* (New York: Citadel Press, 1992), p. 2. For a critical reading of the various interpretations of Columbus, see Margarita Zamora, *Reading Columbus* (Berkeley: University of California Press, 1993).

9 Rev. R. H. W. Shepherd, *The Bantu* (Edinburgh: United Free Church of Scotland Publishers, n.d.), pp. 86–7.

10 A leading figure in the critique of 'economic developmentalism' is Gustavo Gutiérrez. See his *A Theology of Liberation* (Maryknoll: Orbis Books, 1988).

11 John W. de Gruchy and Charles Villa-Vicencio (eds), *Apartheid Is a Heresy* (Grand Rapids: Eerdmans, 1983), p. 150.

12 In fact Homi K. Bhabha, following Lacan, has developed this notion of 'colonial mimicry' and recast it as a space for resistance and a site of colonial desires. See Jacques Lacan, *The Four Fundamental Concepts of Psycho-analysis* (New York: W. W. Norton, 1981), pp 67–104, and Homi K. Bhabha, 'The Other Question', *Screen*, 24:6 (1983).

13 Rev. Francis Wrangham, *A Dissertation on the Best Means of Civilizing the Subjects of the British Empire in India and of Diffusing the Light of the Christian Religion Throughout the Eastern World* (London: R. Taylor and Co., 1805), p. 5.

14 Gutiérrez emphasises scientific analysis with the following expressions: 'truly scientific methodology,' 'scientific grasp of reality,' 'scientific line of reasoning'. See his 'Liberation Praxis and Christian Faith' in Rosino Gibellini (ed.), *Frontiers of Theology in Latin America* (Maryknoll: Orbis Books, 1979).

15 See Gibellini (ed.), *Frontiers of Theology*, p. 17.

16 Ibid., p. 8.

17 Enrique Dussel, *Ethics and Community* (Maryknoll: Orbis Books, 1988), pp. 22, 23.

18 Gutiérrez, *A Theology of Liberation*, p. 171.

19 Albert Nolan, *God in South Africa* (Cape Town: David Philip, 1988), p. 81.

20 Dussel, *Ethics and Community*, p. 34.

21 Nolan, *God in South Africa*, p. 58.

22 Dussel, *Ethics and Community*, p. 55.

23 Gibellini (ed.), *Frontiers of Theology*, p. 1.

24 See Dussel, *Ethics and Community*, pp. 21, 22.

25 Ibid., p. 22.

26 Ibid, p. 24.

27 See Paulo Freire, *Pedagogy of the Oppressed* (New York: Seabury, 1973).

28 Gibellini (ed.), *Frontiers of Theology*, p. 9.

29 Ibid, p. 9.

30 G. Gutiérrez, *We Drink from Our Own Wells* (Maryknoll: Orbis Books, 1986), p. 104.

31 Ibid., p. 125.

32 For a further treatment of the notion of 'location' see Adrienne Rich, *Blood, Bread and Poetry: Selected Prose 1979–1985* (New York: W. W. Norton, 1986), pp. 210–231.

33 See Alfred T. Hennelly (ed.), *Liberation Theology: A Documentary History* (Maryknoll: Orbis Books, 1990).

34 See especially De Gruchy and Villa-Vicencio, *Apartheid Is a Heresy*.

35 Gibellini (ed.), *Frontiers of Theology*, p. 22.

[36] G. Gutiérrez and R. Shaull, *Liberation and Change* (Atlanta: John Knox, 1977), p. 84.

[37] Gutiérrez, *A Theology of Liberation*, p. 86.

[38] Ibid., pp. 82, 83.

[39] Dussel, *Ethics and Community* p. 179.

[40] José Miguez Bonino, 'Historical Praxis and Christian Identity', in Gibellini (ed.), *Frontiers of Theology*, p. 263.

[41] Dussel, *Ethics and Community*, p. 179.

[42] Ibid., p. 81.

[43] Gibellini (ed.), *Frontiers of Theology*, p. 23.

[44] Ibid., p. 33.

[45] Ibid., p. 24.

[46] Ibid., p. 33.

[47] See C. Villa-Vicencio, 'Liberation Theology', in the first volume of *Theology and Praxis*.

Select Bibliography

Dussel, E. *Ethics and Community*. Maryknoll: Orbis Books, 1988

Gibellini, R. (ed.) *Frontiers of Theology in Latin America*. Maryknoll: Orbis Books, 1979

Gutiérrez, G. *A Theology of Liberation*. Maryknoll: Orbis Books, 1988

Nolan, A. *God in South Africa*. Cape Town: David Philip, 1988

10

Ethics in Black Theology[1]

MOLEFE TSELE

We live in a pluralistic world of various meaning systems and religious options. Society at the same time poses a host of questions that traditional ethical systems cannot adequately address. As a result there has arisen a serious moral crisis in contemporary ethical debate.

The problem in Black theology is even more acute. Traditional white ethics is by definition unable to provide moral guidance and answers to problems emanating from the life experiences of black people. In the South African context, blacks readily identify with the judgement of James Cone that traditional ethics constitutes 'the cultural values of white oppressors'.[2] Blacks cannot look for norms of fairness from a system that denies them equal treatment as full citizens and valued members of society.

The South African social reality presents intriguing challenges to any student of ethics. On the one hand, it claims continuity with the best moral ideals of Western civilisation and the Christian tradition. On the other hand, it has imposed systematic oppression and suffering on millions of people. It is hard for blacks to associate this inhuman system of human plunder and destruction with any definition of moral good. Herein lies the crisis of the traditional Christian moral value system for those who have seen suffering and death come out of it.

It is within this context of being black and oppressed in a society founded on white morality and rationality that Black theology seeks to construct an alternative moral way of being. In Black theology, the paramount ethical question is: How ought we to behave morally (i.e. humanly) as members of the black and oppressed community? Alternatively, what constitutes moral conduct for those (blacks) who are struggling for their liberation from (white) oppression? This chapter attempts to answer these questions. It explores the elements and characteristics of an ethical system whose primary concern is the humanity of *all* people. More particularly, it is concerned with the liberation of oppressed people who are denied their full humanity — people who are often black.

Given that there is no single school of black ethics, we begin with a survey of four models of doing ethics within the context of Black theology. Two models, those of Allan Boesak and Simon Maimela, originate from South Africa. The other two are those of the North American black theologians, James Cone and Enoch Oglesby. On the basis of this survey, an ethical proposal will be made which takes into account the issues raised by the experience of being black and oppressed. This model is informed by a liberation perspective, that uses the Kairos critique of traditional ethics.

The *Kairos Document* argues that the crisis in which the church finds itself is such that we are 'compelled to analyse more carefully the different theologies in our churches and to speak out more clearly and boldly about the significance of these theologies'.[3] Our conviction is that unless black ethics situates itself within the Kairos (critical) tradition, it is likely to degenerate into a *status quo* morality and become assimilated to the very system it currently finds so objectionable in white ethics. Our aim is to create a black ethics that is radically critical – critical also of black morality. Only by so doing, can it be both creative and liberating.

We begin by clarifying the way in which key concepts used in this chapter might lend themselves to misunderstanding and ambiguity. One concept is 'black', as in the phrase 'black ethics'. We shall inquire into the various levels of meaning of the concept and also its moral relevance and political significance in South African society.

A Definition

No human groups can exist without some explicit or implicit system of values and norms of good and right. Indeed, to be human, as Charles L. Kammer argues, 'is to be moral'. We are all 'inescapably moral persons'.[4] However, our moral codes are not universal. What is moral to us may be immoral to others. To say a particular conduct is immoral simply means it does not accord with our standard of acceptable conduct or of conduct befitting a human being. For example, a marriage of first cousins may be honourable to one community and a disgrace in another. The point we are making is that each group is moral in its own way; and each group's particular construal of what is moral or immoral may conflict with that of others. Ethics, as the systematic reflection on given moral conduct, seeks to identify cohesion and pattern in the way we structure and account for our moral life. The crucial issue is that it is the raw material of moral life that is integrated systematically and critically into a system of ethics. For Black theology, ethics must be attentive to the life choices we make as members of a particular group with given needs and objectives. The specific shapes this systematic formulation takes will be elaborated later. The question we wish to address now is: Why 'black' ethics?

The Moral Significance of 'Blackness'

In theological discourse, there are three levels of meaning in the concept of blackness. First, there is what Maimela calls the ontological or literal meaning.[5] At this level, blackness is a designative category referring to those whose skin is black. It can be used in a value-free manner purely as a descriptive term, in much the same way that other people are tall or short, fat or thin. The second level of blackness is a derogatory category implying deficiency. In this sense, black is that which is not white, or that which is less than white. In this instance, blackness is invoked as an antithesis to whiteness. While whiteness may refer to what is good, pure and innocent, blackness conjures up negative images such as death, evil and impurity.

The third level of meaning in the concept of blackness is its moral and political use. Used morally, blackness is an affirmation of the humanity of the oppressed. It is what Boesak calls 'a state of mind', or the consciousness of those who have chosen to affirm the humanity of blacks contrary to the practices of the *status quo*. It is used in this sense to challenge the dominant creed that only what is white has value; to affirm that black people do not have to deny their blackness as the condition for being human; and that Christian faith is not antithetical to blackness. Put the other way, you don't have to be white, dress white, talk a white language, in order to be Christian.

To be black means to be engaged in a conscious, deliberate struggle against oppression. Boesak calls it having 'the courage to be' in the face of white power, which seeks to reduce blacks to non-being.[6] As a moral category, blackness means authentic humanity, because for blacks, their humanity is inseparable from their blackness. One discovers what it means to be human by engaging in the struggle against oppression and suffering – i.e. by becoming black. As Boesak puts it, blackness is essential to humanity, it is authentic humanity and the totality of our humanity.[7]

Oglesby agrees with this interpretation by declaring that 'blackness is not only a significant part of our humanity, it is our humanity (period)'.[8] Outside the experience of black life, one cannot truly know life's experiences in their totality. White life is not authentic in so far as it is partial and restricted.

We should be cautious in our references to white traditional ethics. To talk of white ethics as if it were homogeneous and monolithic is simplistic, misleading and ultimately ideological. The truth is that there are diverse and contradictory traditions within white ethical theory. One cannot simply equate, for example, Kant's ethics of the 'categorical imperative' with Kierkegaard's 'ethical'. Some of these traditions have affinity with the liberation perspective; within their context they may be viewed as critical of the *status quo*. A case will be made that even within the Black theological tradition, there are diverse traditions, some of them not necessarily liberating, but reformist or even reactionary.

However, for our purpose, and in the context of South Africa, when we talk of white traditional ethics, we are referring specifically to the dominant white culture of apartheid and its theological justification of the oppression of others solely because they are non-Europeans, non-white and poor. White traditional morality as experienced in South Africa means, therefore, the morality and rationality of oppressors who believe in the superiority of their way of life, who despise anything black and who believe whiteness is not only superior but is also religiously nearer to God. To them, Christian ethics and European morality are synonymous and, by the same token, heathenism or paganism and the black moral life are one and the same. To them, you cannot be black *and* Christian. It is this white morality coupled with its rational foundations in Western intellectual history and its theological basis that we shall be challenging in our formulation of a black ethical system.

Surveying Black Ethics

An attempt is made in what follows to identify only the distinguishing marks of the various ethical theories that concern us here.

Cone: Black Koinonia Ethics

The fundamental defect of the white ethical system, according to Cone, is the result of its defective theology. As he aptly alleges, it is ethically wrong in its theories of 'good' because it is 'wrong theologically'.[9] Its theological fault lies in its notion of a God who is identified with the *status quo*, instead of being founded on the God of the oppressed who is historically engaged in their liberation struggle. Its ethics is committed to the preservation of the *status quo* rather than to its transformation.[10] The fact that white ethics is silent on issues of oppression and racism is not an accident nor does it occur by default. It is a logical consequence of a theology that does not know the God of the oppressed. Therefore, in our search for answers to problems confronting the black community, white ethics cannot provide solutions. Its 'rationality' means 'absurdity', and its talk of 'freedom' and 'democracy' has meant unfreedom and slavery to blacks.[11]

How, then, does Cone see black ethics? Two considerations are central to his ethical system. First, ethics cannot be separated from theology. As Cone says: 'The ethical question 'What am I to do?' cannot be separated from its theological source, i.e. what God is doing and has done [to liberate the oppressed].'[12] And since for Cone, theology is God's liberation of the oppressed, ethical behaviour must be about the liberation of the oppressed. The sources for our knowledge of who God is and what God is doing are the Scriptures and tradition.

The second characteristic of Cone's ethics is the fact that it is grounded on the experience of those who are oppressed. When Cone talks of tradition as a source of ethics in addition to the Scriptures, he refers strictly to the tradition of the black community. What we have is a koinonia ethics limited to the black community. As he contends, 'the koinonia is limited to the victims of oppression and does not include the oppressors'.[13]

Cone's black koinonia ethics of liberation is, in our opinion, a justified indictment of white traditional morality and rationality. There is credence, moreover, to his claim that white theology is in no position to write the rules of how its system has to be fought. However, he seems to be uncritical of the unethical conduct that is potentially present within the koinonia of the oppressed. To suggest that by merely being victims of white oppression, blacks are incapable of wrong conduct is to be unrealistic about human nature and the persistence of sin even within a community of angels. This concern should not minimise the central accusation levelled against white traditional morality that it is a morality of conquerors and oppressors. For Cone, white morality is historically indistinguishable from the morality of conquest, colonial rule and domination. Indeed, in the case of South Africa, it is indistinguishable from the morality of criminals, robbers and murderers. Apartheid has kept murderers and corrupt and greedy politicians in positions of honour in the community, and has imprisoned its citizens of conscience.

Boesak: An Ethics of Authentic Humanity

Like Cone, Boesak faults white traditional ethics for its failure to make the life experiences of blacks central to its task and for its false doctrine of God.[14] The crucial determinants of black ethics, according to Boesak, are the black experience on the one hand and the power of the Word of God on the other. These two are dialectically related. The black situation provides the concrete grounding for ethical reflection. And without the Word of God, black ethics would be reduced to *volk* ethics and thus become an ideology.[15]

Hence for Boesak, Cone's koinonia ethics must transcend the narrowness of the base group. As an ethics of liberation, black ethics must not only affirm the humanity of black people but point to the true humanity offered in the Bible. This is an ethical system that engages the situation and the Word of God in a mutually critical encounter. The final judge of what is right or good is not the demands of the situation but the liberating gospel of Jesus.[16] No one situation is absolute, not even the situation of the oppressed. Conversely, the Word of God does not enjoy a privileged position compared with people's experiences of the situation, nor can it be read apart from those experiences. Black ethics is thus an ethics of liberation whose character is 'situational, social and eschatological'.[17]

The situation is an important authenticating factor but it is not the only one. The black experience is also broadly defined to include a wide spectrum of considerations emanating from the past and the present. Thus Boesak sees African tradition as an important element in black ethics. What emerges is an ethics that is comprehensive and sets as its goal the totality of liberation and the wholeness of life. It is in this wholeness that Boesak seeks to discover the meaning of humanity in its fullness, and thus authentic humanity.

Maimela: An Ethics of Creative Activity

For Maimela, ethics seeks to answer the question: How can we be involved in the dynamic of God's creative and redemptive acts? The fundamental error of traditional ethics, according to Maimela, is that it is premised on the notion of a God who is aloof from historical processes. The alternative Maimela proposes is a view of God who acts in freedom, who breaks into history and invites us to be involved in the creative and liberating dynamics of his love in history. Maimela seeks to introduce an ethics that is both Christocentric and theocentric,[18] and that values criticism as much as creativity.

Methodologically he challenges idealistic notions of truth which attempt to serve as the starting point for theology. He contends that the starting point should be the concrete historical experiences of Christians. We shall be making the point that debates on 'starting points' are significant only in systematic reflection. In real life, both experience and theory are intertwined. Maimela may also be faulted for the undifferentiated manner in which he generalises the various traditions of white ethical theory. However, there is merit in Maimela's central claim that white morality is predicated on an anthropology that deifies human agency and valorises achievement and conquest. He thus sees the roots of the current crisis in white traditional ethics, in its anthropology and theology.[19] In contrast, black ethics is premissed on a view of God who identifies with pain and suffering in the world and who enters the world to save it from its predicament. 'What is' is not necessarily 'what must be' and 'what can be'. Human beings must be actively involved in creating the best and ideal conditions in the world. But they are not the primary actors; they are co-actors with God.

Moreover, the models for the life of freedom come from the Bible read from the vantage point of the real life of the poor and oppressed.[20] There is an interaction between the concrete social situation and the Bible. For Maimela, to start with revealed truths, as is customary in white traditional ethics, is to overlook the fact that truth is not disembodied from life. Thus for him, the best route to truth is through historical praxis. Black ethics is methodologically situated in the tradition of historical studies.

Oglesby: An Ethics of Freedom

Enoch Oglesby's point of departure is similar to those of other black ethicists who are dissatisfied with traditional moral systems. His objective is the construction of an ethical system that will be meaningful and relevant to the black condition.[21] However, he takes a radically different route by seeking answers from universally held ethical principles and theological propositions. He also seeks to correct what he perceives as an insufficient appropriation of Judaeo-Christian moral norms by black ethicists.[22] In so doing, he hopes to ground his ethical mandates in 'deeper yearnings of the human spirit': liberation, coherence, divine purpose, human solidarity and self-fulfilment.

Oglesby's ethical system, like those of other black ethicists, takes the black experience as a moral force central to the construction of an ethical system. Black ethics must evolve out of the cultural ethos of this community. The task of ethics is to provide an adequate analysis of the black experience. The ultimate task, beyond that of describing the black situation, is 'the creation of a humane value system'.[23] What emerges is an ethical system that is attentive to the existential needs of the black community, while remaining deeply biblical; one that is thoroughly communal while committed to personal freedom.

Oglesby's concept of freedom is balanced by a theological understanding of responsibility. His theory of freedom seeks to express a convergence of freedom and responsibility construed as freedom 'in community', which he argues 'points to the interdependent character and mutuality of all human existence'.[24] He defines black ethics as

> an ethic of radical freedom for moral life, initiated by the agapeistic love of God disclosed in Jesus Christ, and in his concern for the poor and dispossessed in human community . . . aimed . . . deliberately and forthrightly, at the creation of community wherein persons have the moral freedom and obligation of caring, of sharing and of responding to the needs of others.[25]

Towards a Model of Black Critical Ethics

Drawing on our survey of black ethics, we can now attempt to construct a model of ethics that does justice to the issues raised by the ethicists we have considered.

Black Ethics and Status Quo Ethics

The *Kairos Document* reminds us that theology is most often used to legitimate the *status quo*. *Status quo* theology 'blesses injustice, canonises the will of the powerful and reduces the poor to passivity, obedience and apathy'.[26] It divinises the *status quo* and demonises the forces of opposition or attempts to transform them. Going against the *status quo* is equated with going against the divine will. The Western cultural ethos is presented as both universal and biblical. Non-Western moral systems are regarded as unbiblical and thus immoral. The *status quo* is normative in the sense that 'what is' is 'what ought to be'. This ethics is non-critical, absolutist and intolerant. It is predominantly an ethics of rules that demands obedience. In the language of the *Kairos Document*, it is the ethics of 'law and order'. To black people, it is the ethics of racism, apartheid and slavery.

Our contention is that certain forms of Black theology, especially those which are tribal and absolutist, lend themselves to features similar to *status quo* ethics. This trend is more pronounced in those 'black' ethical systems that tend to demand uncritical loyalty to authority and blind obedience to law and order. However, central to our definition of black ethics is the notion of powerlessness and oppression. There is, therefore, some doubt whether in our situation black ethics can be dominating and oppressive in the same way that white traditional ethics has been experienced. We can, however, say that it remains a theoretical and methodological possibility for black ethics to become a *status quo* ethics.

Black Ethics and Rational Ethics

What Kairos theologians call 'Church Theology', with its characteristic superficial condemnation of injustice and lack of genuine commitment to fundamental transformation of society, has its counterpart in white rationalist ethics. Here, the concrete issues of justice are treated theoretically, and serious social conflicts are personalised. There is an excessive concern with personal morality and individual freedom. Moral virtues are what promote individual happiness or interests. The primary task is to achieve rational coherence. A particular behaviour is right if it is consistent with the rules of logic and corresponds to the ideal virtues. Serious problems are deemed to have been solved if they can be explained rationally and theoretically or if they can be resolved in the mind. Social problems are emptied of real conflict and presented as problems of perception. The solution then rests in reinterpreting the issues and gaining a better understanding. Thus, serious racial conflicts are depicted as problems of approach or of conflicting viewpoints. When this ethics uses the concept of love and reconciliation, it is depoliticised. The problem of violence is likewise treated as an overreaction of the 'system'. There is no serious consideration that the system may be inherently violent and that social problems like poverty, suffering and individual alienation may be the result of an oppressive and unjust system.

Our view is that certain forms of black ethics, because of their insufficient critical practice, may easily become rationalistic. The temptation is real because rationalistic ethics is opposed to absolutism and coercive support of the *status quo*. The 'Africanisation' of white morality without its radical transformation is an example of a black version of rational ethics. According to Oglesby: 'A black Christian social ethics cannot be [and] . . . . must not be a nicely packaged, well thought and rationally construed corollary to counterbalance a white Christian ethic'.[27]

Boesak similarly warns that what is called for is not that blacks should gain equality with whites in this system of oppression,[28] but rather its radical transformation. He says: 'A solution cannot be sought by imitating the American white capitalist system or by creating a better kind of capitalism in the black community.'[29] Gaining equal opportunity in the exploitation of others or 'getting into' the system will not advance the liberating goal of black ethics. Blacks should not aspire to be white or to excel in white morality, neither should the goal be to make whites black. Rather, it is the creation of a new way of being human.[30]

It is our view that certain forms of black ethics are positioning themselves to coexist as equals side by side with white traditional ethics. Within the South African context, this is evident in the moral teachings of mainline churches. It would be a mistake to assume that simply by virtue of being black, the black church necessarily espouses a critical ethics of liberation.

Black Ethics as Critical Ethics

Black ethics grounded in the tradition of liberation theology views traditional ethics as crisis-ridden and desperately in need of reform. The fundamental crisis of white traditional ethics is that it cannot give moral guidance to those who seek answers to questions of oppression and suffering. Admittedly, there may have been a time when ethical theories of utilitarianism or hedonism provided relevant answers to concrete problems. At this juncture in history, however, those who are morally sensitive and who seek moral guidance find traditional ethics confusing and ideologically an obstruction. Because of this moral breakdown, a new, bold and courageous system must be developed. This ethics should be steeped in an awareness of the prophetic judgement of the existing system and the potential for its replacement. The crisis is an opportunity for bold response and fresh creativity. This ethics views crisis as an inseparable part of the historical struggles in life, and is thus welcome. We call this ethical system a black critical ethics of liberation.

The first characteristic of black ethics is that it is a critical ethics of white society in general and of white morality in particular. It is conscious of the crisis in prevailing morality. Not only do we have a multiplicity of answers, but there is also increasingly a lack of consensus as to the definition of problems. Whilst for some, poverty is the primary problem, for others it is loss of meaning. There is also a crisis in traditional institutions that normally provide moral guidance. Some are being contested and others have become irrelevant. In South Africa, white Christians and the church have lost the right to be examples of moral excellence. They are identified with the horrors of apartheid because they failed to distance themselves from its practice. In view of this challenge to white traditional ethics and the general breakdown of its authority, blacks look elsewhere for moral guidance.

Black ethics is, secondly, contextual. It arises out of a given social context, of white oppression and black suffering. This context broadly includes the history, social norms, cultural heritage and traditions, and experiences of struggle that constitute the reality of black life. A definition of the context of black life that only looks at political experiences while overlooking religious practice will fail to understand it in its entirety.

Within a critical tradition, the social context is seen as a dynamic process that is evolving and undergoing mutations. The relationship between ethics and the social context is also dynamic: the situation does not hold an absolute deterministic power on ethics. There is always in the human spirit the power to transcend the limitations of context. Black ethics is, according to Boesak, critical with respect to its own situation.[31] The final criterion of what is ethically demanded in a given situation is the liberation of the oppressed.

Black ethics is pre-eminently a contextual ethics. Cone, reflecting on this issue, argues against a universalist and absolutist ethics, and says there is no point in saying that blacks must be ethical at all times in relation to white people. He goes on: 'What sense would it make for black people to talk about an absolutist ethic in relation to stealing with people who stole them from Africa and enslaved them . . .?'[32] Moral mandates have meaning only within given situations and contexts.

Black ethics is, thirdly, social and, through society, an ethics of individuals. It does not evolve in isolation from the community and its history and tradition. It is an ethics of society and of relations within society. Its concerns and overriding values are authenticated through the community. It seeks personal transformation for the transformation of society. Its social value is justice. Oglesby calls it the 'we-ness' ethics in contrast to the 'me-ness' of white traditional ethics.[33]

There is an inherent danger that the group may swallow the individual, but as Boesak rightly cautions, the personal dimension need not be neglected.[34] One can argue that without the personal dimension there could never be the ethical, because ultimately only persons, not groups, are ethical. It is these persons who constitute groups and form structures.

The social dimension of black ethics also serves to underscore the notion of solidarity and community. The extent to which the community can be closed to others and thus immune to fresh and renewing influences is part of the tension that continues to exist in socialist ethics. As critical ethics, black ethics seeks to be social without being exclusive or parochial.

Black ethics is, fourthly, an African ethics premised on an African world-view and religiosity. To this world-view, the Western dichotomy of the spiritual and the material, the sacred and the secular, is foreign. African virtues of solidarity, respect for elders, human life and nature, hospitality, and veneration of the memory of the dead (ancestors) are central to genuine black ethics.

However, not everything belonging to the African heritage is necessarily liberating and critical. African submissiveness, humility and uncritical respect for authority have resulted in conservatism and passivity. The other problem area is the insensitivity of African male customs to the oppression, dehumanisation and suffering of women. What is needed is a critical appropriation of all that is best in the African heritage. The soul of black ethics is the sacredness of life in its entirety and in all dimensions.

The fifth characteristic of a black ethic is that it is rational and aligned with the Enlightenment tradition in so far as it is critical of absolutism and legalism. This identification of black ethics with what is normally regarded as Western tradition needs qualification. Firstly, unlike the tradition that has used reason to support the *status quo* or to resist change, black ethics uses rationality creatively to deconstruct the old and reconstruct a new meaning system. Inasmuch as we are willing to appropriate what is best in African traditions and heritage, we must be free to do the same with the Enlightenment tradition. Moreover, the rational tradition is not the exclusive property of the West. Black ethics need not be hostile to common sense and reason; indeed, it must be reasonable and coherent. It should simply refuse to use the requirements of formality and consistency to stifle action.

The sixth characteristic of black ethics can be said to be its biblical sources. Black ethics is steeped as much in the black context as it is in biblical sources. There is an effort to interrelate experience with the Scriptures. According to Maimela, Scripture is read from the perspective of the black experience; and according to Boesak, the black experience is interpreted in the light of the Scriptures. For Cone, both Scripture and the black experience have equal weight, and thus we must read each in the light of the other. It is in the dialogue between Scripture and tradition that we must carve out the answer for every new situation. No matter how one construes the nature of the relationship, there is a central desire to make black ethics as consistent with the ethics of the Bible as possible. The scriptural norm used is the liberating message of Jesus and the liberating actions of the biblical God. As Cone summarises it: 'The behavior of Christians is not deduced by rational principles that all people accept as good and right. It is decided by God's act of liberation in Jesus Christ. This divine act of liberation is the ground of the possibility and the actuality of human freedom.'[35]

The seventh characteristic of black ethics is the fact that it is eschatological. It is conscious that 'what is' is not the final word of 'what ought' to be. Indeed, it is this eschatological possibility that generates visions of alternatives. However, this eschatological element also checks any easy identification of the new with the final. There is always room for improvement as long as history has not reached its ending. The eschatological principle also reminds moral agents that they are to become a new community of the *eschaton*, 'an inclusive community wherein freedom, love and justice . . . can be actualised in history',[36] but conscious that the ultimate perfect society will not be of our creation, neither will it be realised in our current phase of history.

The eighth element of black ethics concerns its task, namely the liberation of the black community from white oppression. Black ethics distinguishes different forms of liberation and seeks what is a comprehensive and unified theory of freedom.

According to this notion, one is set free not only from want and oppression but also for others. Freedom is not simply a discretionary choice for those who can afford it, nor a privilege for the select few. Freedom is the essence of morality and humanity. Without freedom, one cannot truly make morally responsible decisions. To be free is to be human and to be moral. Black ethics seeks to realise liberation in community and in solidarity with others. This is not freedom at the expense of others, or freedom over others.

The ninth characteristic relates to the methodological elements of black ethics. Black ethics employs the simple yet critical method of See—Judge—Act. In some sources it is simply referred to as the action—reflection method. The idea of this method is that it highlights important stages of theoretical reflection without necessarily making one stage primary. The *see* stage of the method serves to highlight the descriptive and analytic task of ethics. One needs to gain a clear understanding of all the various forces that impact on moral decision-making. To aid this descriptive—analytic work, the tools developed by the social sciences may be used.

The second stage of this process is that of integrating and evaluating the situation. This is the *judging* task. The concern here is not only with gaining clarity, but also with seeing how things come together, and why they work or do not work. The ultimate purpose of this method is to be able to do something; thus the *act* stage. At this level, black ethics works for the creation of a humane value system and for the transformation of what devalues black life and humanity.

The tenth characteristic of black ethics is that it is historically conditioned and assumes the limitations imposed on all human systems. Critical black ethics is suspicious of those black ethical systems that do not take serious account of the power of negativity in life. In other words, critical black ethics is aware that ethical systems are neither unambiguously good nor evil; that most systems that pass for good are nevertheless capable of being corrupted or becoming ideological. It further recognises that every new creative achievement of ours in history is not beyond corruption. Implicit here is the claim that ethical mandates are tentative, provisional, historical and limited in their scope and applicability. What may be the most virtuous act in the black community today may not be the same tomorrow.

In the case of South Africa, the ethical imperatives of previous years may have dictated that armed struggle be waged as a means of liberation. Today, the imperative may dictate a different strategy. Central to this argument is the claim that under conditions of history, no single community, even the oppressed community, has a monopoly of morality. Theologically we may say a black critical ethics takes seriously the existential fact of sin in all human structures. It dismisses as utopian and idealist those systems that claim to be perfect or immune from criticism. By the same token, a critical black ethics does not dismiss as demonic those systems that are different from its own. It recognises that the struggle for an ethics of total liberation continues in various shapes in every phase of history.

[1] See also Barney Pityana, 'Black Theology' in the first volume of *Theology and Praxis* (Maryknoll: Orbis Books and Cape Town: David Philip, 1994).

[2] James Cone, *God of the Oppressed* (New York: Seabury, 1975), p. 200.

[3] *The Kairos Document – Challenge to the Church: A Theological Comment on the Political Crisis in South Africa* (Braamfontein: The Kairos Theologians, 1985), p. 2.

[4] Charles L. Kammer, *Ethics and Liberation: An Introduction* (Maryknoll: Orbis Books, 1988), p. 8.

[5] Simon Maimela, *Proclaim Freedom to My People: Essays on Religion and Politics* (Braamfontein: Skotaville, 1987), p. 71.

[6] Allan A. Boesak, *Farewell to Innocence: A Socio-Ethical Study on Black Theology and Black Power* (Maryknoll: Orbis Books, 1977), p. 51.

[7] Ibid., p. 27.

[8] Enoch H. Oglesby, *Ethics and Theology from the Other Side: Sounds of Moral Struggle* (Lanham: University Press of America, 1979), p. 13.

[9] Cone, *God of the Oppressed*, p. 200.

[10] Ibid., p. 198.

[11] Ibid., p. 205.

[12] Ibid., p.197.

[13] Ibid., p. 206.

[14] Boesak, *Farewell to Innocence*, p. 124.

[15] Ibid., p. 181.

[16] Ibid., p. 143.

[17] Ibid., p. 144.

[18] Maimela, *Proclaim Freedom*, p. 17.

[19] Ibid., p. 13.

[20] Ibid., p. 75.

[21] Oglesby, *Ethics and Theology*, p. 23.

[22] Ibid., p. 5.

[23] Ibid., p. 13.

[24] Ibid., p. 158.

[25] Ibid., p. 142.

[26] *Kairos Document*, p. 3.

[27] Oglesby, *Ethics and Theology*, p. 142.

[28] Boesak, *Farewell to Innocence*, p. 150.

[29] Ibid., p. 133.

[30] Ibid., p. 128.

[31] Ibid., p. 193.

[32] Cone, *God of the Oppressed*, p. 208.

[33] Oglesby, *Ethics and Theology*, p. 13.

[34] Boesak, *Farewell to Innocence*, p. 144.

[35] Cone, *God of the Oppressed*, pp. 206–207.

[36] Oglesby, *Ethics and Theology*, p. 146.

Select Bibliography

Boesak, Allan. *Farewell to Innocence: A Socio-Ethical Study on Black Theology and Black Power.* Maryknoll: Orbis Books, 1977

Cone, James H. *God of the Oppressed.* New York: Seabury, 1975

Goba, Bonganjalo. *An Agenda for Black Theology: Hermeneutics for Social Change*. Braamfontein: Skotaville, 1988

Jones, Major J. *Christian Ethics for Black Theology*. Nashville: Abingdon Press, 1974

Kammer, Charles L. *Ethics and Liberation: An Introduction*. Maryknoll: Orbis Books, 1988

Maimela, Simon. *Proclaim Freedom to My People: Essays on Religion and Politics*. Braamfontein: Skotaville, 1987

Oglesby, Enoch H. *Ethics and Theology from the Other Side: Sounds of Moral Struggle*. Lanham: University Press of America, 1979

11

Ethics in African Theology

PETER KASENENE

Africa is not a homogeneous society. Like any other society, it embodies different perspectives. Africa has experienced profound and radical changes as a result of colonialism, the impact of foreign religions, Western education and technology, and the contact with West and East, as well as numerous changes from within. These forces have undermined and disrupted the traditional ethos. There are remarkable differences in values among Africans — between urban and rural, educated and illiterate, Christian, Muslim and traditional. Several sub-cultures are emerging, including an urban sub-culture and an 'educated' sub-culture. A single African world-view or culture simply does not exist.

African theologians cannot ignore this in any attempt to evolve a theology which speaks one language. African theology involves more than excavating or resuscitating the past. It must be a *relevant* theology, which takes seriously the reality of the different African contexts in which people live. It is within these different social contexts that the past, the present and even the future of Africa are to be found.

This having been said, African traditional values, attitudes, ideas and norms are still alive — albeit within the matrix of the heterogeneity already described. New or adapted institutions have been introduced and some new social patterns have emerged, but the traditional ethos has survived. It is this African ethos which is defined in what follows. To do so is not, however, a simple exercise.

Apart from recent changes in Africa, the continent has always been home to a variety of people with different cultures.[1] There are many cultural divergences and even dissimilarities among African societies. The Banyankore of Uganda, for example, are a patrilineal, patriarchal and patrilocal society emphasising male dominance, while the Manga'nja of Malawi are matrilineal, matriarchal and matrilocal. Inevitably, the customary ethics of the two societies differ. It would be misleading to overlook such cultural differences, but it would, however, be equally wrong not to recognise the common values and, at times, uniformity that exists within this diversity, south of the Sahara. There is a common Africanness, which must not be lost sight of.

In identifying the salient African ethical principles in what follows, an attempt is made to integrate the positive values in the African heritage into biblical faith. This is essential for the growth of an African Christian theology. In so doing, my assumption is that the God of the Scriptures is present in African cultures, and that this revelation is to be taken seriously by the African church.

Defining Concepts

Ethics

Ethics refers to principles of right or wrong in people's conduct and to a code or set of principles which may be used to evaluate the norms (such as customs and laws) by which people in a given community live. It is the standard by which people's morality is judged. Ethical systems, however, do not evolve in a vacuum. The criteria which people use in making ethical judgements are influenced by several considerations, one of which is context.

Whereas it is true that there are universal ethical principles such as charity, honesty and justice, these too are influenced by context in their application. Thus in African theology, the African heritage and experience influence and shape ethical reflection and conclusions.

African Theology

The term 'African theology' refers to African Christian theology, not African traditional religion. As an introduction to the discussion on African theology, we need to make three important observations about Christian theology in general. The first is that ethics is part of Christian theology. There is an inseparable link between the vertical relationship between a person and God and the horizontal relationship between a person and his or her neighbour. This is emphasised in the Bible (Matt. 25:41–43; James 1:22–26, 2:14–24). Faith and action are intertwined.

The second observation is that Christian theology is a reflection on Christian faith – listening to God through the Scriptures, which speak of the liberation of people from all forces which dehumanise them. Thirdly, whereas the Christian faith is universal and the gospel of Christ is the same for all churches, societies, communities and times, the language and mode of proclaiming the gospel must be suited to the culture, thought-system and experience of the people who profess it. Thus we have Western, Oriental and other theologies.

When the gospel is applied to a specific situation, it produces a relevant theology for the local people. African theology must be understood in this context, as incarnating the Christian faith in the culture and situation in which African people live. African people have problems and concerns, cultures and world-views which are unique to them. Theology made elsewhere cannot provide relevant and meaningful answers to Africans.

Differently stated, African theology refers to the expression of Africans' response to God in their context and experience, based on the Scriptures, Christian tradition and the African heritage. African theology is the Christian faith as understood, communicated and lived by Africans and applied to issues which concern them profoundly. It takes seriously the aspects of continuity between the Christian faith and African religious beliefs and practices in understanding what God is saying to African people in their situation. Given the nature of African society and African religiosity, the Christian faith in Africa necessarily produces a different set of ethics from Western individualism and materialism.

There are thus essentially three aspects to African theology: it is Christian, it is African, and it addresses the issues which are felt by African people today. The contemporary African experience is wide and varied. It includes political oppression, cultural deprivation, economic exploitation, racial segregation and sexism. Different African theologians emphasise different concerns, depending on their personal and contextual experiences. Cultural, Black, feminist and liberation theologies have emerged out of these various experiences. The common denominator in each case is the African heritage, which is tapped and used to inform these theologies.

Ethics in African Culture

African ethics is deeply religious, being influenced by a belief in an all-pervading Supreme Being who controls the universe and social relationships through a number of intermediaries. African religion is, in turn, an inherent part of social relations. It is believed that the Supreme Being is interested in the way people relate to one another. A number of taboos, regulations and prohibitions exist in every society to ensure mutual coexistence. Violation of these is punishable by God. In African religions there is no separation between religion and ethics, between one's beliefs and one's actions towards others. Ethics is an integral part of religion and of theology.

There are three basic principles around which African ethics is built. These are communalism, vitalism and holism. From these three are derived secondary principles such as benevolence, hospitality, respect for seniors, charity, honesty, bravery, sharing and fairness. The challenge facing African theologians is to determine the form which these values will take in African theology.

Vitalism

In African societies, emphasis is put on vitality. Life is regarded as the most precious gift of God. 'An African is born, brought up, trained and led into maturity so as to attain and live the fullness of life undisturbed.'[2] Rites of passage are performed from the time a person is conceived to ensure that vitality is promoted, maintained and strengthened. These rites and rituals accompany a person through life. Everyone strives to make life stronger and to be protected from misfortune or from a diminution of life or of being.[3] Supreme happiness is to possess the greatest vital force, and the worst misfortune is the diminution of this force through illness, suffering, depression, fatigue, injustice, oppression or any other social or physical evil. This vital force is hierarchical, descending from God through the ancestors and elders to the individual.

In ethical terms, any action which increases life or vital force is right, and whatever decreases it is wrong. Sin and moral evil manifest themselves in any attempt to diminish, threaten or destroy the life of another person. As Maimela rightly puts it, sin and evil in the African world-view 'are measured in terms of the life of individuals who suffer injustice, oppression and destruction at the hands of their fellows'.[4]

Human society is organised on the basis of vital force: life growth, life influence and life rank. This structure must be respected, and individuals are good in so far as they fulfil their duties to promote, support and protect the vital force within the community, according to their particular rank. In this connection marriage and procreation are regarded as duties to promote vitality.

Respect for life necessarily entails an ethic of beneficence. A person has a duty to do good to his or her neighbour, especially relatives, clansmen and -women and friends. Strangers, too, must be protected, helped and cared for. As a result generosity, kindness, hospitality, sharing and charity are basic values in African ethics. These are obligations which aim at promoting the well-being of the community.

In African societies, persons are not only obliged to do good, they are also required not to do harm to others, nor refrain from doing what would stop harm being done to others. Witches who are believed to kill or cause other misfortunes that reduce the vital force in society are the most hated in any society.

Respect for human life is a good starting point in African theology in order to address the evil of violence which is eating into African societies. This aspect will be developed later on.

Communalism

In African societies, 'to be' is to belong. An individual exists corporately in terms of the family, clan and whole ethnic group:

> Only in terms of other people does the individual become conscious of his own being, his own duties, his privileges and responsibilities towards himself and towards other people. . . The individual can only say 'I am, because we are; and since we are, therefore, I am.'[5]

The African community is a religious one, at the centre of which are the ancestors. Communal life is a single entity with religious and moral obligations. A person finds meaning in life through and in the community, which is bound together and lives together by ancestor veneration, rites of passage, and ritual at key moments of life.

Community is the key to understanding the African view of a person. A person's identity, worth and, indeed, very life are valued through membership of a group. According to the Sotho saying, *Mothoke motho ka batho babang*, 'A person is only a person through people', and according to the Venda saying, *Muthu u bebelwa nunwe*, 'A person is born for the other'. This shows that according to African philosophy, a person is a person through, with and for the community. Individualism is something new to Africa.

An individual who disregards the family or the community and pursues personal interests is viewed as anti-social, and excessive individualism is regarded as being a denial of one's corporate existence. African societies emphasise interdependence and an individual's obligations to the community. An individual is required to work for the promotion of the community's welfare by doing good and avoiding evil.

Communalism involves a high degree of sharing and mutual responsibility. In traditional African societies there was relative economic equality, with no distinction of economic classes. Rich people shared their wealth with their relatives, and the division between rich and poor was slight. The sense of communal solidarity did not permit individuals to accumulate wealth, because on many occasions they had to share their riches with kinsfolk and neighbours. The economic life of the individual was enclosed in the framework of the group.

In addition, mutual aid was emphasised. People came together at different times for collective work such as building a house, growing food and caring for the sick, the poor and the orphans. This was in many ways similar to the early Christian community, in which all believers were united and had things in common, sharing according to each one's need (Acts 2:44–47). Individualism and capitalism, as introduced from the West, have seriously undermined this ethic of sharing and co-operation, and promoted competition and selfishness.

The great value attached to community in African life illuminates in a practical way the meaning of the solidarity of the People of God in the Old Testament, the church as the Body of Christ and an ethic of corporate existence.[6] Missionary theology, on the other hand, emphasised individual and peripheral ethical issues such as polygamy, drunkenness and sex. It did not address social evil manifested, for example, through colonialism, capitalism and racial discrimination. An African theology and ethic must be concerned with such evils in our present, post-colonial society in order to restore community.

Holism

According to African spirituality, there is no dichotomy between the sacred and the profane, the physical and the spiritual, the religious and the moral. The African world-view blends the sacred and the mundane. The religious and the moral intermingle with the physical, material, political and social concerns of the people.

African world-views emphasise the wholeness of life. In all they do, Africans strive to promote the well-being of the members of society, and this is attained when there is personal integration, environmental equilibrium, social harmony, and harmony between the individual and both the environment and the community. Natural and social evils which militate against well-being, such as war, famine, drought, conflict and poverty, are hated. A person must contribute his or her share to promote the well-being of the community, or to restore it when it is disrupted.

Ethics in African theology, drawing on African spirituality, must be holistic, aiming at the liberation of the whole person and whole communities and freeing humanity from political, social, economic, religious, mental, psychological and physical deprivation. Jesus himself said that he came to give life and give it to the full (John 10:10).

African theology emphasises people, not souls. Missionary theology, on the other hand, separated the body from the soul and stressed the salvation of souls while minimising bodily needs. Individual salvation was seen apart from and, in some situations, to the exclusion of the community. According to missionary theology, because the body and material things would pass away, people should seek only spiritual things and heavenly treasures. Spiritual redemption was pursued without due regard for temporal redemption.

This is not a correct biblical understanding of salvation. The Bible upholds the sanctity of the body: 'Don't you know that you yourselves are God's temple and that God's spirit lives in you? If anyone destroys God's temple, God will destroy him; for God's temple is sacred, and you are that temple' (1 Cor. 3:16–17). African theology should be an incarnation theology, which means that Jesus 'came to bring salvation into the very heart of human history, that we have been saved in the totality of our nature and in all the grossness of our earthly existence'.[7] African theology takes people holistically in their spiritual, social, economic and political dimensions.

Two Shortcomings of African Ethics

The incarnation of faith aims at setting Africans free from all that oppresses them. This entails unveiling oppression in African cultures and liberating people from values which oppress them and which are contrary to the gospel. African theology does not mean mere conformity to culture. It involves a critical and prophetic confrontation with the movement of history.[8] This means that only liberating aspects of the African heritage should be used as a basis for making the gospel relevant. On the other hand, the gospel can be used to transform the oppressive dimensions of the African heritage in order to make it more relevant. Let us examine two examples, namely paternalism and sexism.

In African cultures the emphasis placed on communalism militates against individual autonomy. Although African societies respect individuals and members are free to think and act independently, as long as their actions do not harm others or restrict their rights, this autonomy is often disregarded. The good of the group is more important than personal autonomy. This militates against freedom of choice, which is important and must be respected if a person is to be responsible for his or her decisions.

Another aspect of African culture which needs the cleansing power of the gospel is sexism. In most African societies sex forms a basis of differentiation. In patriarchal societies, women occupy a characteristically humble position in most spheres of life, and are denied some rights and privileges which are enjoyed by men. Gender discrimination and oppression cannot be tolerated in African theology.

Christian Ethics in the African Context

We have noted that African theology is concerned with African people's existence in light of the gospel. There are, however, hundreds of Christian denominations in Africa. There is no homogeneous Christian ethical system. It is, however, possible to identify the basis of Christian ethics, in much the same way that it is possible to discern an African ethic within the diversity of Africa.

Christian ethics, like African ethics, is concerned with both the relationships between people and the relationship between people and God. It does not sharply distinguish between people's relationship with God and their relationship with their neighbours. This is clear from the basic Christian ethical principles found in the Bible. A Christian is expected to serve God through righteous living (Rom. 6:13). Although Christian believers are free from the Hebrew law in gaining salvation, they are under the law of Christ (1 Cor. 9:21), through whom the will of God was made known to humanity, and by whom humanity is redeemed. Christ's basic moral principle, on which all other rules and commandments stand, is the double commandment of love: to love God wholly and to love one's neighbour as one's self (Matt. 22:37—40).

This commandment is, however, very general. It has to be interpreted in terms of the context within which it is heard. In African theology, African experience and ethical values help to relate the commandment to love to the context in which Africans live. African theology, therefore, has to evolve an ethic which addresses the context of poverty, violence, oppression, and dehumanisation through ignorance, sickness and disease. The world in which Africans live provides a starting point for African theology.

The Christian ethic requiring the promotion of universal love among all peoples is a demand to recognise God in every person. In African theology, love is expressed not in terms of duty alone, but in terms of affection which builds community. It is a love based on God's love for humanity (1 John 4:19). Jesus as a brother—ancestor is the binding force in the family of humanity. His love takes concrete form in ethical behaviour. Several issues may be addressed by way of illustrating this belief and ethic.

Poverty

Many countries in Africa have attained political independence, but the people still live under conditions of economic deprivation. Millions live in utter poverty and are starving while others are well fed and even overfed; some live under inhuman conditions and are poorly clothed while others have more than they need; some people are landless while others have vast tracts of land or are absentee landowners. These are but a few examples of economic inequalities and exploitation which lead to poverty.

African theology, rooted as it is in the Christian ethic of love and African communitarian living, has a message for all those who are economically deprived. This is not the other-worldly pietism of missionary theology, but a relevant theology of economic justice. Sin in African theology should not be seen in terms of evil directed against God, but also as having to do with all the evil deeds which are directed against our fellow beings in society.[9] In addition, African theology must examine and address existing ideologies in order to be a catalyst for the introduction of a meaningful dispensation which establishes a new social and economic order.

Violence

Africa has experienced and is still experiencing widespread violence committed by individuals, groups and even by states. In addition, injustice in some countries causes suffering, injury and death to many of their citizens. In societies such as South Africa, violence is inevitable when peaceful means fail to bring about the desired change. Yet to Africans, evil is first and foremost that which destroys community, and violence is the greatest evil in so far as it destroys fellowship, harmony and stability.

In Christian terms violence is the result of hate, which is the bitter opposite of love. There is a need for a comprehensive theology of violence. In the past, missionary theology condemned all forms of force. Yet in the Bible force is condemned when it serves social injustice. Force to overcome injustice has, on the other hand, traditionally been legitimated by the dominant Christian tradition. African theologians have not adequately addressed these issues. Force and violence in Africa constitute burning questions which need to be addressed.

Oppression

In the Bible, justice and love go together and constitute the most important dimension of biblical ethics. According to the Christian faith, everyone is created in the image of God (Gen. 1:27). Whoever treats another person as an object or dehumanises him or her in any way defiles God's temple. Injustice is sacrilegious because it is a denial of the sacredness of a person or of a group of people. God is present in each and every person: man or woman, black or white, rich or poor. Injustice to a person is an injustice to God. African theology must proclaim justice for all the oppressed.

Jesus put reconciliation between people as a pre-condition for reconciliation with God (Matt. 5:23—24). It follows that African theology must be a theology of reconciliation. However, reconciliation can only take place when there is conversion and repentance. First, the offender is required to be penitent, then the offended person forgives him or her. In an African theology of reconciliation, it is important to emphasise the removal of oppression which separates people and alienates both oppressors and oppressed. It is only when this is addressed that the community can be restored.

What is happening in most African societies, especially in South Africa, is coexistence without reconciliation — people living together as strangers. There is confrontation and mutual suspicion. What is needed is a society in which African brotherhood and sisterhood are allowed to grow in loving interaction.

Dehumanisation

Dehumanisation happens in many ways. Africa has emphasised colonial and political causes of dehumanisation, correctly so. African theology must reveal the ugliness of ignorance, sickness and disease — evils which dehumanise Africans. It must give the real causes of these evils, not explain them in terms of original sin, but in real concrete terms of the limitations in society. In a prophetic voice, it must call for the transformation and humanisation of African societies by reducing, if not eliminating, these evils.

Challenges to African Theologians

The first ethical task of African theologians is to conscientise people. As Allan Boesak rightly observes, 'Unless one knows that one is oppressed, unless one knows the oppressor, one cannot be liberated.'[10] Many people are still mentally enslaved and do not realise the seriousness and degree of their deprivation. Many even participate in and promote their own oppression. An African woman, for example, prepares her daughter for oppression by emphasising the virtues of obedience, submission and docility as a wife.

Secondly, African theologians must promote the ethic of positive involvement in the liberation of the deprived. African theology cannot afford to be cerebral and abstract. It must lead to positive action, firstly by promoting positive values and attitudes and, secondly, by working for the promotion of justice in society.

Thirdly, there is a need to liberate oppressive and inhuman structures and institutions, both African and those newly acquired. Where African culture has been used by men as an oppressive tool to dominate women, there is a need to reform and liberate it from its oppressive elements. The beliefs and values which play into the hands of the oppressors need to be either discarded or transformed from being tools of oppression into tools of liberation.

Fourthly, African theologians must promote a new way of reading and understanding the Bible in Africa's context and in the context of the total liberatory message of salvation. The Bible has to be 'good news' to the poor peasant in Mozambique, the miner in South Africa, the youth in Soweto, the old woman deserted in the Zambian village, and the prostitute in Nairobi.

Men often find justification for their oppressive actions in the Bible in order to deprive women of their rights. In Ephesians 5:22–23, women are instructed to be subject 'in everything' to their husbands. In his letter to the Corinthians, for example, Paul forbids women to speak in church (1 Cor. 14:34–35). It is easy to use a text like this to ignore Jesus' law of love, which does not discriminate on any ground. In Christ, a Christian is required to put off the old nature with its prejudices and practices and to put on the new nature in which there are no distinctions between slave and free, male and female (Gal. 3:26–28).

The challenge to African theologians is to evolve a dialectical approach to reading and understanding Scriptures and to see the liberatory message and work of Jesus as the saviour who saves all people. Christians should also be reminded that some statements in the Bible are not universal declarations, but answers to specific problems in a specific society at a given time. When circumstances change, such statements cease to bind Christians. African theology, and indeed Christian theology, can have no room for slaves.

Praxis

Being Christian implies being Christ-like and, therefore, speaking out as loudly as one can and acting against evil in society even at the risk of one's life. Jesus is the supreme example. Ethics, therefore, must remain an important part of African theology so that our faith is tested by our actions in real-life situations in which we interact with each other.

Being African requires relevant standards and norms which will lead to appropriate action. Among these are reason and praxis. This demands taking an ethical position to regulate one's actions. It goes beyond making general statements, to making definite connections between words and actions. Relevant ethics in African theology can be a source of energy for involvement in the struggle to liberate Africans from all forces which deprive and dehumanise them. It is here that African and Christian traditions meet.

[1] J. Mbiti, *African Traditional Religions and Philosophy* (Nairobi: Heinemann, 1969), p. 1.

[2] S. Maimela, 'Traditional African Anthropology and Christian Theology', *JTSA*, 76 (1991), p. 5.

[3] P. Tempels, *Bantu Philosophy* (Paris: Présence Africaine, 1959).

[4] Maimela, 'Traditional African Anthropology', p. 12.

[5] Mbiti, *African Traditional Religions*, pp. 118–119.

[6] J. Parratt (ed.), *A Reader in African Christian Theology* (London: SPCK, 1987), p. 8.

[7] L. Magesa, *The Church and Liberation in Africa* (Eldoret: Gaba Publications, 1976), p. 41.

[8] Parratt (ed.), *Reader in African Christian Theology*, p. 2.

[9] Maimela, 'Traditional African Anthropology', p. 12

[10] Parratt (ed.), *Reader in African Christian Theology*, p. 133.

Select Bibliography

Appiah-Kubi, K. (ed.) *African Theology En Route*. Maryknoll, New York: Orbis Books, 1979

Becken, H. (ed.) *Relevant Theology for Africa*. Durban: Missiological Institute, 1973

Harr, G. *Faith of Our Fathers*. Utrecht: University of Utrecht, 1990

Ikenga-Metuh, E. *Comparative Studies of African Traditional Religion*. Onitsha: IMICO Publishers, 1987

Magesa, I. *The Church and Liberation in Africa*. Eldoret: Gaba Publications, 1976

Mbiti, J. *African Traditional Religions and Philosophy*. Nairobi, Heinemann, 1969

Muga, E. *African Response to Western Christian Religion*. Nairobi: East African Literature Bureau, 1975

Nyamiti, C. *The Way to Christian Theology for Africa*. Eldoret: Gaba Publications

Parratt, J. *A Reader in African Christian Theology*. London: SPCK, 1987

Pobee, J. S. *Toward an African Theology*. Nashville: Abingdon, 1979

Setiloane, G. *African Theology: An Introduction*. Braamfontein: Skotaville Publishers, 1986

Tempels, P. *Bantu Philosophy*. Paris: Présence Africaine, 1959

12

Ethics in Feminist Theology[1]

WILMA JAKOBSEN

Feminism is concerned with the unjust treatment that women have suffered throughout history. As such, it is profoundly ethical in character, seeking justice for all women and ultimately for all humankind. It includes a broad spectrum of ideological and philosophical thought and praxis. Feminism has emerged out of the realisation that we live in a traditionally male-dominated world in which women have been devalued and oppressed at work, at home and in society. Put differently, feminism is a liberating praxis grounded in the lived experience of women.

Feminist theology is part of this praxis — seeking to do theology from the perspective of feminist consciousness. While feminist theologians agree on many fundamental principles, there is a variety of feminist theological perspectives. Some find it impossible to remain with integrity as feminists within a fundamentally patriarchal church. Within this group are those who explore Goddess worship and seek a more female-centred religion and faith. Others maintain that feminist commitments are consistent with the basic values of Christianity and Judaism. They remain within the church, seeking to rediscover the accounts of women's experiences which male history has either suppressed or failed to record.[2]

The most important principles in feminist theology can be listed as follows:

— The starting point is always women's experience.[3]
— Patriarchal history and theology are rejected.[4]
— The analysis of Scripture and tradition is done from a woman's perspective.[5]
— The dualisms which are part of Western male thought-systems are rejected.[6]
— Relationality is emphasised as central to all that feminist theology attempts to do.[7]

Feminism and feminist theology have been viewed with a fair amount of suspicion in South Africa and elsewhere by those who are afraid of its inherent challenge to traditional patriarchal culture and the male hierarchy of the church. There has also been a perception among some that feminism and feminist theology are 'bourgeois concepts', important only to white, middle-class, North

American women, and have no real place in an African context.[8] Although feminism and feminist theology have more recently acquired a greater legitimacy within the struggle for democracy in South Africa,[9] the reality is that sisterhood is complicated. Although women are oppressed on the basis of their gender, many more people, not only women, are also oppressed on the basis of race, class, religion and ethnicity.[10]

This has given rise to the distinction that is often made between feminist and womanist theology. The implication is that while the former has to do essentially with fulfilment and meaning, the latter is primarily concerned with survival. Of course, definitions are never precise. There are many feminists who seek to address the issues of womanist theology, but the distinction is nevertheless important for purposes of emphasis.

South African feminists must take extreme care to be as contextual as possible, and not simply to mirror-image white Western thinking. The needs and experiences of first-world women are not necessarily these of third-world women. We must seek that which is uniquely our own in our complex society, and forge a feminist liberation theology and feminist ethic that understand the interstructuring of oppressions in our land.

Ethics in Theological Perspective

Traditionally, ethics has assumed that all people are equally free to make moral choices. This ignores the reality that both society and ethicists themselves have not viewed women as autonomous human beings, capable of making moral decisions. Katie Cannon describes various ways in which dominant ethics employs assumptions which are not valid in situations of race, gender and class oppression: that success is possible as long as one tries; that a moral agent is mostly free and self-directing; and that a person possesses self-determining power.[11]

Beverly Harrison maintains that traditional sex-roles have denied women full moral agency.[12] For the most part, the legacy of sexism has meant that men have made moral judgements and moral decisions on behalf of women, often without even consulting them. Ethics in feminist theology must of necessity challenge this aspect of traditional ethics.

The emphasis of traditional ethics on individuality contrasts with the more social, communal approach of feminist ethics. Traditionally, individuals are seen as independent moral agents, able to make moral choices by themselves independent of other realities or decisions. Feminist ethics, in contrast, emphasises the connectedness of all people and things – although not all first-world feminists would support this communality.[13]

These contrasting views are particularly relevant for us in South Africa where a predominantly affluent lifestyle for whites promotes individualistic tendencies, while a predominantly poor lifestyle for blacks promotes more communal tendencies. This has a profound influence on the way in which moral decisions are made and how they are viewed.[14] Once more, without denying the basic differences in white and black females' experiences, the feminist approach of community seems to be closer to the experience of blacks in South Africa. The distinction between feminist and womanist theology again emerges at this point.

Furthermore, feminist theology challenges traditional approaches to ethical reflection in the way its approach begins with women's experience and moves inductively from there to definitions and conclusions. In contrast, traditional ethics begins with abstract statements that serve as first principles, from which moral actions are deduced.

The Development of Feminist Ethical Principles

That women's experience is the starting point is as essential as it is problematic, precisely because the range of women's experiences is so diverse and so complicated by divisions of race, class and sexual orientation. Some women are doubly and triply oppressed, while others find themselves in the roles of both the oppressed and the oppressor. According to Carol Robb, 'If feminist ethics is to be based upon the experiences of *all* women, then such differences in experiences must be acknowledged and incorporated into feminist theory.'[15] This problem or challenge is particularly significant for us in South Africa where 'the deep divisions among women in this country almost make nonsense of the idea of sisterhood'.[16] We must ensure that no generalisations are made for all women on the basis of white women's experiences.

This means that ethics in feminist liberation theology in South Africa has to be rooted in an ethics of justice which carefully explores and outlines the different expressions of women's oppression within all spheres of life. White feminist women have a responsibility not only to 'feel with' and understand the very different experiences of women of different colour and class, but also to express that in praxis by engaging in actions which address the diverse needs of women, and to build relationships across differences.

Analysis

If women's experience is the starting point for ethics, and if we recognise the diversity of women's experience, then it follows that ethics in feminist theology requires a clear analysis of the roots of oppression. As with all feminist theory, there is no one analysis.

Carol Robb points to at least four different socio-political analyses of the oppression of women which can provide a foundation for feminist ethics: radical feminism; critique of sex-roles; Marxist–Leninist feminism; and socialist feminism. Each of these leads to differences in the way in which ethics is practised. The analysis of the roots of oppression is a key factor in feminist ethics, because 'It has a direct bearing on the way we pose problems, gather data, commit our loyalties, rank values, engage in moral reasoning, justify claims, structure autonomy, and heighten motivation.'[17]

Women as Moral Agents

We live in a society which has continually treated women as inferior or as minors under law. It is therefore imperative for feminist ethics to affirm that women are fully able to make moral decisions as autonomous moral agents.

Affirming that women are made in the image of God[18] and thus moral agents in their own right is particularly relevant to South African society, for African culture has to a large degree succeeded in objectifying women by perceiving them as possessions of men, as the daughter of a father or the wife of a husband. Even if a woman becomes widowed, she falls under the control of a designated brother-in-law.[19] The implications of this principle are enormous, precisely because women are so often not part of the decision-making processes which affect their lives. Women need to affirm their moral agency and not abdicate their responsibility and right to participate in decision-making.

The Integration of Body and Mind, Feelings and Reason

The body—mind split in Western philosophy has affected life at every level. Many theologians believe that it has been a fundamental cause of negative attitudes towards women throughout our society.[20] Feminist theology emphasises our connectedness with ourselves, with each other and with creation. Feminist ethics must therefore affirm that all our knowledge, including our moral knowledge, is rooted in this integration of body and mind, that all power is rooted in feeling. The importance of feelings must be affirmed, not as ends in themselves, but as part of moral actions. As Harrison puts it: 'The moral question is not "what do I feel?" but rather "what do I do with what I feel?" '[21] A feminist moral theology welcomes feeling for what it is: the basic ingredient in our relational transaction with the world.[22]

It must be noted that non-Western cultures have not been affected to the same degree by the body—mind split. It is perhaps at this point that feminist theology and African culture are at their closest.

The Integration of Personal and Political

The phrase 'the personal is the political' is a crucial feminist insight. Women tell their stories and name their experiences with one another. In sharing their stories they discover a commonality of experiences, born out of social structures which perpetuate female subordination. This process of story-telling is described as a moral activity, because it affirms the human worth and dignity of women in a world that does not do so.[23]

Women's personal lives are affected by social and political structures. This can be seen in rural areas and squatter camps in South Africa where women struggle to collect their basic necessities of water and firewood, as well as in the lack of child-care facilities and the negative attitudes of employers towards maternity leave.

Relational Decision-making

In a feminist moral theology, 'relationality is at the heart of all things . . . nothing living is self-contained.'[24] Ethical decisions cannot be made by individuals in isolation, and moral agents are not most effective when they are most autonomous.[25]

An ethic of relationality, or connectedness, also means that our relationships with creation and the environment are as important as our relationships with other human persons.

Women's Sense of Well-being

Feminist ethics, in affirming that women are made in the image of God, will regard the well-being of women as a primary concern in moral decision-making. This is of utmost importance when it comes to ethical thinking about reproductive rights for women, and it will ultimately lead to the well-being of both women and men.

Ethical Issues for Feminist Liberation Theology in South Africa

The ethical task for South African feminist theologians is enormous, given the complexity of South African society.

Women and Violence

The ever-increasing incidence of sexual violence against women and children is cause for urgent ethical concern and action. The long-term effects on victims of rape and battering include loss of faith in God, loss of trust in relationships, and increased fear and anxiety. These in turn lead to the loss of the freedom to live fully and a denial of full personhood, resulting in the further breakdown of family life.[26]

Poverty, unemployment and despair exacerbate the problem of sexual violence. However, the root cause of sexual violence lies in underlying attitudes about male and female sexuality and the power dynamics interwoven as part of these attitudes. Feminist theological ethics views male power and dominance in the light of the devastating violence against women.

The emphasis in feminist theology on the full personhood of women and the interconnectedness of all our lives makes sexual violence one of the most urgent issues of our time. It is an issue which affects all people at all levels of society. Any ethical system that does not take seriously the extent of sexual violence cannot claim to work for a better future and a more ideal society.[27] Yet the issue is often blanketed in silence, despite the fact that at least one woman is raped every 83 seconds somewhere in South Africa.[28]

Women and Work

The area of work raises a number of ethical issues. Women are denied equality of work with men, and lack adequate maternity leave and child-care facilities. The inequality of treatment for the different genders is further complicated by inequalities for different races and classes.

Prevailing cultural and societal norms of sex-roles, especially in South Africa, view women as generally responsible for the maintenance and nurturing of domestic and family life. Yet many women also work in full-time jobs because of economic need. For women to bear the brunt of the burden of domestic labour, as wives, mothers and often as domestic workers as well, is widely regarded as an acceptable practice. Admittedly for some, this area of life is prized as a woman's domain, and therefore some women hold on to it. Perhaps it is the source of what little sense of identity they have, or it could be too threatening for them to imagine the men in their life learning to work in the home and be domestic. Possibly they are afraid of what it might mean for their relationships if they challenge the accepted ways of behaving.

Feminist ethical reflection and action must work side by side with the efforts of trade unions. Questions must be raised about the 'capacity of capitalism to respond to the human needs of wage-earning women and their families'.[29] Women bear the brunt of the effects of the high rate of unemployment in South Africa, particularly in the rural areas, where their lives are a day-to-day struggle for the survival of their children and themselves.[30]

Sexual Ethics

Centuries of patriarchal ethical and theological thinking have dominated the field of sexual ethics. The people most affected by decisions and norms about sexual morality have for the most part been left out of the process of ethical reflection and decision-making. Harrison calls for a re-evaluation of the connection between our human capacity for intimacy and love, and our aspirations for a just social order.[31] To some degree this has led to the 'trivialization of sexuality by those whose concerns are presumably focused on the more substantive questions of social justice'.[32] Harrison appeals for 'an approach to sexuality that aims to be holistic, that sets what we know of ourselves as sexual persons in the broadest possible context of our lives within our existing social order'.[33] She appeals for an ethic of maturity in this area as in other areas of ethics, one that accepts and expresses women's power as responsible moral agents without needing prohibitive rules.

For others, it has led to an over-emphasis on the genital expression of sexuality as the totality of sexuality. This influences, in particular, people's attitudes towards gay men and lesbians who wish to live in committed relationships. Sexual ethics from a feminist perspective must also address the social oppression and injustice experienced by gay men and lesbians. This is a complex issue in South Africa because of the interweaving of oppressions. It is also a matter for the churches, where there are few spaces of welcome and affirmation for lesbians and gay men. In addition, the agenda for discussion about homosexuality has been dominated by white gay men. Feminist ethics challenges all of us in our society to consider how heterosexuals can overcome their homophobia and how we can affirm lesbians and gay men as fully human, made in the image of God.

Prostitution. Throughout the world, prostitution is increasing at an alarming rate. Growing numbers of young girls and boys are drawn to it. On many continents, economic hardship and the struggle to survive in the most appalling conditions of poverty force many into the trade. The dramatic increase in numbers in the last three years has in part been due to increasing disparities in wealth world-wide, the collapse of Communism and increased global mobility.[34]

Most feminists are opposed to the idea of legalising prostitution, because this would imply a public approval of the purchase of women's sexual services and would denigrate women and children as sexual objects for gratification and profit. Yet it is recognised that for some women, prostitution has often been their only option for economic survival. Many argue for a social policy of 'de-criminalising' prostitution, removing all laws which prohibit its practice, as opposed to legalising it.[35]

Pornography. It is difficult to define exactly what pornography is, as opposed to appropriate sexually explicit material. South Africa has had a history of strict censorship laws which have infringed the individual's right to make his or her own moral decisions. Although there has recently been a definite relaxation in the legal enforcement of censorship, it is still difficult to determine the official criteria for distinguishing between what is obscene and what is acceptable. It is also difficult to determine just who is responsible for those decisions.

However, there can be no doubt about the need to condemn the kind of pornography which dehumanises women as 'masochistic objects of male sexual sadism'.[36] Anything which directly or indirectly communicates that women actually enjoy male control and exploitation and that women exist to be used by men is morally unacceptable in feminist ethics. Harrison points out that objections to pornography should focus on aspects of violence and control rather than on the explicitness of sex acts or genitalia. It is 'the sadism of pornography — the imposition and enjoyment of another's suffering — that is morally reprehensible, not the explicitness of sexuality'.[37]

Female Circumcision. Female circumcision has historically been practised in countries throughout the world. Although it was known to occur in the Cape as recently as fifty years ago, it has now fallen away here.[38] From a medical point of view female circumcision is a health hazard. Considered in ethical terms, it encourages the notion of women's sexual passivity for the enhancement of male sexual pleasure.

Health

The area of health is exceedingly important for women and provides much scope for feminist ethical reflection, especially in South Africa. The diversity of women's experiences affects how they perceive their health needs. For instance, at a conference on national health at the University of the Witwatersrand in 1992, rural women named clean water as their most important health need. Lack of access to clinics and even primary health care are other issues which beset women and their children in rural areas and urban informal-housing settlements. These services and facilities, on the other hand, are taken for granted by upper and middle-class urban women. Their ethical concerns in health are very different, focusing more on reproductive rights such as abortion, *in vitro* fertilisation and surrogate motherhood.[39] Reproductive rights are, however, also a crucial issue for black rural women.[40]

Contraception. Although most Christian theological opinion accepts contraception as part of the freedom to engage in family planning, a line is usually drawn between contraception and abortion. However, the official teaching of the Roman Catholic Church forbids contraception. This is a matter of great ethical debate in feminist theology, especially in the socio-political and cultural context of South Africa and in the context of increasing AIDS and HIV awareness. Feminist theologians must respond to the enormous role the church has played in shaping negative attitudes towards contraception.[41]

Abortion. In a country like South Africa where there are an estimated 300 000 illegal abortions a year and where thousands of women die from back-street abortions, it seems clear that the issue of abortion needs attention. The difficulty is that it raises vehement reactions and negative responses from many people who find it difficult to accept that abortion can ever be morally justified.[42]

Feminist women are not simply asking for abortion on demand but for the right to make choices about their own bodies and their own lives. Feminist women want to have the right to have an abortion, in certain circumstances. It is never an easy decision for a woman, and always a second choice or last resort after the failure of contraception. No contraceptive method is completely safe or reliable, and contraception is not available to many women in rural areas and urban informal-housing settlements. Moreover, with the widespread occurrence of AIDS, increasing numbers of babies are being born with this syndrome.

In addition to the practical difficulties, cultural myths about male and female sexuality, traditional male expectations about women's submission, and notions about women being created for sex and child-bearing, all combine to create a much more complex issue than has been admitted when it comes to the decision to have an abortion.[43]

The problem from a feminist perspective is threefold. Firstly, the debate is not as simple and clear-cut as it may seem, because of patriarchal attitudes which creep into the arguments. Secondly, women are quite capable moral agents, but their right to make moral decisions about their own procreative choice is not acknowledged. Thirdly, the principle of the sanctity of human life is also affirmed by those who believe abortion is sometimes or frequently justified. They ask only that this principle also includes 'genuine regard and concern for every female already born'.[44]

In conclusion, abortion is an issue which affects all women in South Africa. There is a pressing need to examine the regulations controlling legal abortions.[45]

The Environment

The feminist principle of relationality and the connectedness of all things has broadened the focus of debate on ethical issues to include ecological concerns. A holistic, relational approach to all of life makes it morally necessary to develop a 'non-exploitative attitude toward the natural environment and to ourselves as creatures whose well-being is intertwined with the rest of nature'.[46] We need to recognise that the cosmos and our whole planet form an interdependent ecosystem in which all our actions have consequences for the environment that are reflected back to us. This provides humanity with a moral obligation to treat the environment with the sensitivity with which we treat other people.[47]

The Law

Since 'the personal is the political', the law is touched and challenged in every way by feminist ethics. Susan Bazilli reminds us that 'because the law reflects the interests of the dominant or ruling class in both practice and theory, it therefore reflects the interests of patriarchal control over women's lives. In fact, all notions of what 'law' is can be reduced to one: power.'[48]

Feminist ethics in South Africa must analyse how the law discriminates against women in obvious ways, by what it omits or by lack of its enforcement. In particular, laws affecting women and divorce, and women and property, marital laws treating women as legal minors, and laws concerning sexual violence, abortion, lesbianism and homosexuality, health care, administration of welfare benefits, and women in the workplace, must be included in the long list of statutes which at present discriminate against women as of inferior value to men.[49]

It is therefore crucial during this stage of political transition in our country to work to ensure a clear constitutional commitment to women's rights in a democratic South Africa. But even though constitutional rights for women may create a more ethically moral system of laws, they will not guarantee a changed situation for women. It will take continued efforts by women for the dream of a transformed life to become even partially realised.[50]

The Family

Within traditional theology, there has been much teaching about authority and submission, including stereotyped roles of husband and wife, which has perpetuated oppression and denied countless women the possibilities of developing their potential.

In South Africa, the family has to be a central focus for feminist ethical reflection because it is an area where all forms of oppression — racial, gender and economic — occur. Nolulamo Gwagwa refers to the family as the place where 'one can begin to understand the true meaning of "triple oppression," that oft-used term to describe the levels of oppression of black women in South Africa'.[51]

Many women are not as willing as before to participate in traditional oppressive family structures where they were viewed only as procreators. As it is still socially unacceptable in many black communities to be childless, some women prefer to become single parents rather than enter into a marriage in which it is seen as the husband's right to have intercourse with his wife whenever desired, and his right to 'discipline' her if she refuses. But in many other cases, women are economically and emotionally trapped in oppressive or abusive marriages.

There are customs within traditional African systems which deserve attention. These may include the practices of polygamy, *lobola* (bridewealth), the levirate, the sororate, child betrothal and mourning taboos.[52] Thandabantu Nhlapo, in exploring the ways in which sex discrimination appears to be such an enduring feature of African traditional systems, concludes that 'It is everything that emanates from an attitude to women in marriage and in the family which sees them solely as adjunct to the group, a means to the anachronistic end of clan survival, rather than as valuable in themselves and deserving of recognition for their human worth in the same terms as men.'[53]

In many different ways, and across cultures and groups, the family is a site of struggle.[54]

The Church

The church is the birthplace and the custodian of traditional theology, and is notorious for the slow pace of change within its life and its structures. The church interacts with each of the areas we have outlined, in different ways. These include the lack of women's participation in decision-making bodies and in decision-making processes about moral issues which affect women; the lack of women in equal partnership with men as priests and bishops;[55] a hierarchical structure which consciously and subconsciously attaches different values to people, creating differences of worth between lay people and clergy; and an all-too-often inconsistent praxis of social justice *within* its own life and structures.[56]

The Ethic of Self-Sacrifice

Traditional theology has commonly taught the Christian ideal of self-sacrificial love. Women have been socialised to believe that in order to be 'good Christian women' it is necessary to sacrifice oneself for others, particularly one's husband and one's children. This teaching needs to be re-evaluated in the light of the feminist perspective that women's self-sacrifice has on many occasions led to their abuse and the perpetuation of their oppression.

This question has been explored by Patricia Jung, who condemns as 'demonic' the 'ethic of self-sacrifice which demands that one person (frequently a woman) regularly give the interests of others priority over their rightful concerns'.[57] It is an important issue in the analysis of domestic violence and the perpetuation of sexist attitudes and practices.

Conclusion

It should be clear by now that ethics in South African feminist theology has everything to do with social justice. There are basic ethical principles arising out of feminist theology which fundamentally affirm the centrality of women's experience and the value of women as fully human, equal partners with men in an interdependent society. These ethical principles also affirm the relationality and connectedness of all things, as well as the integration of the personal and political, body and mind, reason and emotion. Traditional ethics is challenged by ethics in feminist theology as to its approach, its assumptions and its method.

Ethics in feminist theology can dream of a transformed future in which women and men live together in mutuality and interdependent partnership and community, despite the realities of the differences in race, class and gender; a future in which individuals and society work together to attain this goal; a future dream of a world of celebration, justice and equality, shared pains and burdens, mutuality and interdependence.

It is towards this dream that we in South Africa can direct our energy and our passion, as we engage in the reflection and praxis of feminist theological ethics.

'Keep in mind always the present you are constructing,
it should be the future that you want' (Alice Walker).

[1] See Denise Ackermann, 'Faith and Feminism: Women Doing Theology' in the first volume of *Theology and Praxis* (Maryknoll: Orbis Books and Cape Town: David Philip, 1994).

[2] B. H. Andolsen, C. E. Gudorf and M. D. Pellauer (eds), *Women's Consciousness, Women's Conscience: A Reader in Feminist Ethics* (Minneapolis: Winston, 1985), pp. xxi–xxiii, gives a concise summary of feminist religious options and their connection with ethics. See also Carol P. Christ and Judith Plaskow (eds), *Womanspirit Rising: A Feminist Reader in Religion* (New York: Harper and Row, 1979).

[3] For a fuller discussion see Ackermann, 'Faith and Feminism'.

[4] For a fuller discussion see J. Draper, 'Oppressive and Subversive Moral Instruction in the New Testament' in D. Ackermann, J. Draper and E. Mashinini (eds), *Women Hold Up Half the Sky* (Pietermaritzburg: Cluster, 1991), pp. 37–54.

[5] R. R. Ruether, *Sexism and God-Talk* (Boston: Beacon 1985).

[6] B. Harrison, *Making the Connections: Essays in Feminist Social Ethics* (Boston: Beacon 1985), p. xix.

[7] Ackermann, 'Being Women, Being Human' in Ackermann *et al.*, *Women Hold Up Half the Sky*, pp. 100–103.

[8] Rhoda B. Kadalie, 'The Importance of Feminism for the Women's Movement in South Africa', *JTSA*, 66, p. 48. I also base this comment on the experience of myself and other women in the church, especially in the debates at synods and workshops, and in informal discussions around the ordination of women as priests.

[9] Ibid., p. 48. This was noted by the national executive committee of the ANC on the 'Emancipation of Women in South Africa' in May 1990, and quoted by Jacklyn Cock in 'Putting Women on the Agenda' in S. Bazilli (ed.), *Putting Women on the Agenda* (Johannesburg: Ravan, 1991), p. 28.

[10] Kadalie, 'Importance of Feminism', p 5.

[11] K. Cannon, *Black Womanist Ethics* (Atlanta: Scholars Press, 1988), p. 3. 'Womanist' is a term coined by Alice Walker, used by women of colour who wish to distinguish themselves from feminist, as that term has been perceived by them to have racist connotations.

[12] Harrison, *Making the Connections*, p. xvi.

[13] C. Keller, 'Feminism and the Ethic of Inseparability' in Andolsen *et al.*, *Women's Conscience*, pp. 251–259.

[14] J. Kotze, 'Science as Effective Social Communication: Subjectivity and a Possible World of Common-sense Reality', *Communicare*, 9:2, pp. 40–62.

[15] C. Robb, 'A Framework for Feminist Ethics' in Andolsen *et al.*, *Women's Conscience*, p. xv.

[16] Kadalie, 'Importance of Feminism', p. 51.

[17] Robb, 'Framework for Feminist Ethics', pp. 219–231, gives a fuller outline of the way in which the different socio-political theories affect the manner in which ethics is approached and engaged in, providing examples.

[18] For a fuller discussion see Ackermann, 'Being Women, Being Human', p. 99.

[19] M. Ramphele, *A Bed Called Home* (South Africa: David Philip, 1993), p. 70.

[20] Harrison, *Making the Connections*, p. 12.

[21] Ibid., p. 14.

[22] Ibid., p. 14.

[23] Andolsen *et al.*, *Women's Conscience*, p. xv.

[24] Harrison, *Making the Connections*, pp. 15, 16.

[25] This does not negate the principle of women as full moral agents in their own right; rather, women exercise their moral agency within the context of their relationality.

[26] Domestic violence and unhelpful attitudes towards sexuality can contribute towards some women's preference to be single parents.

[27] For a fuller discussion, including facts and figures, see D. Hansson, 'Working Against Violence Against Women' in Bazilli (ed.), *Putting Women on the Agenda*, pp. 180–193. See also *Co-ordinated Action for Battered Women, Battering Is a Crime: An Information Booklet for Battered Women* (Cape Town, 1990).

[28] See Ackermann, 'Faith and Feminism'.

[29] B. Andolsen, 'A Woman's Work Is Never Done' in Andolsen *et al.*, *Women's Conscience*, p. 3.

[30] For a fuller discussion see I. Obery (ed.), *Vukani Makhosikazi: South African Women Speak* (London: Catholic Institute for International Relations, 1985), pp. 5–94.

[31] 'Sexuality and Social Policy' in Harrison, *Making the Connections*, p. 83.

[32] Ibid., p. 85.

[33] Ibid., p. 86.

[34] *Time* magazine, 21 June 1993, pp. 22–41.

[35] Harrison, *Making Connections*, p. 102.

[36] Ibid., p. 102–103.

[37] Ibid., p. 102.

[38] For a fuller discussion see O. Koso-Thomas, *Circumcision of Women: A Strategy for Eradication* (London: Zed, 1987). See also R. Shell, 'Rites and Rebellion: Islamic Conversion at the Cape, 1808–1915', in C. Saunders (ed.), *Studies in the History of Cape Town*, Vol. 5 (Cape Town: UCT, 1984).

[39] Surrogate motherhood has existed in different forms in South Africa, especially in the custom in early Cape history of women who employed slave-women as wet-nurses for their babies, so that they did not need to breastfeed their babies. In a different way, the employment of black women nannies to care for white women's children, often in a full-time capacity, is surely an interesting phenomenon of surrogate motherhood in the complex race and class dynamics of South Africa. See Ignacio L. Gotz, 'Surrogate Motherhood', *Theology Today*, XVL: 2 (July 1988), pp. 189–195.

[40] At the Conference on Health Policy organised in Johannesburg in December 1992, the issue of legalised abortion almost failed to get the necessary two-thirds majority required to pass a controversial motion. Black women present ensured that it eventually passed, as it was seen by them as a vital health necessity for women.

[41] Harrison, *Making Connections*, pp. 116–117.

[42] For a fuller discussion see H. Rees, 'Women and Reproductive Rights' in Bazilli (ed.), *Putting Women on the Agenda*, pp. 209–216.

[43] Harrison, *Making Connections*, p. 115.

[44] Ibid., p. 116.

[45] For a fuller discussion, with facts and figures, see Rees, 'Women and Reproductive Rights', pp. 213–214.

[46] Harrison, *Making Connections*, p. 175.

[47] For further reading see Matthew Fox, *Creation Spirituality: Liberating Gifts for the Peoples of the Earth* (New York: Harper Collins 1991); Sallie McFague, *Models of God: Theology for an Ecological Nuclear Age* (London: SCM 1987); Walter B. Gulick, 'The Bible and Ecological Spirituality', *Theology Today*, XLVIII: 2 (July 1991), pp. 182–194.

[48] Bazilli (ed.), *Putting Women on the Agenda*, p. 15.

[49] Ibid., pp. 15–17.

[50] For further reading see C. Murray and C. O'Regan, 'Putting Women into the Constitution' in Bazilli (ed.), *Putting Women on the Agenda,* pp. 41–50.

[51] N. Gwagwa, 'The Family and South African Politics: Conceptualising Progressive Change' in ibid., p. 125.

[52] Any assessment of polygamy etc. is affected by cultural bias, which affects the way these practices are viewed ethically. I make the suggestion tentatively, as I understand that these practices are designed to uphold certain values which are not a part of my own culture.

[53] T. Nhlapo, 'Women's Rights and the Family in Traditional and Customary Law' in Bazilli (ed.), *Putting Women on the Agenda,* p. 114.

[54] Gwagwa, 'The Family', p. 125.

[55] Although women may be ordained priests and bishops (only a few, recently!), there is a long way to go before the church will reflect an authentic mutual partnership between women and men in leadership.

[56] See the statement by women delegates to the Rustenburg national conference of church leaders in South Africa in L. Alberts and F. Chikane (eds), *The Road to Rustenburg: The Church Looking Forward to a New South Africa* (Cape Town: Struik, 1991).

[57] P. Jung, 'The Ethic of Self-Sacrifice: A Feminist Reassessment', Unpublished paper presented at Wartburg Theological Seminary, Iowa.

Select Bibliography

Ackermann, D., J. Draper and E. Mashinini (eds.) *Women Hold Up Half the Sky: Women in the Church in Southern Africa.* Pietermaritzburg: Cluster Publications, 1991

Andolsen, Barbara H., Christine E. Gudorf and Mary D. Pellauer (eds.) *Women's Consciousness, Women's Conscience: A Reader in Feminist Ethics.* Minneapolis: Winston, 1985

Bazilli, Susan (ed.) *Putting Women on the Agenda.* Johannesburg: Ravan, 1991

Cannon, Katie G. *American Academy of Religion No. 60: Black Womanist Ethics.* Atlanta, Georgia: Scholars Press, 1988

Fabella, Virginia and Mercy A. Oduyoye (eds.) *With Passion and Compassion: Third World Women Doing Theology.* Maryknoll: Orbis, 1988

Harrison, Beverly W. *Making the Connections: Essays in Feminist Social Ethics.* Boston: Beacon, 1985

Obery, Ingrid (ed.) *Vukani Makhosikazi: South African Women Speak.* London: Catholic Institute for International Relations, 1985

Oduyoye, Mercy A. and Musimbi R. A. Kanyoro (eds.) *The Will to Arise: Women, Tradition and the Church in Africa.* Maryknoll: Orbis, 1992

Ruether, Rosemary R. *Sexism and God-Talk: Toward a Feminist Theology.* Boston: Beacon, 1983

Thistlethwaite, Susan B. *Sex, Race, and God: Christian Feminism in Black and White.* New York: Crossroad, 1989

PART FOUR
Some Ethical Issues

13:1

Medical Ethics

GILBERT LAWRENCE

In the preamble to the constitution of the World Health Organisation, health is defined as a state of complete physical, mental and social well-being and not merely the absence of disease or infirmity.

The large discrepancies in the provision of health care to different populations in our world belie the assumption that good health is enjoyed by many. In reality many people suffer severe hardship through ill health. Can medicine as practised world-wide meet the needs of the people? If not, why not?

Many ethical challenges and moral dilemmas are facing modern medicine. This has been particularly so over the last thirty years. High-technology health care, super-specialisation of health-care personnel, the high cost of health care, and spectacular clinical interventions (especially at the beginning and the end of life) confront health-care providers as well as society at large.

Scientific medicine has been used to advance the power and authority of the physician. This has led to the promotion of a religious aura around the doctor. The physician has become the one who holds the rational and objective knowledge that may save lives. Given this understanding of their practice, it is not surprising that some physicians arrogate to themselves the power of life and death.[1]

All that medical power cannot prevent is the eventual death of patients. Doctors are preoccupied with death. Death is the enemy for both patient and doctor, and yet it will win in the end. Fundamental questions are thus presented to society, questions such as: Who shall live? Who shall die? Who shall decide? How will the decision be made? No consensus has been reached on these questions.

The term 'medical ethics' is currently being used in a variety of ways. In one of its oldest but still current usages, medical ethics refers to the body of thinking and codes of conduct developed by the medical profession. Self-conscious reflection on standards of conduct is one of the defining characteristics of a profession. Thus it is not surprising that the development of medical ethics as a form of professional self-regulation has a history as long and as venerable as the history of medicine itself. The Hippocratic Oath and modern codes of medical ethics are evidence of this.

As early as the sixteenth century BC, papyri documents mention priest—physicians, with rules laid down on how and when to treat patients. Jewish medical tradition was based on Mesopotamian precepts, and later included the Egyptian system after the period of servitude in Egypt. Greeks traded with Egyptians and Babylonians and consequently were influenced by them. Hippocrates (440—377 BC) brought scholarship and observation to medicine. The Hippocratic Oath and corpus stressed that a person had to be regarded as an individual. A strict moral code was also adopted. The Hippocratic Oath also dealt with the doctor's relationship with the patient, 'to help if at all possible but at least to do no harm'. Another important aspect is the whole question of regarding as confidential any information gathered from the patient. 'And whatever I shall see or hear in the course of my profession, as well as outside my profession in intercourse with man, if it be what should not be published abroad, I will never divulge, holding such things to be holy secrets.'

Five analogical models of the patient—physician relationship have been described.[2] Firstly, in the commodity model, the delivery of health care constitutes a sale of services in the market place, with health-care providers pursuing their own interests. This is an issue facing us in South Africa as we assess health strategies advocating the privatisation of health-care facilities and services. Wealthy patients are able to purchase and demand better services. Secondly, a covenantal model provides for a relationship in which the health-care provider's obligation to the patient transcends science and human contracts and involves a trusting relationship with strong religious overtones. Thirdly, the applied biology model depicts a professional relationship under the influence of the scientific and technological revolutions. It emphasises the causes of disease and technological curative processes to the neglect of other vitally important, humane aspects of medicine. Fourthly, the doctor, in the social functionary model, is depicted as social functionary, primarily for the benefit of maintaining a healthy society. The efforts and responsibilities of the doctor are directed towards the society in which he or she works.

Finally, in the contractual model the physician—patient relationship is reduced to a mutually acceptable legalistic engagement. This model focuses on legal and institutionalised rights as a minimalist form of ethics, and underplays the more humane or human moral rights. This relationship encourages a litigious atmosphere if contracts are broken or complaints arise.

None of these models alone or in combination adequately describes the internal morality of medicine itself. This focuses on the nature of illness and the relationship between physician and patient; and the obligations of medicine which arise within this context and which are built into the nature of the healing process. The emphasis here is on beneficence, trust, fidelity to promises, and effacement of the physician's self-interest. These comments apply to all members of the health-care team and not merely the doctor.

The doctor—patient relationship has been extended in our modern society into a health-care team—community relationship. Issues of empowerment, democratisation and justice also enter this relationship.

Concepts of what constitutes and drives a community and its needs are vital in our current situation. The democratisation process has questioned and rejected the top-down approach of even the health-care provider. This raises questions of what constitutes a community, how does the community decide, and what should it decide and for whom.

E. H. Loewy has outlined two alternative concepts of community.[3] Each would reflect very different health-care systems. For example, community A is perceived as a group of individuals bound together by duties of non-maleficence (refraining from harming each other). Health care in such a community would be seen as an individual responsibility. There would be minimal obligation to cater for the less fortunate, who would be denied adequate access to health services. Many wealthy countries and communities adopt this view, with serious consequences for the marginalised.

Community B, on the other hand, is perceived as a group of individuals bound together not only by non-maleficence but also by mutual beneficence. Health care would become a social goal. The natural lottery which makes some persons more fortunate than others confers on them duties and obligations towards others in that community. This would be a more Christian viewpoint, but the dilemma is how far should such beneficence extend and the degree to which altruism and self-sacrifice are to be considered the norm.

In the context of its views on the nature of medicine and the nature of community, each society will decide what kind of health system it wishes to have and all the related ethical issues.

Medical ethics will test our faith. Christians will be presented with ethical challenges long before the legal system or the community at large has had an opportunity to make up its mind on a particular issue. Medicine is breaking new frontiers and forcing humankind to take heed and to make decisions. Examples are questions related to surrogacy, treatment of AIDS patients, invasive research, organ trafficking, definitions of death, and abortion.

Another major concern in medical ethics is the question of health care as a right, entrenched in a Bill of Rights. Some analysts feel that health care should not be a right, as it would require state involvement in health-care provision. For those persons, health is a matter of self-determined action, full autonomy exercised by free individuals, the seeking of services by persons (patients), and the provision of services by doctors and other health-care providers. State involvement, it is felt, is coercive of both patient and provider.

But we may ask: Can patients and doctors truly behave as autonomous individuals? There are many interfering bodies and organisations such as professional associations, medical aid societies, private hospitals as well as state fiscal constraints and state policies on health. Health may well have to be a right to ensure some measure of justice and equity for all people, especially the disadvantaged.

Shriver argues that Western religion makes a contribution to medicine precisely at these points.[4] Medical practitioners are reminded that human life is worth caring for, even when it proceeds under the shadow of death. This feature of human life means that physicians must explore with patients the meaning of their life and must care for more than the body. It is a person who is the object of care. It seems obvious that care-givers must be technically competent. But what other characteristics must they possess so that they will continue to care for patients when they are very ill, in pain and unpleasant to be with?

In conclusion, theological reflection on issues raised by advances in medical research and technology is critically important.[5] Firstly, it is important for communities of faith with visions of what it means for human beings to flourish and to live with integrity, and secondly, it is important for the broader community. A pluralistic society requires the candid expression of different perspectives. Frank attention to the religious dimension of morality, including medical morality, could prevent morality being reduced to a set of minimal expectations. This would remind all participants in the public debate of broader and more profound questions about what human beings are meant to be and to become.

[1] See S. E. Lammers and A. Verhey (eds), *On Moral Medicine: Theological Perspectives in Medical Ethics* (Grand Rapids: Eerdmans, 1987).

[2] E. D. Pellegrino, 'The Anatomy of Clinical Perinatology and Neonatology: A Substantive and Procedural Framework', *Seminars in Perinatology*, 11 (1987), pp. 203–209.

[3] E. H. Loewy, 'Communities, Obligations and Health Care', *Social Science and Medicine*, 25 (1987), pp. 783–791.

[4] D. W Shriver, 'The Interrelationship of Religion and Medicine', in Lammers and Verhey, *On Moral Medicine*, pp. 11–20.

[5] Ibid., p. ix.

13:2

Abortion

DOT CLEMINSHAW

Ethics assumes that life is good and worth living:

> Even the most wretched cling to it . . . the will to live is instinctive and
> Christian insight has built on this basis the belief that life is also the gift of
> God . . . to be held in trust until taken away. . . Christians, like
> members of other faiths, do not claim infallibility in all these matters.
> Some simplistic people would say it's all in the Bible. If only it was. But
> little direct guidance is given to us in the Scriptures or indeed from the
> tradition of the church as we face new and perplexing situations. . .[1]

What, then, of abortion, the destruction of foetal life? Regrettably, religious,
medical and political leaders — those best qualified to influence ethical
behaviour — often shrink from publicly debating abortion. Conflicting beliefs
divide people into two hostile camps inaccurately labelled 'pro-life' and 'pro-
choice'.[2]

The abortion debate is about a seemingly insoluble conflict between two
fundamental values: the right of a foetus to live and the right of a woman to
determine her own fate. Is the foetus essentially tissue belonging to the woman, or
is it a human being? The first view absolutises the rights of the woman; the second
view does the same for the foetus. 'Competing values' are often overlooked in the
process, and circumstances surrounding each particular case are ignored. Between
the advocates of these two positions stand those who are committed to finding a
more nuanced point of view.[3]

Until the 1960s little moral philosophy on abortion appeared in recognised
journals.[4] By the end of the 1960s it had become a popular topic for discussion (in
the centuries-old tradition) by male theologians and philosophers, with attention
being focused almost exclusively on the foetus.[5] We still at times read ethical
writings on abortion without learning anything about the emotional and physical
involvement of the mother in the reproduction process. This suggests abortion
can be discussed as an isolated event, 'as though abortion is the same as any other

166

form of killing'.[6] Pregnancy and abortion are the lot of women, yet until recent times their voices have been significantly silent. Male legislators made the laws on abortion, and male-dominated religions laid down moral codes about it.

Abortion Within the Christian Tradition

Ancient Attitudes

Early Christians rejected the prevalent codes of sexuality in the ancient world, where abortion and infanticide were relatively commonplace. The theological ground for the new ethic was God's hallowing of life through sex and pregnancy within the family.[7] The third-century theologian Tertullian, for example, added the idea that the foetus is 'the fruit already existing in·the seed'. Some Roman Catholic moralists still operate within a natural law framework which assumes that the organic structure of things not only shapes but predetermines actuality. It presupposes that human rationality must accept, not transcend, the limits that 'nature' supposedly 'dictates'.[8]

The abortion debate has been significantly influenced by the Christian appropriation of the body—soul dualism, which came to dominate Western philosophy and theology. This resulted in a notion of higher and lower forms of being and a commitment to some moment of 'animation', when animal tissue becomes 'ensouled', at which point it needs to be defended.[9] The obvious question is: Precisely when does this moment occur?

The early Catholic position was that a foetus was not a human being until animated with a soul (at forty days after conception if male, but eighty if female!). Although the church disapproved of abortion, abortion as murder was not yet part of official teaching. Today, of course, there is a range of options which suggest when the foetus becomes a person. We return to this discussion later.

Differences Within Christianity

It was only in the late nineteenth century, after scientific insights emerged about the process of fertilisation, that the church moved towards the view that human life begins at conception. In 1869 an encyclical by Pope Pius IX ceased limiting excommunication for abortion to those who aborted 'ensouled' foetuses. In 1965 the Second Vatican Council affirmed that 'from the moment of conception life must be guarded with the greatest care, while abortion and infanticide are unspeakable crimes.'[10] The Catholic Church's substantial conviction now is that abortion is tolerable only when it is a life-saving, and therefore also life-serving, intervention. In other words the church permits abortion only to save a woman's life endangered by the pregnancy, accepting that the *indirect* result is the death of the foetus.[11]

In the United States[12] (as in South Africa)[13] it was medical and political groups in society which moved to criminalise abortion. Organised religions were not at the forefront. However, today the Protestant religious right has become a coalition partner with Catholicism in the struggle against abortion.[14] Different opinions continue to exist among various Protestant denominations, as well as within the Roman Catholic tradition. For example, there are 'Catholics for

Choice', and in the United States Catholic women are about as likely to obtain an abortion as other women. Catholic women are in fact 30 per cent more likely than Protestants to have abortions, while Jewish women are less likely to have an abortion than Catholics.[15]

Prior to the passing of the British Abortion Act of 1967, Lord Fisher, former archbishop of Canterbury, in a letter to *The Times* opposed the view that personal life begins at conception, and expressed the opinion that abortion is permissible under certain medically and morally justifiable conditions.[16] The Methodist Church in England stated in 1976 that 'Man is made for relationships'. An American Lutheran statement declared that, because the nature of being human is to be in relation to others, the unborn foetus cannot be considered fully and properly a human being. For these and related reasons, some churches have come to regard abortion as legitimate in certain circumstances. Put differently, the ecumenical pattern world-wide on ethical questions challenges the existing traditional teaching of the church on abortion. Around this, suggests Ellingsen, a new consensus on abortion may be evolving.[17]

Some Arenas of Argument

In the interest of promoting debate, a number of issues on abortion are raised for discussion.

An Emerging Consensus

There seems to be general agreement among ethicists that while abortion is not morally innocuous, it is justifiable in certain circumstances. Not all will agree on the grounds for abortion. Those grounds suggested variously include a situation where pregnancy endangers the woman's life, in cases of rape, incest or serious ill health (physical or mental), where there is severe foetal defect (with the caution that many handicapped people lead worthwhile lives), abandonment by the father, excessive poverty, failed contraception, gross adverse effect on an existing family, or where the woman is too old or too young.[18]

On the other hand, there is agreement that abortion is not morally justifiable after viability (when the foetus could survive if born) unless for some higher ethical purpose, such as saving the life of the mother. There is also consensus that abortion for some entirely personal whim would be selfish, callous and wrong. The consensus further suggests that abortion, used as a substitute for birth control, would be immoral. Women have, however, resorted to it in countries where contraception has not been readily available (as in Russia, Romania and many third-world countries). It is, further, generally regarded in the West as immoral for the state to compel women to have abortions, as in China.

Status of the Foetus

We return to the question about the beginning of human life, which is pivotal to the debate about the morality of abortion. In Harrison's words, 'When shall we predicate full human value to developing foetal life?'[19]

Morwitz and Trefil argue that humanness lies in our verbal intellectual abilities or rational capabilities, located in the cortex of the brain. Since the cortex only becomes operative in the foetus's twenty-fourth week of development, it is argued that the destruction of the foetus in the first two trimesters (six months) does not destroy a distinctive human being. Prior to this point, the foetus is only a 'form of life',[20] not a complete human being.[21] Dr J. C. Wilke, on the other hand, argues that the embryo must be regarded as a separate human person, not simply living tissue, from the moment of conception, since the crucial 46 chromosomes are all present in the fertilised egg. Following Tertullian, he says: 'Contained within the single cell who I once was, was the totality of everything I am today.'[22]

But cell biologist Charles A. Gardner contends that a person's constitution is not merely determined by DNA genetic material. Cell division is also affected by the pattern of cells and molecules in the preceding cell division, with each cell responding to new information in a random way. A mixture of chance and planning is what makes each of us a unique person. In other words, the foetus is not a small person that simply has to grow larger. Identical twins can grow from the same egg, have the same DNA, yet have different fingerprints. If a thing as simple as a fingerprint is not genuinely present in some programmed sense in the fertilised ovum, how could anything as subtle and unique as the individual human brain or the individual personality or psyche be regarded as present from the moment of conception?

A single embryo may split at a very early stage into two or more identical embryos, yielding identical twins or triplets. Is the pre-twinning embryo one distinct person or two? The particular person that it might become is not yet there. Therefore, it is argued, abortion is not murder. At most it is the termination of a particular form of potential early existence. A newly fertilised ovum is not fully equivalent to a baby about to be born. This realisation persuades many ethicists that abortion of the former does not, therefore, present the same moral issues as abortion of the latter.

It can, of course, be argued that scientific 'disproof' of separate embryonic personhood cannot be said to prove that the embryo is less a human being than any of us, because we ourselves are constantly changing, and the particular person we might still become is 'not yet there'. This is dependent on the path we take. We are, nevertheless, already human persons.

In brief, ethicists argue that the question whether it is morally right or wrong to destroy an *embryo* (whatever status we may ascribe to it) cannot be answered on the basis of scientific analysis alone. Ethics involves more than this.

Personhood

The philosophical and medical debate continues on the point at which an embryo can be said to be a human person. It is also addressed at a legal level. Here, the distinction between moral rights and legal rights is important. Some maintain that the foetus from conception is a 'person' with absolute rights, such as the right to life, on a basis of equality with the mother. If the embryo, on the other hand, is not recognised as a person in the legal sense, it cannot be a bearer of full human rights.[23] In this situation the mother, as an existing human person, is seen to have full legal rights, including the right to privacy and decision-making over her reproductive system.[24] From the time the foetus is accorded legal status and the right to life, it (she or he) is accorded rights equal to the mother. What this means is that an abortion would be impermissible after this time even if it is necessary to save the mother's life.[25] Those advocating that the unborn child prior to viability should not be accorded legal status, argue that other rights of the unborn, such as the right to inherit property or claim damages, need to be protected by declaring that the child, once born, be accorded legal rights to exercise such claims.[26]

The USA Supreme Court in *Roe* v. *Wade* (1973), for example, declared that the word 'person' refers to an individual already born. 'It declared unconstitutional all state laws that prohibit abortion during the first six months of pregnancy or regulate the physician's practice of abortion during the first three months of pregnancy.'[27] Subsequently, despite various state Supreme Court rulings requiring, for example, spousal and parental consent, waiting periods, or regulation for fertility cases, the core of *Roe* v. *Wade* remains intact at the present time.

Women's Rights

Harrison contends that the controversy over abortion is to be located in the broad world-historical struggle to enable women to 'become the subjects of our lives'.[28] Her argument is that before we evaluate the act of abortion, we have first to grant recognition of women's 'capacity for full moral agency'.

Wahlberg, in turn, contrasts the vulnerability and responsibility of the female with the freedom of the male. When the adult male deposits millions of sperms inside the marriage (or non-marriage) partner, the danger of pregnancy is for him removed. The male may feel concerned, but essentially it is the woman's problem. It happens to *her* body. Therefore she has the right and responsibility to make the decision whether or not to bear a child.[29]

Feminism has created an increasing awareness of the rising demands of oppressed women for justice, equality and dignity in terms of Article 1 of the Universal Declaration of Human Rights. Article 12 of the Declaration goes further. It protects privacy, family and home from interference. These articles strengthen a woman's claim to exercise control over her reproductive system. Many countries recognise a legal right to reproductive choice and personal autonomy, and by 1992 almost two-thirds of the world's women had access to legal abortion services. On the other hand, one-quarter of all women still have to seek help from unskilled, illegal abortionists to exercise this right.[30]

Abortion, Ethics and Theology in the South African Context

In addition to wrestling with these issues, theology on abortion in South Africa must face the reality of women struggling with poverty, hunger, unemployment, crime, violence, disease and breakdown of family life, not to mention male domination. How shall we intelligently and responsibly address the issue of abortion within the context of enabling people to live well?

Hursthouse offers some ideas.[31] She finds all rather bald the arguments for abortion based entirely on the theoretical concept of when a foetus can be regarded as a person, as well as the pro-abortionist stance based exclusively on women's rights. Such arguments, in her opinion, tend to support a too permissive line on abortion. At the same time she argues that abortion is morally justifiable when a higher ethical motive is involved. Her argument is essentially that people should try to 'live well' by following the teaching of Aristotle to acquire and practise the virtues of courage, justice, honesty, fidelity, generosity and compassion. This focuses the abortion debate on what has earlier been described in this chapter as 'an emerging consensus': the complexity of the debate needs to be faced in relation to the issues included in the 'consensus'. It needs also to address the competing values for and against abortion in a sensitive manner, rather than ignore some in affirming others.

Hursthouse argues that if bearing children is essentially worth while (which society suggests it is), then abortion must be assessed in relation to the goodness of life. It follows that because abortion is the destruction of life, it must always be regarded in a most serious light. To think of abortion as the killing of 'something' that does not matter, or as nothing but the exercise of the rights of a woman, or as the incidental means to some desirable end, is for her unacceptable.

Abortion need not, however, necessarily indicate a callous attitude to human life. Hursthouse considers a number of arguments advanced in favour of abortion. One might, for example, genuinely desire that new lives should not begin disabled. Young girls may decide on abortion out of fear or from an inability to cope with the responsibilities of motherhood. Later they may develop into serious-minded women who become marvellous mothers. An older woman, with several children, may well fear that another child will seriously reduce her capacity to be a good mother to her family. Her concern is primarily to address these issues. The decision to abort is not in all cases (and perhaps rarely) by definition a callous disregard for life. On the contrary, in these circumstances it may even constitute an affirmation of 'quality life'. In brief, Hursthouse argues that there are no simple answers to the abortion debate. To face the issues involved leads people to reflect seriously about the meaning of life. This, in turn, opens up a space within which the abortion debate can be approached in a less vindictive, judgmental and moralistic manner than has hitherto been the case. We should recognise that the former ways of dealing with the problem have not done a great deal to resolve the matter in either one direction or the other.

In South Africa, diseases such as HIV infection and tuberculosis are spreading at an alarming rate. Additionally, there is reason for concern about the increasing incidence of rape, child abuse and child abandonment. There are approximately 3 323 births a day in South Africa, one every 26 seconds, 30 per cent occurring to teenagers.[32] Our current population (excluding the 'homelands' of Transkei, Bophuthatswana, Venda and Ciskei) is 32.6 million and is expected to grow to 80 million by 2020. Approximately half of this population is under 21 years old. Some 66 per cent of black and 61 per cent of coloured women have never been legally married.[33] At just one hospital, some 300 women a month are treated for failed or life-threatening abortions. On average each day two women attending the antenatal clinic at this hospital prove to be infected with the AIDS virus.[34] The estimated number of illegal abortions per annum ranges between 42 000 and 200 000, with attendant deaths and serious complications, including sterility.[35]

Ethicists are compelled to respond to the contribution of women's experience and eco-feminist insights regarding the abortion debate. Politicians will have to grasp the nettle of rapid population growth. We need to develop a new ethic based on quality of life, not only for the individual but for the collective community and the environment.

All this challenges religious leaders to support at least open debate on sex education, contraception, condom usage, sterilisation and early abortion on request. The best contraceptives are not 100 per cent reliable. Should abortion be allowed as a back-up method in cases of contraceptive failure?[36] Should the French abortion pill, RU.486 (mifepristone), now in use in Britain, Sweden, China and elsewhere, be made available in South Africa? This would make the abortion decision a 'private' one and end the stigma attached to doctors who perform surgical abortions.

It is futile asking women to control their fertility without also addressing the problem of poverty. Money needs to be spent on water supply, housing, sanitation, education and literacy. The raising of the status of women and increased help to single mothers can contribute to a climate which provides alternatives to abortion. Gender equity and women's participation in decision-making on abortion are essential. This would happen much more easily if religious institutions were to promote open and serious inquiry into abortion and related matters. Moralistic attitudes on abortion have not adequately addressed the dilemma.

Those of us who have the time to read and think about the ethics of abortion are very privileged. It would be morally untenable if we were not to show compassion and to seek to assist those desperate thousands who wretchedly cling to life – often having both children and abortion thrust on them by the circumstances of life.

[1] E. L. King, Contribution to Symposium, *Ethical and Moral Issues in Contemporary Medical Practice*, ed. S. R. Benatar (Cape Town: Dept. of Medicine, University of Cape Town, 1985), p. 23.

[2] R. A. McCormick, 'Abortion: Rules for Debate', in P. T. Jersild and D. A. Johnson (eds), *Moral Issues and Christian Response* (Austin: Holt, Rinehart and Winston, 1982), p. 368.

[3] Ibid., p. 365.

[4] R. Hursthouse, *Beginning Lives* (Oxford: B. Blackwell and the Open University, 1987), p. 5.

[5] J. Glover, 'Matters of Life and Death', *New York Review of Books*, 32 (1985), p. 1.

[6] Hursthouse, *Beginning Lives*, p. 179.

[7] A. C. Outler, 'The Beginnings of Personhood: Theological Considerations' in Jersild and Johnson (eds), *Moral Issues*, p. 384.

[8] B. W. Harrison, *Our Right to Choose: Toward a New Ethic of Abortion* (Boston: Beacon Press, 1983), p. 212.

[9] Outler, 'Beginnings of Personhood', p. 386.

[10] 'S.A. Catholic Bishops' Conference Statement on Abortion', *Southern Cross*, 16 (1972), p. 16.

[11] McCormick, *Abortion*, p. 374.

[12] L. Tribe, *Abortion: The Clash of Absolutes* (New York: W. W. Norton, 1990), p. 30.

[13] H. Bradford, 'Her Body, Her Life', *Cosmopolitan* (August 1991), p. 128.

[14] M. Ellingsen, 'The Church and Abortion: Signs of Consensus', *The Christian Century*, 3–10 January 1990, reproduced in *South African Outlook*, October–November 1990, p. 316.

[15] Alan Guttmacher Institute, *Facts in Brief: Abortion in the United States* (New York: c. 1989).

[16] M. Potts, P. Diggory and J. Peel, *Abortion* (Cambridge: Cambridge University Press, 1977), p. 7.

[17] Ellingsen, 'The Church and Abortion', p. 318.

[18] E. Nash, 'Teenage Pregnancy: Need a Child Bear a Child', *South African Medical Journal,* 77 (3 Feb. 1990), p. 151; N. L. Geisler, *Ethics: Alternatives and Issues* (Grand Rapids: Zondervan, 1971), p. 220.

[19] Harrison, *Our Right to Choose*, p. 193.

[20] H. J. Morowitz, and J. S. Trefil, *The Facts of Life: Science and the Abortion Controversy,* reviewed by E. Fox-Genovese in *The Washington Post,* 4 October 1992.

[21] See also C. Wellman, *Morals and Ethics* (Glenville, Illinois: Scott Foreman and Co., 1975).

[22] Tribe, *Abortion,* p. 117.

[23] For an examination of the validity of the right to privacy, see Wellman, *Morals and Ethics,* p. 180.

[24] Ibid.

[25] D. Shelton, cited in S. J. Frankowski and G. F. Cole, *Abortion and Protection of the Human Fetus* (Boston: Martinus Nijhoff, 1987), p. 9.

[26] Wellman, *Morals and Ethics,* pp. 165, 175.

[27] Ibid., p. 159.

[28] Harrison, *Our Right to Choose*, p. 196.

[29] R. C. Walberg, 'The Woman and the Fetus: "One Flesh?"' in Jersild and Johnson (eds), *Moral Issues,* p. 377.

[30] E. Ketting, 'Global Overview of Abortion', *Planned Parenthood Challenges,* 1 (1993) (Public Affairs Dept., International Planned Parenthood Federation), p. 27.

[31] Hursthouse, *Beginning Lives,* p. 330.

[32] Population Development Programme, 'Women of the 90s — Poor, Powerless and Pregnant?' (Pretoria: Dept. of National Health, 1990), p. 6. See also the editorial in *Cape Times,* 21 June 1991.

[33] Central Statistical Service, *Statistical Report 03-01-00 (1991)* (Pretoria: CSS, 1992).

[34] Dr J. McIntyre, Baragwanath Hospital, Johannesburg, in a letter to D. Cleminshaw dated 26 May 1993.

[35] Dr. M. Dyer, Address to Human Rights Lobby Group for the New Constitution, Port Elizabeth (2–3 June 1992). See also 'Backstreet Slaughter', *Weekend Argus* (1 February 1992).

[36] Potts *et al., Abortion,* p. 528.

Select Bibliography

Harrison, B. W. *Our Right to Choose: Toward a New Ethic of Abortion.* Boston: Beacon Press, 1983

Jersild, P. T. and D. A. Johnson (eds.) *Moral Issues and Christian Response.* Austin: Holt, Rinehart and Winston, 1982

Wellman, C. *Morals and Ethics.* Glenville, Illinois: Scott Foreman and Co., 1975

13:3

AIDS

WILLEM SAAYMAN

As AIDS is a sexually transmitted disease and as sexual behaviour patterns are mainly culturally determined, AIDS must be thought of as a sociocultural disease. Any discussion about AIDS in an ethical perspective must therefore take the social epidemiology of the AIDS epidemic very seriously.

The Social Epidemiology of AIDS

Poverty

In Africa south of the Sahara, AIDS is spread mainly (in as many as 80 per cent of all cases) through heterosexual contact. Many scholars agree that the social, economic and political structures of African countries, which were basically inherited from the colonial powers, contribute directly to the rapid heterosexual spreading of AIDS in Africa.[1] As Waite puts it, the causes for this rapid progress should not be sought primarily in 'aberrant' or 'promiscuous' sexual behaviour, but much rather in 'the aberrant nature of the African economies'.[2] Schoeman confirms this view with his statement that 'poverty is the most important "co-factor" influencing the spread of the virus'.[3]

Any ethical reflection on AIDS should therefore not be undertaken from a narrowly 'moral' or 'religious' viewpoint, but within the social, political and economic structures of Southern African society.[4]

Migrant Labour

Migrant labour is an enduring heritage from colonial times in the political economies of many Southern African countries. Even where racist laws which institutionalised migrant labour have been revoked, the material conditions pertaining to it still remain. The long periods of enforced separation between sexual and/or marriage partners which result from migrant labour serve to encourage open sexual relationships.[5] Migrant labourers' needs for sexual expression while away from their regular partners also encourage the growth and continued existence of prostitution, especially in situations where social security measures such as unemployment benefits are basically non-existent.

Ethical Reflections from a Communal Perspective

If one takes the social epidemiology of AIDS in Southern Africa as seriously as it ought to be, it becomes clear that a narrowly moralistic or 'religious' premise for ethical reflections on the epidemic is inadequate. It is for this reason that we propagate rather a communal perspective. In general, the African concept of community is still centred on the extended family and the village community, as the majority of African people are still rural.

Furthermore, many urban people in Africa keep their rural links alive and will, in times of crisis (such as serious illness), turn to their village or extended family for support. Those African people who have become permanently urbanised have created various alternatives to the extended family or village community, such as African-initiated churches, women's church associations, burial societies, stokvels, labour unions and political organisations. In urban as well as rural areas these communities are vibrantly alive. Community is the predominant root-metaphor in African views on sickness and well-being.[6] Ethical decisions on important issues, such as compulsory HIV testing and the follow-up of sexual partners of HIV positive people, should therefore be the responsibility of the community. In various African communities, differing mechanisms will have to be found for such a communal decision-making process. In Zimbabwe, for example, a successful communal tree-planting campaign has been undertaken, involving modern Western governmental structures, traditional African socio-political authorities, traditional African spirit mediums, associations of ex-guerrilla fighters and African-initiated churches.[7]

That such an approach is possible also in matters relating to medical ethics has been proven by a pioneering approach to caring for AIDS patients at the Salvation Army's Chikankata Hospital in Zambia. The programme entails home-based care and prevention. Every patient who is diagnosed as HIV positive (often in antenatal clinics) or has already developed AIDS in the acute form is admitted to home-based care. The whole family are informed about the consequences of the disease, and counselled by a team of trained counsellors, who visit members at home. In this way the sexual contacts of the patient are followed up and, in the community context, persuaded to go to the hospital for testing. Eventually the whole community in which the family lives are involved in the programme of prevention, decision-making and care. The aim of this programme is to raise community-awareness of the problems associated with AIDS, and the need for changes in sexual behaviour. The aim is to empower people to develop a sense of collective responsibility for dealing with AIDS, and instil the conviction that something positive can be done about this life-threatening disease.[8]

The most important ethical decision which the community will have to take in consultation with health workers concerns the epidemiology of AIDS. I have pointed out that the rapid heterosexual spread of AIDS in Africa is linked to open sexual relationships. The only way, in my opinion, in which the AIDS epidemic will be broken is by the vigorous propagation of closed sexual relationships. Such relationships can be either homosexual or heterosexual, monogamous or polygamous. As long as they are closed and involve lifelong faithful relationships, AIDS cannot enter. If it does enter a closed sexual relationship by way of an opportunistic infection (such as the transfusion of infected blood), it cannot infect the community further.[9]

Obviously the whole community will have to be informed about the ways AIDS is spread before one can hope to establish such closed relationships. This will be very difficult in Africa, not (as I have already stated) because Africans are more inclined to open sexual relationships, but because AIDS 'is a disease, invested with foreign concepts of causality. It is devoid of symptoms or signs appropriate to its nature as a sex-related disease. It requires methods of management which clash with many traditional societal norms of sexual activity' (e.g. the use of condoms).[10]

An educational programme based on the biomedical model (which is the prevailing model in South African AIDS education programmes at present) will thus, in my opinion, have only limited success. It does not fit the traditional African concept of sickness, and is predicated on the decisions of individuals. New models of educational programmes to inform communities about the clinical and social epidemiology of AIDS, as well as the possibility of breaking the epidemic by way of closed sexual relationships, will have to be devised. In this way communities will have to be informed about the fatal threat of AIDS to their communal life force, so that communal decisions can be taken about sexual mores.

Central to such a communal approach to ethical decision-making is the notion of the reclamation of cultural sexual mores by the whole community. These mores can be inspired by a vision of being fully human, by a specific religious ethos, or by both. I would argue that African tradition (in conjunction with the Judaeo-Christian and the Islamic traditions, the other two predominant religious traditions in Africa) provides people with such a vision and such mores. What is needed is, however, not simply a return to some romanticised concept of an idyllic past, but rather reclaiming dimensions of living in community which have been forgotten or repressed because of economic and social devastation. Reclaiming the fullness of these traditions can contribute to moral and humane ethical decision-making in respect of the life-threatening reality of AIDS in Africa.[11]

Conclusion

The spread of AIDS throughout the world, but especially in Southern and Central Africa, is forcing the whole community to reconsider many generally held assumptions about sickness, well-being, and how epidemics should be fought.[12] We will need all available resources if fullness of life for all is to be maintained. The protective and regenerative power of the African concept of human community will most probably play a decisive role in determining what kind of society survives the epidemic.

[1] See, for example, N. Miller and R. C. Rockwell (eds), *AIDS in Africa: The Social and Policy Impact* (Lewiston/Queenstown: Edwin Mellon Press, 1988), pp. 57–68; S. Schoeman, 'AIDS – The International Malady', Paper read at the Africa Studies Forum, University of South Africa, 21 June 1990.

[2] In Miller and Rockwell (eds), *AIDS in Africa*, p. 151.

[3] Schoeman, 'AIDS', p. 4.

[4] Miller and Rockwell (eds), *AIDS in Africa*, pp. 167–173.

[5] I.e. sexual relationships in which at least one of the partners maintains sexual relations with at least one other person. Cf. W. Saayman and J. Kriel, *AIDS: The Leprosy of Our Time?* (Johannesburg: Orion: 1992), pp. 21ff.

[6] W. Saayman, 'Some Reflections on AIDS, Ethics and the Community in Southern and Central Africa', *Theologia Evangelica*, XXIV:3 (September 1991).

[7] M. L. Daneel, 'The Liberation of Creation and African Traditional Religious and Independent Church Perspectives', *Missionalia*, 19:2 (August 1992).

[8] *Contact: Journal of the Christian Medical Commission*, 117 (Dec. 1990).

[9] An infected mother can, of course, pass the epidemic on to her unborn baby, but this way of communicating the disease cannot sustain a major epidemic.

[10] Mokhobo, cited by J. Kriel, 'AIDS Is Not a (Medical) Disease', in A. van Niekerk (ed.), *AIDS in Context* (Cape Town: Lux Verbi, 1991), p. 16.

[11] Cf. Saayman, 'Some Reflections on AIDS'.

[12] Saayman and Kriel, *AIDS*, pp. 11–13.

Select Bibliography

Contact: Journal of the Christian Medical Commission No. 117 (December 1990). Geneva: World Council of Churches

Daneel, M. L. 'The Liberation of Creation and African Traditional Religious and Independent Church Perspectives'. *Missionalia*, 19:2 (August 1992)

Kriel, J. R. 'AIDS Is Not a (Medical) Disease', in A. van Niekerk (ed.), *AIDS in Context*. Cape Town: Lux Verbi, 1991

Miller, N. and R. C. Rockwell (eds.) *AIDS in Africa. The Social and Policy Impact*. Lewiston/Queenstown: Edwin Mellon Press, 1988

Saayman, W. 'Some Reflections on AIDS, Ethics and the Community in Southern and Central Africa'. *Theologia Evangelica*, XXIV:3 (September 1991)

Saayman, W. 'Concepts of Sickness and Health in Intercultural Communication in South Africa: A Semiotic Approach'. *Journal for the Study of Religion*, 5:4 (September 1992)

Saayman W. and J. Kriel. *AIDS: The Leprosy of Our Time?* Johannesburg: Orion, 1992

Schoeman, S. 'AIDS – The International Malady'. Paper read at the Africa Studies Forum, Unisa, 21 June 1990

13:4

Euthanasia

DAWID OLIVIER

Euthanasia is about the pursuit of a 'good death'. A report on the views of doctors and the decision of a judge witness to this effect. In its June 1992 issue, *Modern Medicine of South Africa* published the findings of a survey of 9 000 general and family practitioners and specialists concerning the question of a person's right to die, and whether the patient should be assisted to do so. The scope of doctor-assisted death in South Africa is said to go 'beyond the expected terminal-illness/intensive-care specialities and situations'. Nearly one in ten doctors, it is claimed, have deliberately taken clinical actions that would directly cause the death of a patient. About half of this number are said to have intentionally taken clinical actions that would indirectly cause a patient's death, while 6 per cent indicated that they have provided next-of-kin with information to be used for suicide. This report also claims that over four in ten of the respondents said that there were circumstances in which a medical doctor would be justified in deliberately causing a patient's death. Findings are also said to show that situations in which patients ask for death are a common aspect of today's medicine.

In July 1992 the accepted position of the South African legal system on euthanasia was challenged by a bold decision handed down in the Supreme Court in Durban by Mr Justice Thirion in the case of *Clarke* v. *Hurst NO and Others*.[1] In terms of this decision it was judged not to be either wrongful or unlawful to discontinue the nasogastric feeding of a Dr Clarke who, at that stage, had for four years been in a persistent vegetative state.

The World Medical Association and Euthanasia

The debate on the rights and wrongs of euthanasia concerns the kind of medical action ethically acceptable to promote the optimal well-being of persons who find themselves in situations such as terminal illness involving a painful and drawn-out death or a permanent comatose state or total paralysis. What action is ethically permissible in the case of severely handicapped new-borns or senile dementia in geriatric wards, where a meaningful life no longer seems possible? Life in such a state, it can be argued, is deemed by either the patients themselves or by others with whom they are involved, to be no longer worth living. Views in this debate, each in their own way, express a concern for enabling persons beyond any therapeutic hope to experience a humane death, to end their lives, or have their lives ended, in such a way that it is not an affront to human dignity, theirs and that of others.

The World Medical Association opts for a passive voluntary-type of euthanasia. In its declaration on euthanasia, adopted at the 39th World Medical Assembly in Madrid in October 1987, the Association states that euthanasia, 'the act of deliberately ending the life of a patient, even at the patient's own request or at the request of close relatives, is unethical'. This does not 'prevent the physician from respecting the desire of a patient to allow the natural process of death to follow its course in the terminal phase of sickness'.

This statement reflects the views of an earlier declaration on the treatment of terminally ill patients adopted in October 1983 at the 35th World Medical Assembly in Venice. Treatment of these patients may be withheld with their consent or that of their immediate family if they are unable to express their will in this regard. Withholding such treatment, however, does not free the doctor from the obligation to assist the dying person and give that person the necessary medication to ease the terminal phase of his or her illness. What about the comatose person, the person in a permanent vegetative state? The World Medical Association clearly would not endorse any direct measures to end such a life, irrespective of whether the patient wants to die or not. It appears, however, to agree that the death of a terminally ill or irremediably injured patient should not be unreasonably prolonged.

These precepts of the World Medical Association are endorsed by the Medical Association of South Africa. Their approach — a voluntary indirect or voluntary passive euthanasia — is the form which presently enjoys the widest professional and public acceptance. This differs from an active voluntary approach (where death is hastened at the request of the patient), an active involuntary approach (the death of the person is brought about regardless of that person's wishes) and a passive involuntary approach (all means to keep the person alive for as long as possible are terminated irrespective of whether the person has expressed any desire for this to be done or not).

The official positions of the two medical bodies aside, there are, broadly speaking, three positions advanced on the issue of euthanasia. There are those who would argue that even in the circumstances we have sketched, people should be kept alive at all costs; the moment of death should be postponed for as long as possible. Others would allow for therapy to be rejected or withdrawn, and then only for such medical care to be given that would ensure, so far as possible, the patient's comfort. Still others argue that well-guided, controlled, positive and direct steps to end a person's life are permissible.

Arguments against Euthanasia

What arguments are advanced for opposing euthanasia? To begin with, human life, created in the 'image and likeness of God' (Gen. 1:26), is sacred, requiring unqualified protection. In this view voluntary active, involuntary active and passive euthanasia contradict the principle of the inviolability of human life. To practise euthanasia is, in other words, a transgression of God's commandment 'You shall not kill' (Exod. 20:13), and a direct affront to God's lordship over human life.

Another argument against euthanasia avers that the practice of euthanasia goes against the grain of the professional code of doctors and nurses. Their duty is to preserve the life of the patient and to relieve, to the best of their ability, any suffering. Where it is impossible to preserve a person's life, the principle of doing no harm comes into effect. Any doctor or nurse who actively causes the death of a person resorts to actions which violate his or her profession and vocation. Doctors and nurses are healers, not executioners.

Opponents of euthanasia also argue that to allow voluntary active euthanasia in the case of terminally ill patients is to open the door to possible abuse. Such a step could lead to involuntary acts of killing the weak, the helpless and the unwanted. There is no other way, it is argued, of preventing abuses than to legislate against euthanasia.

Opponents of euthanasia also point out that people ask for their lives to be taken, not because they desire to die, but for other reasons. These include their fear of having to face a painful and drawn-out death, or of being a burden on their family and friends. Such fears could also impair not only their judgement but also that of close relatives and friends. It is said that once these fears are identified and allayed, their desire to have their lives taken diminishes. Attending to the psychological and spiritual as well as the physical needs of such people, as is done in the hospice movement, is what is needed, not euthanasia.

One cannot be sure that cases are as hopeless as often claimed. Numerous examples are cited where surprise recoveries have taken place. Mistakes can also be made by doctors in their diagnosis of a patient's condition. Once a life is terminated, it is then obviously too late to rectify matters. By taking a life, one could also rob a person of any chance of profiting from possible new discoveries and cures that might later appear.

Finally, in certain cases suffering might be ennobling and a means of God's grace. Suffering, it is emphasised, should not always be necessarily shunned.

Arguments for Euthanasia

A number of reasons are often given in favour of euthanasia. It is argued that where persons clearly do not enjoy an adequate quality of life, the practice of euthanasia should not be excluded. Quality of life is concerned with personal well-being, with a sense of worth and dignity. It implies a capacity for consciousness, for interpersonal relationships and self-transcendence, and the ability to take decisions and exercise a reasonable degree of self- and body control.

Those who argue for euthanasia often ask whether there really is any moral difference between voluntary passive and voluntary active euthanasia. Can one really claim that to stop treatment once it has been started, or not starting it at all, is ethically better than actively ending the life of a person who wants to die? Is it not more humane to end the life of a person in severe, irreversible pain or in a coma than simply to let the person slowly die? What is the real difference between accelerating death using drugs that are meant to kill the pain, and administering a direct lethal dosage that will end it all quickly?

Another argument concerns two basic values that are honoured when voluntary active euthanasia takes place. The first is that of compassion for those suffering, and the second, that of personal autonomy or self-determination. A person has the right to choose death, and that right should be respected.

Keeping people alive who really have no chance of recovering has emotionally negative effects on relatives and friends, who are required to watch these people die slowly. Financially this could also become an extreme burden for family and society, if one takes into consideration the enormous costs of hospitalisation.

Taking the Debate Further

Is it ethically acceptable for doctors and nurses to actively cause the death, or assist in causing the death, of terminally ill patients, the severely debilitated or those in a persistent vegetative state where life has become unbearable?

One's answer to this question is influenced by one's views on three issues: (1) the factors that contribute in a specific case towards a patient's well-being (the principle of beneficence); (2) the patient's right to refuse treatment and also to choose to end his or her life or have it ended (the principle of self-determination); (3) the integrity of health-care professionals and the health-care system (the principles of justice, equity and social responsibility). Any attempt to address these issues confronts one immediately with numerous questions about God's sovereignty over human life, the meaning of life and death, and the meaning of human suffering. The focal point of these questions and issues is, however, that of coming to some understanding of what our responsibility should be towards God and our fellow human beings in such circumstances.

The principles of the sanctity of life and of quality of life focus attention on the need to respect life and to ensure that the potential for a meaningful life experience is, as far as possible, protected and allowed to develop. It must be remembered that in the debate on euthanasia, the concern is not to prolong unnecessarily the suffering of people in situations where, as a result of progressive and irreversible somatic or psychological degeneration, hope for life in any meaningful form, humanly speaking, does not exist.

Over the last few decades, phenomenal progress been made in the various fields of medicine and related technology. Doctors and specialists have not only been able, through the development and improvement of drugs, surgical skills and technology, to improve the quality of life for many terminally ill patients. They have also acquired the means and skills to keep the basic biological functions of the human body operating in cases where in the past it would have been impossible to do so.

Progress in medicine, which promotes the care of patients through countering somatic dysfunctions and their effects, has often prompted doctors to prolong the life of people. Respect for life and concern for its quality might, however, require us, in certain cases, not to do everything possible to keep people alive, but to do what is necessary to ensure a humane existence. This concern will inevitably require that we let go of life or in certain cases terminate it.

Although it may be difficult in specific cases, one has to distinguish between personal human existence and a kind of human existence which could well be described as 'post-personal'. The latter is an existence which has irretrievably lost its capacity for personhood as we know it, having become no more than an expression of physiological life. In brief, life vitality and personhood can no longer be accepted as coterminous or synonymous concepts. More than organismic vitality is at stake, as far as humans are concerned. In everyday life this is clear in the concern expressed that people have sufficient nutrition and an income to enable them to have decent housing and education and the opportunity to engage in socio-political and cultural activities of their choice. Does mere physiological life have meaning apart from personal life? To say 'no' introduces the Nazi option. This is why the ethicist is obliged to affirm respect for all forms of life.

There is always the danger that to maintain a distinction between physiological and personal life can become a contradiction of the basic tenets of the Christian faith regarding God's sovereignty over human life. This is not necessarily the case. God's involvement in the history of humankind moves from creation through salvation into consummation. The triune God, as creator, redeemer and consummator, involves us as humans in this process in a fundamental way. Humans have a specific responsibility towards God, themselves, their fellow human beings and creatures of this world, as expressed in not only Genesis 1:26 but also in the Sabbath reality (Gen. 2:2f; Exod. 20:8; Lev. 25; Isa. 61; Luke 4:18ff). It is a responsibility to enhance and develop life in all its facets though our actions, as guided by God in precepts such as found in Exodus 20:1–17 or Matthew 5:3–12. In certain circumstances, this holistic approach to life requires death.

Every facet of our lives (including our death) is drawn into this mission of God, which is to affirm the fullness of life for all of God's creation. If a life is taken, Exodus 20:13 reminds us, it should not be an act which arises out of feelings of hatred and malice. Motives are important. If euthanasia is not rooted in a genuine compassion for the person, it is murder. Real compassion seems to be the only ground for euthanasia in its different forms.

In the light of what has been said about God's will and our responsibility to share in the work of God, the mere desire to terminate life in order to escape pain and suffering or even the humiliating experience of total dependence and helplessness is not enough. Theologically, it can only be justified when a person can no longer experience and contribute towards life-enrichment. And it is not always easy to know when that time has come. Nevertheless, perhaps I have the right to ask for my life to be ended in such circumstances. When others are asked to judge when I have reached this stage presents an even more awesome decision.

Are we not playing God when doing so? Two comments must suffice. First, if taking a life is to be forbidden on the grounds that only God has the right to determine how long a person shall live and when, where and how a person should die, then clearly any medical intervention that saves life is also forbidden. Secondly, this kind of thinking equates God's will with natural processes. It leaves no room for human responsibility.

[1] 1992 (4) SA 630 (D).

Select Bibliography

Anderson, J. K. 'Euthanasia: A Biblical Appraisal'. *Bibliotheca Sacra,* 144 (1987), pp. 208–217

Hamel, R. (ed.) *Choosing Death: Active Euthanasia, Religion, and the Public Debate.* Philadelphia: Trinity Press, 1991

McCormick, R. A. 'The New Medicine and Morality'. *Theology Digest,* 21 (1973), pp. 308–321

Nelson, J. B. and J. S. Rohricht. *Human Medicine: Ethical Perspectives on Today's Medical Issues.* Minneapolis: Augsburg, 1984

Rachels, J. 'Active and Passive Euthanasia'. *New England Journal of Medicine,* 292 (1975), pp. 78–80

Skoglund, E. R. *Life on the Line: Critical Choices You Must Face.* Minneapolis: World Wide Publications, 1989

Smith, H. L. *Ethics and the New Medicine.* Nashville: Abingdon, 1979

Vorster, W. S. *The Right to Life: Issues in Bioethics.* Pretoria: Unisa, 1988

Wennberg, R. N. *Terminal Choices: Euthanasia, Suicide, and the Right to Die.* Grand Rapids: Eerdmans, 1989

14:1

Political Ethics

CHARLES VILLA-VICENCIO

Does theology have a constructive contribution to make to the political process? The track record of the church is not a good one in this regard. Its history is shot through with examples of theologically legitimised political triumphalism and economic greed. When Constantine managed to grab the imperial throne from his political rivals, Christians rewrote their political theology in response to the Emperor's willingness to open up the political sphere to Christians, who had hitherto been regarded as politically undesirable. Medieval Europe was conquered in the name of Christ, and the Protestant Reformation was as much a theologised struggle for independence as it was a religious movement.

Columbus colonised the Americas bearing the cross and the sword, and the conquistadores, blessed by the church, slaughtered the Aztecs, Mayas, Incas and other indigenous nations. Kaiser Wilhelm sent his troops into battle with *Gott mit Uns* inscribed on their buttons. 'German Christians' promoted the ideals of Nazism. British soldiers fought and died 'for God, Queen and country' in British colonies scattered across the globe, and Christian symbolism is today still part of the United States of America's ideology of global conquest. In South Africa apartheid was underpinned by a theological justification.

On the other hand, there are examples of individuals and groups throughout the history of the institutional churches who have fought against oppression. In Latin and Central America some within the church have been directly involved in the liberation struggle of their countries. In South Africa some Christians have similarly been at the forefront of resistance against apartheid. There is not, however, a great deal of evidence of effective *liberatory* church-based participation in nation-building and reconstruction.[1]

Bluntly stated, theology sometimes works well in combating political abuse, but can become a dangerous device in the arena of power. Paul Tillich has suggested that while 'a mighty weapon in warfare', theologies of resistance are often 'an inconvenient tool for use in the building trade'.[2] His concern was with Barth's insistence that the most important theological contribution to be made, not only in oppressive regimes but in *all* political situations, was to say no to all political endeavour that could give rise to a sense of human pride and achievement.

Reflecting on reconstruction in Europe after the First World War and the failure of the 1918 Russian Revolution to realise what he and many European socialists had expected, Barth feared that a theological 'yes' might be the first step down the slippery slope to political triumphalism and tyranny. 'Grace', said Barth, 'is the axe laid at the root of the good conscience which the politician and the civil servant always wish to enjoy . . .'[3] 'God's revolution', he thought, not only condemns the tyranny of unjust rulers, it also demands more than what even the most socially responsible governments can offer.[4] This is the source of what Paul Lehmann has called Barth's theology of 'permanent revolution', giving rise to a political incentive which powerfully militates against any tendency to sacralise or absolutise any political ideology.[5]

This kind of theology was an important political incentive in oppressive situations, such as Nazi Germany, within which Barth wrote. It has also been a powerful ingredient in theological resistance in South Africa. Furthermore, it has a significant contribution to make in situations of political stability, working against political complacency where the danger always exists of the nation being elevated to the level of an absolute. The existence of national security ideologies, which dominate in many first and third world situations, locating the state 'beyond the reach of judicial norms, beyond good and evil', is a stark vindication of a theology of radical critique.[6] Differently stated, the eschatological dimension of theology provides an important contribution to any political process. It provides an incentive to vigilance against tyranny, and promotes continuing political renewal.

In emerging nations and situations of reconstruction, however, sometimes plagued as they are by internal divisions or suffering in the aftermath of prolonged and exacting wars, the primary theological task is often a different one. Here the church is frequently required to share in the creation of a culture of national unity, one given to tolerance, compromise and moderation. History suggests that in this situation resistance theology more often than not surrenders its prophetic task, becoming yet another legitimating theology. Alternatively, being an 'inconvenient tool in the building trade' (Tillich), it destabilises the emerging new society, and sometimes becomes an instrument in the hands of reactionary forces.

Having learned how easy it is for theologians to provide theological legitimation to political ideologies, some within the church are reluctant to leave the realm of theory, in concretising their ethical proposals. Karl Rahner identified a related risk. He warned: 'The church can be wide off the mark in such imperatives and directives' and 'more palpably [so] than in theoretical declarations.' This does not, however, mean that the church dare avoid risking itself in much the same way as any other participant in the political process. 'This', suggests Rahner, 'is a risk that must be taken if the church is not to seem to be pedantic, to be living in a world of pure theory, remote from life, making pronouncements that do not touch the stubborn concreteness of real life.'[7] The essays on violence and the legitimate use of force, human rights, economic justice, ecology, and the use of land that follow in this book all constitute attempts to engage theology constructively in the reconstruction process.

At the centre of the debate on political ethics lies the question of the creative relationship between eschatological critique and concrete proposal. It has to do with learning to know when to say no to political proposals and when to say yes – not because the political initiative is necessarily synonymous with the ideals of the gospel, but because it is perhaps the next logical and tentative step in the continuing process of renewal.

In brief, constructive political theology has to do with Christians being prepared to soil their hands while sharing with others in constructing political, socio-economic and other initiatives that better serve the poor – to whom the Scriptures require us to show a preferential option. We, at the same time, need to ensure that there is at the centre of all political debate what Horkheimer calls the 'theological moment' – a space for critique, openness and continuing renewal within the reconstruction process. Without this, Horkheimer suggests, 'no matter how skilful, [politics] in the last analysis is mere business.'[8] Political theological ethics is ultimately about the promotion of ongoing renewal and change. It has to do with what Lehmann calls the 'permanent revolution'.

[1] See Charles Villa-Vicencio, *A Theology of Reconstruction: Nation Building and Human Rights* (Cambridge: Cambridge University Press; Cape Town: David Philip, 1992). Also James Cochrane and Gerald West, 'War, Remembrance and Reconstruction', *JTSA*, 84 (September 1993).

[2] Paul Tillich, 'What is Wrong with Dialectical Theology?', *Journal of Religion,* 15 (1935), p. 135.

[3] Karl Barth, *The Epistle to the Romans* (London: Oxford University Press, 1960), p. 430.

[4] Ibid., pp. 475–502. Also my 'Karl Barth's Revolution of God: Quietism or Anarchy?' in C. Villa-Vicencio (ed.), *On Reading Karl Barth in South Africa* (Grand Rapids: Eerdmans, 1988), pp. 45–58.

[5] Paul Lehmann, 'Karl Barth, Theologian of Permanent Revolution', *Union Seminary Quarterly Review*, 28 (1972).

[6] *Pro Mundi Vita Bulletin: The Churches of Latin America in Confrontation with the State and the Ideology of National Security,* 71 (March–April 1978), p. 7. Also José Comblin, *The Church and the National Security State* (Maryknoll: Orbis Books, 1979), p. 72.

[7] Karl Rahner, *The Shape of the Church to Come* (London: SPCK, 1974), p. 79.

[8] M. Horkheimer, 'Die Sehnsucht nach dem ganz Andern: Ein Interview mit Kommentaar von Helmut Gumnoir' (Hamburg: Furche, 1975), p. 60.

14:2

War, Violence and Revolution

MALUSI MPUMLWANA

War, violence and revolution can mean both life and death. Where they lead to the restoration of the good life, they are instruments of the common good. Where they lead to absolute misery without prospects for meaningful improvement of the overall situation, they are an agency of death.

In what follows, the traditional theological positions on violence are identified, the limitations of these positions are analysed, and a proposal is made to broaden the theological-ethical discussion on violence.

The Traditional Position

In the history of Christian ethics, three positions have developed on war and violence: pacifism, just war theory, and crusade theology. For the first three centuries of the church, pacifism was the dominant and certainly the only theologically recognised position of early Christians.[1] They refused to serve in the army of a state that did not acknowledge their God. They also refused to resort to violence in self-defence against the persecution of the state.

With the Edict of Milan, the state adopted a new attitude to the church, giving Christians the right to proclaim the gospel in an unhindered manner. Order was established in the empire, and the 'peace' of Constantinian rule prevailed. It was a militarily imposed peace. The church came to terms with this, and changed its hitherto pacifist stance.

Borrowing liberally from the Hebrew Bible and Stoicism, Ambrose of Milan began to develop just war teaching as a Christian ethical position. This holds that force or violence can be justifiably used in certain circumstances. Augustine consolidated the doctrine, and soon the church came to accept those criteria that are today regarded as part of the just war theory. These are that a war should have a just cause (or be a better evil), its end or purpose should be just, it should be declared by a legitimate authority, it should be used only as a last resort, and it should be conducted by just means.[2]

Crusade theology used (or rather abused) just war theory to sanction war as a means of promoting the ideals of the gospel. Already anticipated in Ambrose's notion of the righteousness of war in defence of the empire, the crusades were seen as a means of defending the empire for the sake of the church.

Summing up the three positions, R. H. Bainton says:

> Pacifism has commonly despaired of the world and dissociated itself either from society altogether, or from political life, and especially from war. The advocates of the just war theory have taken the position that evil can be restrained by the coercive power of the state. The church should support the state in this endeavour and individual Christians as citizens should fight under the auspices of the state. The crusade belongs to a theocratic view that the church, even though it be a minority, should impose its will upon a recalcitrant world.[3]

In time, a further theological option on violence emerged, which is the notion of just revolution. Jacques Ellul provides the parameters of what is involved:

> If the prince is a tyrant by reason of the origin of his power (usurpation, violence): in this case, every citizen has the duty of killing him. If the prince is a tyrant by reason of the abuses of power he commits against the 'republic': in this case, the people's representatives must pronounce a judgement (secret, of course!), but private persons will have to carry out the sentence (by assassination). Finally, if the tyrant wrongs private persons, they may not avenge themselves; only the whole people, or the 'public powers', can revolt. In all these cases, the tyrant is a public enemy.[4]

In the South African situation, the question of the theological 'understanding' of the inevitability of armed struggle against the apartheid power structure became a hotly contested issue in the 1980s.[5] However, the real debate was not whether violence was ethically permissible in principle, but whether the South African regime was evil enough to warrant it.

Problems with the Traditional Debate

The traditional Christian ethical debate on violence has mostly centred on war. This has determined what constitutes violence, and has limited effective Christian teaching on a whole range of ethical dilemmas related to other manifestations of violence.

Other Forms of Violence

David Levinson helpfully defines violence as 'an act carried out with the intention or perceived intention of physically hurting another person'.[6] This definition justifies talk of economic and ecological violence, sexual violence and family violence. War is not the only form of violence with which the church should concern itself. *All* forms of violence — whatever hurts people and violates the commandment to love one another — require the theological attention of the church.

Violence is often a socio-psychological phenomenon, manifest in the syndrome of superiority and primacy of interests. This amounts to the 'bullyboy' tendency, whereby an individual or a group becomes preoccupied with its own sense of self-importance and superiority, leaving little room for the humanity of others, except to the extent that they are subordinated to the dominant group.

Violence also manifests itself in the syndrome of self-hate and self-denigration, which is often a direct consequence of the superiority syndrome. In the case of black people in South Africa, self-hate is often projected onto other black persons. One consequence of this is a willingness by blacks to exploit and act violently against other blacks because they are 'black like me'. The root of the so-called black-on-black violence is partly to be found in this phenomenon.

The insecurity syndrome is a further dimension of violence. This is the tendency for people to use power to intimidate and subdue others, out of their own sense of insecurity or inferiority. Feeling insecure, they abuse others.

Finally, we may speak of cultural conditioning as a manifestation of violence. In many cultures around the world, violence is culturally inculcated and legitimised. Such culturally conditioned violence is often of a domestic kind, seen in spouse-beating (usually of women by men), sibling violence and child-beating. Other forms of family violence include incest, the abuse of the aged, and marital rape. There is also corporal punishment and violence applied in various traditional rites and judicial systems. Violence in these situations is culturally and socially legitimised. In some instances the right to inflict violence is seen as a sign of social standing, if not a moral virtue.

The inadequacy of the traditional ethical debate on violence, which is limited to the question of war (to the exclusion of other forms of violence), is a serious indictment on the church. By refusing to concern itself theologically with the forms of violence we have identified, in the same manner in which it has traditionally concerned itself with the question of war, the church fails to give sufficient attention to forces that drive people to violence, revolution and war.

Force and Violence

A further limitation of traditional teaching on violence is contained in Jacques Ellul's observation: 'The *state is invested with force*; it is an organism instituted and ordained by God, and remains such even when it is unjust; even its harshest acts are not the same thing as the angry or brutal deed of the individual. The *individual* surrenders to his passions, *he commits violence*.'[7] As Ellul notes, the violent activities of the state are invested with moral correctness, divesting the individual or group of any moral justification for the use of force. This distinction is challenged by liberation theology.[8] Focusing on human emancipation, liberation theology refuses to exempt the state from the censure on violence which the church directs against individuals and revolutionary groups.

There are three points of concern that need to be looked at in relation to this issue. Firstly, there is the tendency to equate the government with the state. Sovereignty must be unambiguously vested in the nation-state, as represented by a constitution that puts a high premium on human rights. This locates the state above the government. The latter is only a temporal agent of the state, whose sovereignty cannot be reduced to the level of the government. If and when a government violates the well-being of the state, it needs to be censured and, if need be, removed from office.

Secondly, consideration should be given to the role and influence of individuals and lobby groups on government policy, as well as the capacity of the state ideology to conceal such interests. Class, racial, ethnic, gender and party interests are often served in the name of the state.

Thirdly, we need to look out for the bias of ethicists who makes pronouncements on questions of violence, in determining what constitutes legitimate force and what is illegitimate violence. The point of the social location of the ethicist is well summarised by Leonardo Boff:

> The faithful in the church occupy objectively different social positions according to their social class. They perceive reality in a way that corresponds to their social conditions, and so they interpret and live the gospel message out of the needs, interests and behaviour of their particular class. Thus actions that are possible, tolerant, recommended, necessary or demanding vary from one social class to another.[9]

The distinction made between the 'force' of the state and the 'violence' of the individual is directly related to whether one recognises the legitimacy of government — or even that of the state. Suffice it to say, ethical debate on violence must begin with a social analysis of the situation within which the violence occurs and the nature of the violence being perpetrated.

From Pacifism to Realistic Compromise: An Ethical Problem

Concerned with the ethical compromise in the transition from pacifism to just war, Bishop Sigqibo Dwane says:

> History is full of examples of situations in which the church has had recourse to violence and to the doctrine of just war. . . It is important [however] for modern Christians to come face to face with the stark realisation that early Christians found violence and bloodshed shocking and disconcerting. This reality should challenge Christians who serve in both conventional and revolutionary armies.[10]

Dwane's concern is to keep the challenge of the early church before the eyes of present-day Christians. At the same time he realises that 'Once the step of accepting and justifying violence under certain circumstances had been taken, however special those circumstances, the church lost its pristine innocence. Christian identity could never be the same again.'[11]

The theological problem facing the church is how to hold the challenge of the early church and the need to compromise on the use of violence in a creative tension. The logic goes something like this: The Christian church is fundamentally pacifist, but under certain circumstances there may and probably should be a need to consider the use of violence to prevent a greater evil. From a theological-ethical perspective, the pertinent question is whether it is possible to establish viable criteria by which to measure any deviation from the norm of pacifism.

Rather than simply seeking to articulate those criteria (which is essentially what just war theory does), an option for Christians is to promote actively the values of the reign of God — within which human persons are seen to be of inherent worth. This requires a holistic ethical approach to the question of violence, grounded in the conviction that human beings are created in the image of God. This is an image of holiness and love, and also of freedom, for God is under no compulsion. More than that, God's image is an image of creative power.

We consider here only the image of power. To say that God's power is present in human nature is to say that the disempowerment of people is a form of dehumanisation. Paul Tillich identifies power with what he calls the will and the need 'to be'. For him, in order 'to be' one must experience the power of being.[12] To the extent that power is denied or suppressed (prevented from coming to creative expression in society), the will 'to be' is manifest in other ways — through coercion, violence and in other forms of non-social behaviour. The 'will to be' is driven to almost any length to overcome the threat of non-being.[13] In other words, resort to violence is for Tillich a necessary manifestation, in some situations, of what it means to be human. Where human power is denied expression, violence is inevitable. Bluntly stated, an act of violence is sometimes the only course of action open to an abused or oppressed person who either has or knows no other way of giving expression to his or her humanity. 'Human beings', Tillich insists, 'cannot renounce being human.'[14]

Tillich's insights into coercion and violence as human self-expression have obvious implications for the theological debate on violence. The question is: At what point is force illegitimate? Tillich's answer is that compulsion and (where appropriate) violence are a necessity only to the extent that they are essential to overcome non-being. 'Power needs compulsion, but compulsion needs the [limiting] criterion which is implied in an actual power relation. . . If compulsion trespasses this limit, it becomes self-denying and undercuts the power which it is supposed to preserve.'[15]

For Tillich, manifestations of human power are a necessity in the quest 'to be'. Where there are no creative ways for this to be manifest, it will eventually be expressed in violence and non-social forms of behaviour. Herein lies the basis for the argument (often advanced) that violence is necessary for survival, for security and for countering the prospect of annihilation. Herein lies also the basis for a compromise between pacifism and just war or just revolution.

A Theological Epilogue

Through the life, death and resurrection of Christ, the human person, created in the image of God, is given new power. This is the saving and liberating power of Christ, which calls us to act in a life-giving way against all oppressive realities — before they gather enough force to threaten the very being of humanity. This holistic and proactive Christian ethic constitutes the most effective way of countering violence. As a life-empowering ethic, it allows at the same time that sometimes violence — as a means of affirming one's own life — is inevitable.

The approach is holistic because it addresses all possible experiences of violence with the same degree of concern for the dignity and power of being. It can be adequately applied to the concern for environmental violence, marital violence and economic violence. In essence it suggests that where being (whether in humanity or nature) is violated, violence in one form or another is likely to follow.

It is also a proactive ethic because it functions with the energy of an evangelical imperative. It seeks to promote in all situations of social experience — in families, in neighbourhoods, in social, economic and political institutions, in national and international relations, in war and revolution — a stance on violence that is energised by a faith in resurrection, a faith that heralds victory over death, a faith that rebels against the reduction of being to non-being. It is a faith that lifts those reduced to naught into 'being somebody'. To this end it is an ethic that refuses to wait for revolutionary war in order to pronounce and act against the injustices that give rise to revolutions. It seeks to affirm life (being) and oppose death (non-being) as part of Christian living.

[1] See Sigqibo Dwane, 'Early Christians and the Problem of War', in Charles Villa-Vicencio (ed.), *Theology and Violence* (Johannesburg: Skotaville, 1987), pp. 133–146.

[2] For a full treatment of the subject, see Douglas S. Bax, 'From Constantine to Calvin: The Doctrine of the Just War', in Villa-Vicencio (ed.), *Theology and Violence,* pp. 147–172.

[3] R. H. Bainton, *Christian Attitudes Toward War and Peace* (Nashville: Abingdon Press, 1960), p. 15

[4] J. Ellul, *Violence: Reflections from a Christian Perspective* (New York: Seabury, 1969), p. 21.

[5] Charles Villa-Vicencio, 'The Ecumenical Debate: Violent Revolution and Military Disarmament,' in Villa-Vicencio (ed.), *Theology and Violence,* pp. 233–253.

[6] David Levinson, *Family Violence in Cross-Cultural Perspective* (New York: Sage Publications, 1989), p. 11.

[7] Ellul, *Violence,* p. 3, my emphasis.

[8] See Paul Germond, 'Liberation Theology: Theology in the Service of Justice', in Villa-Vicencio (ed.), *Theology and Violence,* pp. 215–232.

[9] Quoted in Frank Chikane, 'Where the Debate Ends', in Villa-Vicencio (ed.), *Theology and Violence,* p. 305.

[10] Dwane, 'Early Christians', p. 137.

[11] Ibid., p. 144.

[12] *Love, Power and Justice: An Ontological Analysis of Ethical Implications* (New York: Oxford University Press, 1954), p. 37.

[13] Ibid., p. 47.

[14] Paul Tillich, *The Socialist Decision* (New York: Harper and Row, 1977), p. 44.

[15] Tillich, *Love, Power and Justice,* p. 48.

14:3

Human Rights

NJONGONKULU NDUNGANE

The notion of human rights has become one of the key elements in the establishment of justice and peace in any society. This is often expressed by reference to international documents such as the United Nations Declaration of Human Rights of 1948, the European Convention for Human Rights of 1956, and the African Charter of Human and People's Rights of 1981. These international instruments, as well as many others like them, are used by human rights groups as a basis for challenging violations of human rights in various countries. They are also used by people who are engaged in nation-building and desirous of lasting peace in their countries.[1]

What lies behind the formulation of these international instruments is an inherent desire of human beings to live in peace with one another. The horror and shock of two world wars prompted people to look for positive and practical ways to establish a lasting world peace. The United Nations organisation is but one result of such an effort. In the preamble to the United Nations Charter, the notion of human rights is 'mentioned almost for the first time in an international treaty'.[2]

> We the peoples of the United Nations
> determined to save succeeding
> generations from the scourge of war,
> which twice in our lifetime has
> brought untold sorrow to mankind
> and to reaffirm faith in fundamental
> human rights, in the dignity and
> worth of the human person. . .
> to practise tolerance and live together
> in peace with one another as
> good neighbours. . .

The inclusion of the notion of human rights in the Charter, as A. H. Robertson suggests, may have been due to the fact that 'the drafters of the Charter were looking behind the facts of war to its causes, one of which had been shown by experience to be the existence of dictatorship. An international order which can effectively secure human rights is thereby taking a major step towards the prevention of war.'[3] A desire for lasting peace is, therefore, one of the fundamental motives behind the advocacy of human rights.

The quest for lasting peace in South Africa has been a major driving force behind the demand for a Bill of Rights to be enshrined in a new, democratic constitution. The history of South Africa has been a very tragic one. It has been characterised by oppression, exploitation and a denial of human rights to the vast majority of its inhabitants. In the transition from apartheid to democracy, it has become necessary to have a Bill of Rights which enshrines fundamental human rights,[4] to enable a nation that has been torn apart to move towards greater justice.

What Are Human Rights?

Human rights are so called because they are the kind of rights that belong to human beings simply by virtue of their personhood.

> The human person possesses rights because of the very fact that it is a person, a whole, a master of itself and of its acts and which is not merely a means to an end but an end which must be treated as such. The dignity of the human person signifies that by virtue of natural law, the human person has the right to be respected, is the subject of rights. These are the things which are owed to man [a person] because of the very fact that he [or she] is a man [person].[5]

> Men [human beings] live surrounded by a pattern of rights and duties whose claims upon them are quite independent of their attitude towards them and which lays upon them obligations which are binding upon them whether they choose to accept them or not.[6]

A human right belongs to all people everywhere regardless of status or position in life. As J. E. J. Fawcett says, 'human rights might be better called "common rights" for they are rights and freedoms which do not depend for their exercise upon the holder belonging to any particular community, group or category; they are the rights of all human beings'.[7] Universality, therefore, is the main feature of a human right.

There are other kinds of rights which we may term 'institutional' or 'professional' rights; that is to say, the kind of rights that belong to people because of their profession or position in society. We talk about 'the rights of students,' 'the rights of judges,' 'the rights of university lecturers' and 'the rights of cricketers'. Similarly, we can talk of 'the right of workers'. These are, however, not human rights, as they cannot meet the requirements of universal applicability.

The Basis of the Notion of Human Rights

The natural law tradition has been closely associated with the notion of human rights, having influenced the conception as well as the development of the human rights idea. There are two main features that are common to all natural law theories. One is that there is a human nature that is shared by all people; the other is that there is an objective moral standard which is accessible to reason and forms the basis of human rights. Human beings are aware that there exists in the nature of things some kind of standard or pattern which is independent of our choices but which has authority over our actions. We are conscious that there are general laws in nature which tell us that some acts are good and others are bad.

One of the classic examples of the application of the natural law concept is found in Sophocles' play *Antigone*. In this play, Creon, King of Thebes, had pronounced an edict forbidding the burial of traitors who die on the battlefield; according to the edict, they were to be left to be eaten by dogs and vultures. One such traitor was Polynices. His sister Antigone revolted against the whole idea and proceeded to bury Polynices. She was, of course, arrested and brought before Creon.

Antigone's claim was that the 'imperative of morality', whose basis is 'the unwritten and unfailing statutes of heaven', lays down some obligations regarding the treatment of human beings. In this particular case, human beings are entitled to a decent burial irrespective of who they are — whether they are traitors or not. The significance of this story is that Antigone established a very important principle that there is a higher law which is above the positive law of the state and which has greater authority. This higher law constitutes a basis for challenging the unlimited powers of states.

Peter and the Apostles applied the same principle when they were brought before the Jewish Council for preaching the good news of the risen Christ, saying, 'We must obey God rather than men' (Acts 5:29). The notion of a higher law that is superior to positive law is therefore, among other things, 'a safeguard against the usurpation by the State of unlimited power'.[8]

Inspired by Stoic philosophy, Cicero described some very significant elements of natural law. In *De Republica* he stated that natural law derives its authority from God. God is its 'promulgator and its enforcing judge'. He speaks of the universal nature of this law: it is applicable to all people, in Rome and Athens alike. Its obligations were binding on all human beings. 'We cannot be freed from its obligations by Senate or people.'

Cicero clearly understood humanity as a universal community bound together by an eternal order, which regulates the affairs of humanity. That is why there is a wide measure of agreement on many moral issues among diverse nations of the world drawn from various social, racial, cultural, religious and political traditions. The existence of international instruments for the protection of human rights is a good example of this.

The biblical tradition also provides a basis for the notion of human rights. It places a high value on a human being's personality, and expresses a person's distinctiveness in the concept of the *imago Dei*. The Genesis narratives describe human beings as having been created in the image of God. God said, 'And now we will make human beings; they will be like us and resemble us' (Gen. 1:26). Although individuals are different from one another, they nevertheless share a common humanity in that they are created in the image of God. The image of God in human beings binds them together, thereby establishing a basis for the obligation for each to care for the other's welfare.

Creation in the image of God is also held to signify that a person is a unique being with intrinsic worth and dignity. 'The dignity of [a person] is the dignity of the image of God.'[9] The idea that a person possesses rights is understood to follow directly from this. This is reflected in the preambles of some international instruments for the protection of human rights.[10]

The book of Genesis depicts human beings as created for a life of fellowship with one another. When the first man was provided with a woman, he burst out in jubilation, saying: 'This at last is bone of my bone and flesh of my flesh' (Gen. 2:23). This kind of formula is common for claiming relationship in the Semitic world. 'What is claimed and recognised is that you and others are all part of one living organism.'[11] The man recognises the woman as a being of the same kind as he is, as someone with whom he can enter into a relationship. Genesis, therefore, gives us a picture of the human being as a social animal with a capacity to enter into personal relationships with other fellow human beings.

The community aspect of our humanity is given much emphasis in the African world-view in expressions like *umuntu ngumuntu ngabantu* (a person is a person through others). Tiyo Soga endorsed this when he said: 'We Africans, by origin, have a deep-rooted sense of relationship and friendship.'[12] In the words of John Donne, 'No man is an island entire of itself: every man is a piece of the continent, a part of the main.' No person can exist without the help, company and co-operation of other persons. As Aquinas says, 'it is natural for a [human being] to be a social and political animal living in community; and this is more true of him [or her] than of any other animal, a fact which is shown by his [or her] natural necessities.'[13]

Mutual interdependence, therefore, is of the very essence of being human. Respect for one another's dignity and personal integrity is an essential ingredient of harmonious relations in every society. There is, therefore, a natural requirement for each society to guarantee basic human rights to its members. For it is in society that a person's dignity and worth as a rational and free being, created and loved by God, is safeguarded, and that people can develop to their full potential.

A Bill of Rights

In the light of all this, it is vital to have a Bill of Rights which enshrines individual human rights and freedoms. However, the effectiveness of any Bill of Rights depends largely on the existence of an independent judiciary that is capable of interpreting not only the letter but also the spirit of the law and of judging the political processes and politicians themselves. Politics and power must be under God and the law.

Furthermore, it is conceivable that some international measures could be established to ensure the protection of human rights. The international instruments for the protection of human rights serve a useful function in so far as they create an awareness of basic human rights. An internationally recognised authority, together with some international committee, possibly under the auspices of the United Nations, might act as a court of arbitration, where citizens or groups acting on their behalf could present complaints of violations of human rights. Such international channels of communication would not only provide the people of South Africa with a much needed guarantee and protection by the international community; they would also act as a deterrent against any government's misuse of power.

[1] See Charles Villa-Vicencio, *A Theology of Reconstruction: Nation Building and Human Rights* (Cape Town: David Philip, 1992).

[2] A. H. Robertson, *Human Rights in Europe* (Manchester: Manchester University Press, 1977), p. 2.

[3] Ibid., p. 2.

[4] See for example Albie Sachs, *Protecting Human Rights in a New South Africa* (Cape Town: Oxford University Press, 1990).

[5] J. Maritain, *The Rights of Man and Natural Law* (London: The Centenary Press, 1944).

[6] H. P. Owen, 'Nature and Morality', in G. R. Dunstan (ed.), *Duty and Discernment* (London: SCM Press, 1975), p. 29.

[7] J. E. S. Fawcett, 'Human Rights: The Applicability of International Instruments' in F. E. Dowrick (ed.), *Human Rights: Problems and Perspectives* (Westmead: Saxon House, 1979), p. 78.

[8] J. Macquarrie, *Three Issues in Ethics* (London: SCM, 1970), p. 99.

[9] *Acta Apostolicae Sede*, XXXVII (1945), 15, p. 29.

[10] See preambles to the *Canadian Bill of Rights*, the *Universal Declaration of Human Rights* and the *American Declaration of the Rights and Duties of Man*.

[11] T. W. Manson, *Ethics and the Gospel* (London: SCM Press, 1960), p. 16.

[12] *Intlalo Ka Xhosa* (Lovedale: The Lovedale Press, 1974), p. 102.

[13] Quoted from F. C. Copleston, *Aquinas* (Harmondsworth: Penguin Books, 1955), p. 236.

14:4

Economic Justice

JAMES COCHRANE

In economics, we are dealing with fundamental ways in which humans organise their life in the world, and profound realities which hurt or destroy millions. If our lives are to be shaped by our Christian commitments and values, we need to take economics seriously.

Economic justice has been at the forefront of ecumenical theological concern in the last four decades. But the roots of modern concerns with economic justice lie deep in the nineteenth century with the original 'Christian socialists' (Kingsley, Maurice and Ludlow) who emerged as a group in England at about the time Karl Marx and Friedrich Engels were drafting the *Communist Manifesto*. Witnessing the horrors of early industrial capitalism, especially in its harsh effects on children and women and on the urban environment, these Christian socialists were among the first to treat economics as a particular realm of life and a branch of knowledge. Later, other theologians elsewhere picked up the same concerns: Ragaz in Switzerland, Rauschenbusch in the USA, the early Tillich in Germany in the 1930s, and Oldham in England in the 1940s.

The impact of industrial capitalism and the rationalist movement of the Enlightenment had been to separate secular life from the authority of Christianity and the church. Now it became necessary to say why those in charge of the economy should have to listen to theological concerns, especially in view of the claim that economic policies and practices are secular matters best left to 'those who know'. It has become necessary, therefore, to show why theology should bother itself with economics, a human science which requires no god to explain such things as supply and demand laws.

However, we will find important articles of faith in Scripture which have everything to do with what we now call economics: 'If we find no ready-made economic solutions to our dilemmas, we nevertheless find in the biblical traditions the shape of God's economy to which, for Christians, our economic systems should correspond as much as possible under the conditions of history . . . God's 'law of the household' [*oikonomia*] is the economy of life against death. . .'[1]

What Are We Dealing With?

But first let us ask: What is economics? Perhaps it is easiest to recognise that economics deals with three processes which affect every human being in every age: production, distribution and consumption. What is produced, distributed and consumed? The answer in its simplest form is material goods. The science of economics is concerned with how we obtain, share out and use material goods. Human beings – and perhaps the machines they invent to extend their capacities (technology) – are the agents of economic processes.

Economics is a science which attempts to understand how economic processes can be regulated to achieve the best possible match of needs and scarce resources. This gives rise to a key concept in all modern economic theories: in all real societies there are always more needs than there are means to fulfil them. In other words, economics is the theory of scarcity. How can the limited goods that are available meet the always greater needs that are there?

Decisions about activities of production, distribution and consumption deeply affect the lives of anyone touched by them (most obviously those in unemployment). Who is to make such decisions? In simple societies, where productive processes are closely linked with distribution and consumption, this is an easier question to understand and resolve.

In a peasant farming community, everyone works together in small family units on a limited piece of land, to produce little more than is sufficient for their own needs, and perhaps enough surplus to barter for things they cannot produce themselves. What they produce is distributed within an extended family who consume it and, if there is a surplus, within a clan to which the family belongs. Ownership of the land, of the labour and technology to work it, is local and shared among the same people. Production processes are local, distribution of the products is local, and consumption is local. In order to survive, the scarce resources and the most important needs have to be organised communally. This kind of economy lies behind much of the teaching about sharing, communal ownership of goods and so on, which we find in the Bible.

But in a complex, increasingly industrialised society, production processes are unavoidably removed from local control, as is ownership of them. The same is true for labour and technology. Distribution processes are highly complex, and have given rise to a different form of exchange from direct barter of goods – namely money. Money is not a product but a symbol of value. Those who make the products do not own them or usually the right to distribute them (whether in a capitalist market economy or a centrally planned socialist economy). What those who make the products get is money which they can exchange for products in order to consume them. What they can consume depends upon the value of the product they want and how much money they have.

Economic processes in a complex society clearly no longer operate under local controls but in a highly differentiated, multi-level system of interlocking mechanisms of production, distribution and consumption which no society is fully able to control. Questions of who owns what and why, on what basis decisions are made to produce things and for whom, which needs are most important to fulfil with available resources, how and to whom available goods should be distributed, and what consumption patterns are beneficial for whom, do not disappear. They do become much more difficult to grasp as a whole, and much more resistant to the challenges of those who feel that injustice is done to them.

Why Deal with It?

Nevertheless, one only need think briefly about these questions to realise that they have everything to do with justice. Justice is so important to the God of the Bible that it cannot be imagined that theology should leave economics to the scientific experts and the politicians. As Duchrow says, for Christians not to involve themselves in economic matters 'amounts to a *de facto* abandonment of the economy to an autonomy exempted from any scrutiny in the light of Jesus Christ and the God revealed in him, in respect of love to God and the neighbour'.[2] Or, as Boesak argues, 'In the end God is tolerated in his area: that of religion. The other areas become completely autonomous, with their own laws, their own way of doing things, completely shut off from the Torah and the prophets.'[3]

Duchrow notes that Matthew 25:31—46 answers Bonhoeffer's important question, 'Who and where is Jesus Christ for us today?' Jesus comes to us in persons who are hungry, thirsty, homeless, naked, sick and imprisoned. Precisely those things which in economics would be called basic human needs are listed here — food, clothing, shelter, health care and, by implication, the basic political need for human dignity and integrity.

As in Old Testament prophetic literature, and in many things Paul writes about, God's justification is directly linked to God's justice. Yet human beings do not always, or even frequently, serve God's justice. Mammon, the god of wealth, and other similar gods may be an even greater attraction. Economic realities are as easily subject to idolatry as they are subject to the justice of the God of the Bible. As Frostin puts it, the spiritual problem in Western industrial capitalism 'is not that Westerners have lost interest in gods, but that they have vested their interest in a different god, most clearly seen in the economic system. Theologically speaking, the God and Father of Jesus Christ has been dethroned by Mammon.'[4]

In concrete contexts, such as ours, a theology of economic justice will have to do several things simultaneously: first, to recognise that in a world defined in economic terms as permanently faced with the problems of access to, use of and competition for scarce resources, we will not be able to meet all the needs of everyone at the same time, and we will have to make hard decisions about whose and which needs should be met and how; second, to avoid sinking into passive or reactionary attitudes and behaviour simply because this is so; and, third, to continue to proclaim and live out the profound Christian hope for something completely different, for a 'city of Jerusalem' on earth in which there will be no tears.[5]

Solidarity and Empowerment

Christian response-ability in a context where there has been an extreme skewing of productive resources, distribution channels and consumption capacities towards the white, rich inheritors of conquest and colonisation requires that questions of a new economic system, a new value for work, a new concept of labour, and a new understanding of the ownership of such things as land, must be taken with utmost seriousness.[6]

The witness of the church to economic reality requires it to enter into solidarity with those who suffer economic injustice. In doing so, it is called to unmask the idols whose interests are served by decisions taken concerning who produces, distributes and consumes what for whom, who has the right to make such decisions, and who owns the resources and the products of economic activity.

There is no necessary reason to accept that all these decisions are made best by experts, the wealthy, the powerful or anonymous market forces. There is every reason to believe that God's justice requires the church to understand the material aspect of redemption as including the task of empowering the poor, the oppressed and the marginalised. They must be able to take part in economic decisions which affect their lives, and those who are powerful, wealthy and expert should be unable to ignore the reality of their needs in managing God's 'household' (*oikonomia*). This is the concrete meaning of justice for the poor.

Unemployment: Example of Economic Devastation

We will explore the issue of unemployment to make the task of Christian economics clear, because it is a major impediment to justice, dignity and integrity for so many people in our land, and because it shows clearly the effects of an unjust economy on people.

The biblical witness is that 'creativity belongs to the essence of the human being . . . [In the fellowship of God] human beings are meant to participate in God's creative authority, God's redemptive love and God's comprehensive vision for a restored universe.'[7] This implies that humans are meant to contribute actively to the well-being of society, and that those who cannot will be deeply and badly affected. They will suffer, materially and spiritually.

Those who are unemployed may survive, but to be fully human, in God's image, they need empowerment and confirmation of the right of existence and of the meaningfulness of their lives.[8] What unemployment produces, however, is suffering in virtually all dimensions of life: physical, psychological, social and political. The effect of large numbers of unemployed people on society is also negative, for example in a rapid rise in crime. In essence, unemployed people are deprived of everything that God's economy demands.

What, then, does economic justice, understood as God's righteousness, require of us in the face of massive unemployment in South Africa? There are numerous practical responses to the problem of unemployment that might be considered,[9] but whatever one may try, 'the basic problem is how to harness the productive powers of technological advance and accumulating capital in such a way that it fulfils the needs of the suffering majority instead of the luxury consumption of the rich.' This in turn requires policies, and institutions at local, regional and national levels which embody these policies, 'directed against the concentration of both production and consumption in an elite and towards the spreading of both productive capacity and purchasing power in the population as a whole . . .'[10]

The witness and activity of the church means solidarity with the unemployed to facilitate and strengthen processes of empowerment within decision-making bodies at every level of economic life, and a prophetic challenge to the powerful and the affluent to understand the way in which their wholeness and redemption are linked to the good of the community as a whole. The church has the task of proclaiming God's economy of righteousness to all, of supporting initiatives and movements whose intentions approximate the concretisation of God's right-eousness in history, and of naming and unmasking the idols against whom the biblical God stands.

In sum, we may say with strong biblical and theological justification that 'economy exists for the sake of the human community and its relationship to God and the creation. The criterion of a just economic system will be whether it serves the life and future of this community.'[11] As Meeks points out, the biblical testimony to God the economist uncovers a radically different assumption from what we take as normal in our time: 'If the righteousness of God is present, there is always enough to go around.'[12]

[1] Douglas M. Meeks, *God the Economist: The Doctrine of God and Political Economy* (Minneapolis: Fortress Press, 1989), p. 3.

[2] *Global Economy: A Confessional Issue for the Churches?* (Geneva: World Council of Churches, 1987), p. 196.

[3] *The Finger of God* (Johannesburg: Ravan, 1979), p. 12.

[4] 'The Spiritual Crisis in the Metropolis of Capitalism'. Unpublished paper given at the Liberation Theology Seminar in the West European Context, Agape, Italy, 6–14 September 1986.

[5] J. R. Cochrane and G. O. West (eds), *The Threefold Cord: Theology, Work and Labour* (Pietermaritzburg: Cluster Publications, 1991), p. 280.

[6] See Charles Villa-Vicencio, *A Theology of Reconstruction* (Cape Town: David Philip, 1992) for a discussion of economic rights.

[7] K. Nürnberger, *The Scourge of Unemployment* (Pietermaritzburg: Encounter Publications, 1990), p. 8.

[8] Ibid., p. 9.

[9] See ibid. for some examples.

[10] Ibid., pp. 17–18.

[11] Meeks, *God the Economist*, p. 9.

[12] Ibid., p. 12.

Select Bibliography

Boesak, A. A. *The Finger of God*. Johannesburg: Ravan, 1979

Cochrane, J. R. and G. O. West (eds.) *The Threefold Cord: Theology, Work and Labour.* Pietermaritzburg: Cluster Publications, 1991

Duchrow, U. *Global Economy: A Confessional Issue for the Churches?* Geneva: World Council of Churches, 1987

Frostin, P. 'The Spiritual Crisis in the Metropolis of Capitalism.' Paper given at the Liberation Theology Seminar in the West European Context, Agape, Italy, September 1986

Meeks, M. Douglas. *God the Economist: The Doctrine of God and Political Economy.* Minneapolis: Fortress, 1989

Nürnberger, K. *The Scourge of Unemployment*. Pietermaritzburg: Encounter Publications, 1990

Tawney, R. *Religion and the Rise of Capitalism*. Harmondsworth: Penguin, 1972

Villa-Vicencio, C. *A Theology of Reconstruction*. Cape Town: David Philip, 1992

14:5

Ecology

JOHN DE GRUCHY AND DAVID FIELD

The current environmental crisis is the culmination of a number of interwoven factors. These include the poisoning of our planet through pollution; the degradation of the land through incorrect farming methods, resulting in soil erosion and desertification; the wasting and excessive use of the earth's non-renewable resources, particularly fossil fuels; the destruction of the earth's delicate ecological balance through the devastation of natural forests, resulting in increasing levels of carbon dioxide and major changes in weather patterns; and the daily extinction of plant and animal species, which affects the complex ecosystems of the planet and deprives us of potential resources of food and medicine. On top of all this, the exponential growth of the human population constantly multiplies the effect of all the other dimensions of the crisis.[1]

In South Africa, the problem has been exacerbated by apartheid. The 'homelands' have become ecological deserts as a result of overpopulation. The failure to provide basic water and energy supplies to urban and rural blacks has led to increasing pollution and deforestation. People were forcibly removed from areas to create nature reserves, and permission was given to pursue environmentally destructive projects despite the protests of those affected.[2] Grinding poverty and endemic violence have turned the life of the majority of South Africans into a struggle for survival. As a result, a concern for the environment is often seen as a pastime of the affluent. Yet no one can afford to ignore the destruction of the environment. The future survival of all is dependent upon our care and protection of the earth and its resources.[3]

The exact relationship between Christianity and the environmental crisis is a matter of debate.[4] But the complex interrelationship between Christianity and the expansion and hegemony of Western culture raises serious challenges for Christian theology and ethics. Two propositions are of particular significance in this regard. The first is that modern science, technology, capitalism and the ideology of progress, which provided an environmentally devastating combination in the eighteenth and nineteenth centuries, were often encouraged and legitimated by certain forms of Christian theology. At the same time, those elements within the Christian tradition which opposed the exploitation of the environment were suppressed by the dominant culture.

The second proposition is that interpretations of Christianity were ambiguous in their approach to issues involving the environment, and did not facilitate the development of a Christian environmental ethic.[5] This ambiguity has enabled some Christians to oppose the environmental movement,[6] and others to become active in Green politics.[7] In the light of this ambiguity and the environmental crisis facing us, it has become essential to critically re-examine the Christian tradition, and to develop a theological basis and framework for the development of a Christian environmental ethic.

Theology and Ecology

God and Creation

Some 'Green' thinkers and feminist theologians have proposed that Christianity's emphasis on a transcendent God, distinct from creation, has legitimated the exploitation of nature.[8] This is often contrasted with other religions which regard nature as in some sense divine or intimately linked to God or the gods. It is, of course, true that the biblical accounts of creation were deliberate attempts to combat such a deification of nature.[9] But this was not intentionally destructive of nature itself. The prophetic view of creation within the biblical tradition is a positive and holistic one. Regardless of the validity of the critique, however, a theological ethic of the environment will need to re-examine this relationship.[10]

Lawrence Osborn has proposed that one of the fundamental problems in Western Christianity's view of this relationship is that it has understood it in a monotheistic rather than in a trinitarian manner.[11] A fully trinitarian view of God's creative and providential activity enables one to see God as both distinct from creation and yet actively involved in it. This is problematic because it suggests that before a trinitarian theology developed, there was no concern for nature and the environment within the biblical tradition. That is patently not so. By the same token, trinitarian doctrine is no guarantee of a sound environmental ethic, though in principle it is more able to relate God and creation in ways which avoid the dangers of pantheism and deism.

Of particular importance in this regard is the recognition that creation is not to be understood only as an event in the past, but as an ongoing process. This means that God is actively involved in the life of the complex ecosystems of the earth and wider cosmos, as creator, renewer and sustainer. The doctrine of the Holy Spirit is pertinent, for it is the Spirit who is present within creation itself, seeking to sustain and renew it. Understood in this way, creation is not only a gift which points back to its giver, but is infused with God's presence. The ethical implication is that creation cannot be treated as though it were at the disposal of humanity to use and abuse as it likes.

Creation and Redemption

Much traditional Christianity has viewed salvation as an escape from the material universe to enjoy eternal bliss in heaven. Related to this has often been the conviction that the earth will soon pass away in some kind of apocalyptic cataclysm. This being so, there is no need to preserve and care for the environment. Over against such a distorted understanding of salvation, an ecological ethic will have to recover a sense of the cosmic scope of redemption.

The whole created order praises God (Ps. 148), and the vision of the messianic age encompasses all living creatures (Isa. 11:6–9; 41:17–20). Paul speaks of the created order groaning in anticipation of its liberation (Rom. 8:18–25), and the Colossian hymn to the cosmic Christ (Col. 1:15–20) describes salvation as a cosmic event. The Johannine Apocalypse depicts the *eschaton* as God coming to live within a renewed creation rather than as humanity growing to live with God (Rev. 21:1–4). God's covenantal purpose in both creation and redemption will only reach completion when the whole of creation unambiguously displays God's glory.

Thus redemption is not the negation of creation but the process through which it is brought to its fulfilment. The New Testament portrays Christ as the centre of both creation and redemption, for it is through his mediatorship that God's purpose for creation is achieved. In the same way, the Spirit's work in both creation and redemption is to draw the cosmos forward to its sabbath rest — its perfection. God's intimate concern for all of creation is demonstrated in God's entering into the suffering of creation in order to redeem it. Nowhere is this more dramatically portrayed than in the eucharistic celebration where bread and wine become a means of God's grace through the Spirit, mediating to believers the redemptive work of Christ.

Humanity and Nature

On the basis of a distorted reading of Genesis 1:28, the so-called cultural mandate, much Christian teaching has portrayed human beings as having a right to dominate the rest of creation. The created order, it has been argued, was made for us and only has significance in relation to us. Human beings thus have the right to do as they please with nature. More than that, it is their God-given duty to use it for their own benefit. In view of this anthropocentric attitude, it is not surprising that Christianity has been subjected to severe criticism by those who are rightly convinced that the degradation of the environment will only stop when we realise that we are not distinct from or superior to the rest of nature.

The Genesis narrative portrays the created order as having its own dignity and value even before the creation of human beings. It is this creation which declares 'the glory of God' (Ps. 19:1), and thus has the capacity to reveal God to humanity. Genesis affirms the value not only of human life but also of animal life (Gen. 9:4–6). Biblical anthropology locates human beings within this created order as an integral part of it, even though it also recognises an important distinction (Ps. 8). Human beings are embedded within a complex network of relationships with the rest of creation, but have the special responsibility to be the stewards of creation.

In view of this, Douglas Hall has proposed that the *imago Dei* is not something that humans have but rather something that they do.[12] The fact that we are accountable for the way in which we care for the earth implies 'that God has given humanity what it needs for actually being accountable'.[13] The abilities which distinguish human beings from the rest of creation and which enable them to modify their environment are the tools which make accountability possible. It is the abuse of this position which has resulted in the destruction of the environment. Biblically speaking, human will-to-power or sin — that is, a perverted sense of dominion — is the reason for the destruction of the environment. Hence the liberation of the environment is linked to the salvation of humanity (Rom. 8:18ff).

In environmental-exercising stewardship, we recognise creation as belonging to God, and accept accountability for our own role within it. This means further that we cannot exploit the environment for the benefit of a few, or even for our own generation. The human community extends to future generations, and thus in modifying or using creation with reference to it we should bear in mind the impact this may have on future environmental conditions.

Contours of an Ecological Ethic

The recognition that human life occurs within a complex web of ecological relationships provides the starting point for a fundamental revision of all ethical systems. The comprehensive nature of environmental considerations raises a new set of ethical norms, and demands the restructuring of the traditional relationships between them. All that can be attempted here is a brief sketch of the contours of such an ethic in the light of our previous theological discussion.

An Ecological Perspective

Fundamental to all else is the need to develop an ecological perspective on reality which views all of God's creation as an interconnected and interdependent system.[14] Individual creatures form part of complex ecosystems; individual ecosystems are connected in complex ways to other ecosystems. What takes place in one ecosystem can have diverse effects on other ecosystems right across the planet. From a theological perspective, this set of complex relationships is a manifestation of God's care for creation. Christian theology has traditionally recognised the interdependence of the human community. What now needs to be done is to extend this recognition to the rest of creation. Human sociality needs to be located within the ecosystem.

The Ethical Status of Non-Human Life

An ecological ethic would re-evaluate the ethical status that is given to non-human and particularly animal life. While there has been a growing rejection of cruelty to animals, they are still widely viewed as at the disposal of human beings. Cruelty that is seen to benefit humanity is regarded as legitimate, even if this involves merely the development of a new cosmetic. The ethical valuation of animal life is a complex issue,[15] but it must be affirmed that animals have an inherent ethical status which is not simply determined by their relationship with humanity. This must result in a re-evaluation of numerous activities which directly or indirectly affect the lives of animals, including such obvious issues as vivisection, farming and wildlife conservation. But it will also extend to any activities which affect the lives of animals. While plant life obviously falls into a different category, it too must be perceived to have ethical value as species and as components of ecosystems. The destruction of plant species and important components of ecosystems is not an ethically neutral activity.

Ecological Economics

Traditional economics views natural resources in purely financial terms. An ecological perspective proposes that natural resources and other components of the environment have a value that should not be measured in this way. The concept of value in economics must be expanded to include ecological value and should not be confined to monetary value. The use of natural resources must be seen in terms of its impact on the limited resources of the earth and on other aspects of the environment. Economic development which is financially profitable but environmentally expensive, whether through the destruction of local ecosystems, pollution or the radical depletion of non-renewable resources, must be rejected. This obviously raises complex issues in relation to human development. Nonetheless, individual development projects need to be seen in relation to the broader ecological reality. What might be of benefit to a small group of people in the short term may be disastrous for the planet and thus the human race. Policies of sustainable development must be pursued within an ecological framework.

This approach requires that non-renewable resources, such as fossil fuels, must be conserved, and alternative renewable resources found. These alternatives must not have a destructive impact on the environment. The financial cost of such development is justified by its ecological benefits for the present and the future. Renewable resources must be used in ways which enable them to be renewed, even if this is financially expensive. Agriculture, for example, needs to be pursued in such a manner that it does not destroy the fertility of the land. Every effort must be made to restore damaged ecosystems. All this obviously has serious implications for poor and developing countries, and therefore cannot be dealt with in isolation from a more just restructuring of the world economy. Such issues demonstrate how important it is that a Christian ethic for the environment be pursued ecumenically and internationally, for environmental issues transcend national boundaries.

Critique of the Consumer Society

While liberation theology calls for a lifestyle of solidarity with the poor, an ecological ethic recognises that the earth cannot sustain the consumer society of the 'developed' nations. Moreover, it is not possible to extend this lifestyle to all the inhabitants of the earth. All human beings bear the image of God and therefore all have an equal right to the earth's resources and a sustainable lifestyle.

The present inequalities are a violation of the creator's mandate. By the same token, all have an equal responsibility for the earth: the ideas and agendas of the 'developed' nations must not be imposed on the 'developing' nations.

Reproductive Responsibility

The earth's resources cannot provide for the exponential growth of the human population. A healthy environment with a substantial bio-diversity can only be maintained if the size of the human population is limited. An understanding of God's concern for and involvement with all of creation requires the recognition that the human population cannot be allowed to expand at the expense of the rest of creation. Respect for the value of the human person must be expressed through attempts to provide quality life for all human beings. An essential dimension of this is that human beings exercise reproductive responsibility.

Ecology and Christian Mission

If this framework is valid, ecological issues cannot be viewed as peripheral to the church's mission, but must rather be regarded as an integral part of its witness to the creative and salvific reign of God. As the church has been forced to re-examine its witness in relation to the oppression of human beings, so it is now called to do so in the light of the devastation of the environment. In doing so, the church needs to get its own house in order, as well as to issue a prophetic call to society.

[1] For a detailed investigation of the crisis and its implications for human life and development, see the report of the World Commission on Environment and Development, *Our Common Future* (Oxford: Oxford University Press, 1987).

[2] For an analysis of the environmental crisis in South Africa see Mamphela Ramphele and Chris McDowell (eds), *Restoring the Land: Environment and Change in Post-Apartheid South Africa* (London: Panos, 1991).

[3] See especially the work of Farieda Kahn in helping to bridge this gap between social deprivation and environmental concern in South Africa, e.g. 'Targeting Environmental Poverty: The Role of Community-based Greening Projects', *Veld and Flora*, 78:1 (March 1992).

[4] See for example L. White, 'The Historical Roots of Our Environmental Crisis', *Science*, 155 (1967), pp. 1203–1207; L. W. Moncrief, 'The Cultural Basis for Our Environmental Crisis', *Science*, 170 (1970), pp. 508–512; G. Osborn, *Guardians of Creation: Nature in Theology and the Christian Life* (Leicester: Apollos, 1993), pp. 24–40.

[5] See H. Paul Santmire, *The Travail of Nature: The Ambiguous Ecological Promise of Christian Theology* (Philadelphia: Fortress, 1985).

[6] An example of this approach is Calvin E. Beisner, *Prospects for Growth: A Biblical View of Population, Resources and the Future* (Westchester: Crossway, 1990).

[7] An example of this approach is found in Tim Cooper, *Green Christianity: Caring for the Whole of Creation* (London: Spire, 1990), Cooper is a prominent member of the British Green Party.

[8] Carol P. Christ, 'Rethinking Theology and Nature', in Judith Plaskow and Carol P. Christ (eds), *Weaving the Visions: Patterns in Feminist Spirituality* (San Francisco: Harper and Row, 1989); Sallie McFague, *Models of God: Theology for an Ecological, Nuclear Age* (Philadelphia: Fortress, 1987).

[9] There is, however, no evidence that this was linked to a greater degree of environmental exploitation in ancient Israel. See James Barr, 'Man and Nature: The Ecological Controversy in the Old Testament', *Bulletin of the John Rylands Library,* 55 (1972), pp. 9–32.

[10] An early but still relevant discussion of the issues is George S. Hendry, *Theology of Nature* (Philadelphia: Westminster, 1980).

[11] See Osborn, *Guardians of Creation,* pp. 101–115.

[12] Douglas John Hall, *Imaging God: Dominion as Stewardship* (Grand Rapids: Eerdmans, 1987). See also L. Wilkinson *et al.*, *Earthkeeping in the Nineties: Stewardship of Creation* (Grand Rapids: Eerdmans, 1991), pp. 308–311.

[13] Wilkinson *et al.*, *Earthkeeping,* p. 311.

[14] On a scientific level this been most powerfully advocated by James Lovelock in *Gaia: A New Look at Life on Earth* (Oxford: Oxford University Press, 1979). This scientific theory needs to be distinguished from the mystical and religious personification and divinisation of Gaia, which has been practised by some members of the environmental movement.

[15] See Tom Regan, *The Case for Animal Rights* (Berkeley: University of California Press, 1983); Andrew Linzey, *Christianity and the Rights of Animals* (New York: Crossroad, 1987); Wolfgang Huber, 'Rights of Nature or Dignity of Nature?', *The Annual of the Society of Christian Ethics* (1991), pp. 43ff.

Select Bibliography

Birch, C., W. Eakin and J. B. McDaniel. *Liberating Life: Contemporary Approaches to Ecological Theology.* Maryknoll: Orbis, 1990

Cooper, T. *Green Christianity: Caring for the Whole of Creation.* London: Spire, 1990

Hall, D. J. *Imaging God: Dominion as Stewardship.* Grand Rapids: Eerdmans, 1987

Moltmann, J. *God in Creation – An Ecological Doctrine of Creation,* trans. M. Kohl. London: SCM, 1985

Osborn, L. *Guardians of Creation: Nature in Theology and the Christian Life.* Leicester: Apollos, 1993

Primavesi, A. *From Apocalypse to Genesis: Ecology, Feminism and Christianity.* Minneapolis: Fortress, 1991

Ramphele, M. and C. McDowell (eds.) *Restoring the Land: Environment and Change in Post-Apartheid South Africa.* London: Panos, 1991

Robb, C. S. and C. J. Casebolt. *Covenant for a New Creation: Ethics, Religion and Public Policy.* Maryknoll: Orbis, 1991

Santmire, P. H. *The Travail of Nature: The Ambiguous Ecological Promise of Christian Theology.* Philadelphia: Fortress, 1985

Wilkinson, L., P. de Vos, C. de Witt, E. Dykema and V. Ehlers (eds) *Earthkeeping in the Nineties: Stewardship of Creation.* Grand Rapids: Eerdmans, 1980

World Commission on Environment and Development. *Our Common Future.* Oxford: Oxford University Press, 1987

14:6

Reparation and Land

WELI MAZAMISA

The land problem in South Africa is not only a political, economic and emotional reality; it is also an ethical issue of significance. The core issue involved is grounded in a universal reality articulated by Walter Brueggemann: 'The sense of being lost, displaced, and homeless is pervasive in contemporary culture. The yearning to belong somewhere, to have a home, to be in a safe place is a deep and moving pursuit. Loss of place and yearning for place are dominant images.'[1]

Contemporary South African culture is dominated by landlessness, home-lessness and the yearning for place, for land. This yearning and despair is subtly expressed in the pathos of freedom songs like *Sikhalela umhlaba wethu owathathwa ngabelungu* [We cry for our land that was taken by white people]. (Remarkably the same fear of losing the land and the yearning for place are much in evidence among whites.) The dominant image among blacks is one of rootlessness. Yet in an African world-view there is no meaning apart from roots. This sense of belonging is a primary concern of black people and a central tenet of *ubuntu-botho* (of being truly human).

There can be no political, economic and racial solution in South Africa if the land problem is not tackled. Land is particularly important for those who have lost it through colonialism and resettlement programmes. We cannot allow the current land distribution between black and white to remain unchallenged.

In one sense, reparation and restitution are two sides of the same coin. Reparation 'addresses the losses or injuries inflicted through deliberate forms of injustice such as dehumanisation, underpayment and exploitation of the people beyond the people's capacity to be human'.[2] Restitution 'arises from forms of land dispossession in which the indigenous people have been rendered landless'.[3]

However, it is also necessary to distinguish between 'reparation' and 'restitution' of land. The Development Strategy and Policy Unit of the Urban Foundation makes a useful dinstinction. 'Restitution' is the more restricted of the two concepts for the following reasons:

— The remedy is the granting of land rather than something else of economic value, such as money.

— It must be the same land of which people were originally dispossessed.

— The individual or the community dispossessed must be the claimant or must still exist as a cohesive group.

— The land must be given back by the same agency that originally took it; i.e. the State must still be the owner of the land (or be able to re-acquire it) in order to give it back.[4]

'Reparation', on the other hand, does not necessarily include any of the restrictions discussed above. 'Reparation' implies the following:

— The remedy is not limited to the restitution of the same land. It seems appropriate to speak of 'reparation' or 'redress' in cases where remedies take the form of involvement in rural development programmes, sharing the use of land, the payment of money, etc.

— The wrong or disadvantage deserving reparation could also have been suffered indirectly, for example by the descendants of those originally dispossessed or by individual members of a community which no longer exists.

— Similarly, the call for reparations is not dependent upon the question as to whether or not the original wrongdoer (e.g. the State) still has the land in order to give it back.

— The concept of reparations is not confined to dealing with claims based solely on history; it can also denote a process that takes cognisance of current interests.[5]

Reparation has legal and theological dimensions. This means that the issue of land redistribution or reparation in South Africa has to be analysed politically as well as theologically. In an attempt to facilitate this, models of land redistribution as identified in the Bible are discussed in this chapter. Some of the political models of land redistribution proposed in South Africa are then weighed against the models.

Biblical Teaching

The Bible uses 'land' both literally and symbolically. Literally, land refers 'to actual earthly turf where people can be safe and secure, where meaning and well-being are enjoyed without pressure or coercion'.[6] Symbolically, land expresses 'the wholeness of joy and well-being characterised by social coherence and personal ease in prosperity, security, and freedom'.[7]

In an African setting, land has both literal and symbolic significations. On the one hand, land is fully historical, while on the other it bears a wealth of meaning known only to those who lose and yearn for it. The hunger for land is at once a concern for actual historical placement, and at the same time a yearning for meaning. This dialectic belongs to *ubuntu-botho*. *Ubuntu-botho* is essentially about historical placement on the earth, but that historical placement subsumes meanings both rooted in and transcending literalism.

The Hebrew Bible proposes a number of theologies of the land. The first theology of land is announced in the Pentateuch,[8] when God promised to give Abraham land (Gen. 12:1). The theology of land that emerged from the first generation of former Hebrew nomads who settled on agricultural land legitimised the privilege of the occupation of land, and was only rarely a reflection on the justice of such occupation. Klaus Nürnberger maintains that there was no Israelite theology that took the interests of the original natives of Palestine, the Canaanites, seriously.[9] A legitimating theology or religious ideology of the land thus emerged as a result of conflict over land occupation.

When the Israelites settled permanently in Canaan, a hierarchy of social classes emerged. Diferences between the poor and the rich surfaced, particularly during the reign of the kings. The prophets spoke against the unjust socio-economic relations and the dispossession of the land of the poor by the ruling classes. The story of Naboth and Ahab is a case in point (1 Kings 21). The theology of land thus became a crude defence of the collective self-interest of the privileged classes.

A Model of Redistribution of Land and Reparation

Because the biblical God is a God who demonstrates a 'preferential option for the poor and oppressed', a Year of Jubilee was promulgated (see Leviticus 25). The Year of Jubilee provides a model of land redistribution and reparation. Its distinctive features included the restoration of social and economic justice and the return of property to the landless and non-propertied classes. Israel was forbidden to sell land in perpetuity; land could only be leased temporarily, because it belonged to God.

The purpose of returning land to its original owners was to break the cycle of poverty and dependence. Jubilee was regarded as a major redress of injustice. K. Lebacqz articulates the importance of land restitution expressed in the Jubilee motif as follows:

> It is an image of reclamation. Reclamation means both the returning of something taken away and the action of calling or bringing back from wrongdoing. What is reclaimed is set right, renewed. It [Jubilee] shows clearly the centrality of economic injustice and its relation to loss of political power.[10]

It is not certain whether the law of Jubilee was ever applied in Israel, but Leon Epstein argues that the Jubilee law had two objectives: 'the freedom acquired at the exodus from Egypt must be rediscovered by all the children of Israel and the property received in common on the entry into Canaan cannot be alienated for ever'.[11]

Whether or not the Jubilee was applied in Israel, it is attractive as a model for the redistribution of land in South Africa. But the debate on the redistribution of land has just started in this country. The historically dispossessed people can only participate 'in the creation of their own future, both economically and politically' if they are given access to land.[12]

The Political Ethics of Reparation

According to Albie Sachs, emphasis in the debate on the land question must be laid on principles and procedures rather than outcomes. The land issue must be situated 'in the context of democracy, human rights, and the Rule of Law rather than the context of race'.[13] Land redistribution can only function when human rights are applied. Large tracts of land were reserved historically for white ownership. Black people as a result own less than one per cent of land in South Africa. This has far-reaching implications for the political economy and human relations in this country. It highlights the absence of black people's property rights and the general denial of human rights. The exclusion of blacks from land ownership has been undergirded by the Afrikaner land theology, which has preached racial hegemony over land. Afrikaner land theology does not question the legitimacy of white land ownership, because God himself gave the land to his chosen people. This idea is articulated in the preamble of the South African Republic constitution:

> In humble submission to the Almighty God, who controls the destiny of nations and the history of peoples, who gathered our forebears from lands and gave them this their own; who has guided them from generation to generation; who has wondrously delivered them from the dangers that beset them . . .

Sachs proposes three phases of land redistribution. The first phase would involve the symbolic and publicised return of land recently expropriated. The major benefactors of this phase would be black. Black farmers have demanded: 'First give us back what we held until recently in terms of the white man's law itself and of which we have been robbed, then we can start talking about sharing the land as a whole with the whites.'[14] The second phase would stabilise and create defensive rights in relation to land. The major aspects of this phase would be to pass legislation that protects occupants against eviction, and create conditions for eliminating physical and human rights abuses.[15] The third phase would entail the establishment of a land court or similar institution. In order to ensure a measure of success for this phase, Sachs proposes that the following would have to be addressed:

— The farmers themselves, both black and white, must be actively involved in the processes at every stage.

— While the criteria and procedures should be firmly based on well-established principles, their application in particular cases should be flexible and rooted in local reality, taking account of local patterns of land use and tenure.[16]

Sach's solution to the land question is consistent with an ethos which claims that South Africa belongs 'to all'. However, it is necessary to point out diverging political perceptions on the restoration of land.

The National Party 'believes that the restoration of land tenure rights resulting from past policies could be considered in cases where it would not entail the dispossession of existing land tenure rights; that is to say, in cases where land is still in possession of the state and where it has not yet been developed or allocated for a specific purpose'.[17] The implication is that Trust Land held by the state would be used for resettling black people.

According to the African National Congress's policy guidelines: 'It is the ANC's view that the legacy of forced removals must be addressed as a fundamental point of departure to any future land policy for our country.' Claims of communities to land would be settled by a Land Claims Court.

The Pan Africanist Congress's position on the restoration of land 'is that the land and all natural resources belong to the African people as a whole, and therefore, all benefits, financial and otherwise, accruing from them must be shared equitably among the people'.[18] The original position of the PAC on the restoration of land was nationalisation. However, the PAC now advocates a policy of socialisation of the land.

The Azanian People's Organisation asserts that the land question must be central in any future economic dispensation in South Africa. AZAPO's vision of the land is formulated thus: 'It is clear that because land is the primary means of production, it belongs to the people and cannot become the property of individuals.'[19]

The Democratic Party maintains that land must be restored to victims of the Group Areas Act. In order to address imbalances in land ownership, the state must assume responsibility for the redistribution of land. Land that is owned by the state must be distributed on the principle of 'willing seller, willing buyer'.[20]

To the Inkatha Freedom Party, redistribution of land is secondary to the independent status of KwaZulu. On the land question, the IFP shares the view of the National Party — namely, that land must be subjected to prevailing market forces: 'we believe in the desirability of a market economy, of private ownership of property, and in rewarding initiative and enterprise.'[21]

The Conservative Party does not embrace the concept of redistribution of land. What is central in its political agenda is the self-determination of the white people in a white homeland. The vision of the Conservative Party is the old-fashioned ideology of 'separate homelands for separate nations'.

The Afrikaner Volksunie likewise does not advocate redistribution of land, but, unlike the Conservative Party, it stands for the establishment of an Afrikaner state and not a white homeland. It asserts that this is not a racist but a cultural dispensation. The Afrikaner Volksunie argues that the priority for the state is not redistribution of land, but providing houses for the black people, because 'Land is not a basic need for any individual'.[22]

The Urban Foundation, which represents big business in South Africa, is critical of the proposals of the National Party. It argues that there are two issues which are important for future policy, namely consideration of the victims of forced settlements, and the imbalance in land ownership. The redistribution of land must be based on the principle of equity. The Foundation proposes that two million hectares of Trust Land must be made available to about one thousand black farmers in order to include them in the commercial agricultural sector.[23]

Probably the most difficult aspect of any proposed redistribution concerns the allocation of land to people who were dispossessed long ago. Some of these people are the homeless who live in ghettos in the townships and in the homelands. They are people who can no longer motivate claims for specific portions of ancestral land. Aninka Claassens proposes that 'Affirmative state policy for this vast category of people should be directed by the demands expressed in the struggles of these communities.'[24]

Conclusion

Land is theology. It is the blanket that covers the nakedness of the ancestors and incarnates their soul. It provides the basis and context of *ubuntu-botho*. Mosoma is right when he states that 'for black people, the struggle is not based on some formal abstract principles. It is essentially expressed and concretised in land . . . To be sure, without land restitution, the conditions necessary for the actualisation of a just democratic social and political order cannot be attained.'[25]

In our view, the model of the Jubilee provides a sound foundation for constitutional and ethical thinking in South Africa today. If the principle of the Jubilee Year were applied in this country, then no family would be landless. Residential land would be freely redistributed among the dispossessed; mortgages would be renegotiated, and debts would be forgiven. This would give a democratic South Africa a new start.

Charles Villa-Vicencio maintains that 'the redistribution of the ownership of land and the means of industrial production is as much a remedial ingredient . . . as is any talk of democratic and political control over the use to which it is put in a new South Africa. Theologically, the ownership and the use of God's creation is to be used for the benefit and well-being of all God's children, especially those who are at any point in time in most need of empowerment.'[26] This in an ethic of reparation in a nutshell.

[1] *The Land* (Philadelphia: Fortress Press, 1977), p. 1.

[2] Klaus Nürnberger, 'Theses on the Theology of Land in Its Overall Context', in E. M. Conradie (ed.), *Church and Land* (Stellenbosch: The Stellenbosch Economic Project, 1992), p. 18.

[3] Ibid., p. 18.

[4] K. Beavon, *U. F. Research: Summaries on Critical Issues* (Johannesburg: Urban Foundation, 1993), p. 7.

[5] Ibid., p. 7.

[6] Brueggemann, *The Land,* p. 2.

[7] Ibid., p. 2.

[8] Ibid., p. 86.

[9] Nürnberger, 'Theses', p. 2.

[10] K. Lebacqz, *Justice in an Unjust World: Foundations for a Christian Approach to Justice* (Minneapolis: Augsburg, 1987), p. 127.

[11] L. Epstein, *Social Justice in the Ancient Near East and the People of Israel* (London: SCM, 1986), p. 134.

[12] C. Villa-Vicencio, *A Theology of Reconstruction* (Cape Town: David Philip, 1992), p. 201.

[13] A. Sachs, *Protecting Human Rights* (Cape Town: Oxford University Press, 1990), p. 106.

[14] Ibid., p. 129.

[15] Ibid., p. 130.

[16] Ibid., p. 131.

[17] *Barometer on Negotiations,* Vol. 5 (Clubview: Regional Research and Report Commission, 1993), p. 7.

[18] Ibid., p. 5.

[19] E. Harsch, 'Land Reform in South Africa: On Whose Terms?', *Transafrica Forum,* 8:4 (Winter 1991/1992), pp. 31–32.

[20] Ibid., p. 9.

[21] Ibid., p. 9.

[22] *Barometer on Negotiations,* p. 17.

[23] Beavon, *U. F. Research.*

[24] A. Claassens, 'For Whites Only: Land Ownership in South Africa,' in M. de Klerk (ed.), *A Harvest of Discontent: The Land Question in South Africa* (Johannesburg: IDASA, 1991), p. 60.

[25] D. L. Mosoma, 'Justice, Peace, Reparation and Restitution', *Journal of Black Theology in South Africa,* 5:2 (1991), pp. 26–27.

[26] Villa-Vicencio, *Theology of Reconstruction,* p. 204.

Select Bibliography

De Klerk, M. (ed.) *A Harvest of Discontent: The Land Question in South Africa.* Johannesburg: Institute for a Democratic Alternative for South Africa, 1991

Lebacqz, K. *Justice in an Unjust World: Foundations for a Christian Approach to Justice.* Minneapolis: Augsburg Publishing House, 1987

Conradie, E. M. (ed.) *Church and Land.* Stellenbosch: The Stellenbosch Economic Project, 1992

Mosoma, D. L. 'Justice, Peace, Reparation and Restitution', *Journal of Black Theology in South Africa,* 5:2 (1991), pp. 12–28

Sachs, A. *Protecting Human Rights.* Cape Town: Oxford University Press, 1990

Villa-Vicencio, C. 1992. *A Theology of Reconstruction: Nation Building and Human Rights.* Cape Town: David Philip, 1992

Index